Redefining Citizenship in Australia, Canada, and Aotearoa New Zealand

"The diverse array of citizens of settler colonizer nations need to know their full story. This clearly written and courageously comparative history demonstrates how at the end of the British world, three nation-states redefined citizenship from a concept based upon race, status, and links to Britain to one based upon civic rights and responsibilities. This meticulously researched book will be a must-read for scholars interested in national identity, political and legal history, and the history of indigenous resistance."

—Ann McGrath (AM, FASSA, FAHA), Kathleen Fitzpatrick Australian Laureate Fellow and W.K. Hancock Professor of History, School of History, Australian National University

"This book is a groundbreaking comparative study of Canada, Australia, and Aotearoa New Zealand and the shift from ethnic forms of British-based national identity to civic and potentially more inclusive varieties during the 1960s and 1970s. This crucial shift in identity has been inadequately studied until now. Jatinder Mann's insightful and impeccably researched book, based on a wealth of primary sources, casts new light into the connections between national identity and citizenship in settler states. It correlates major changes in conceptions of national self and other with the rise and decline of the British imperial system. An impressive addition to the literature on citizenship studies, Indigenous peoples, and racialized peoples."

—David B. MacDonald, Professor and Research Leadership Chair for the College of Social and Applied Human Sciences, Department of Political Science, University of Guelph

"At a time when a disunited Kingdom is engaged in an almost byzantine debate about Brexit in which some protagonists are seeking to rekindle the flames of empire, Jatinder Mann's impressive book offers a rigorous analysis of how the relations between Britain and its closest dominions became severely weakened if not entirely severed.

Carefully examining the way citizenship was redefined in Australia, Canada, and New Zealand between the 1950s and 1970s, Mann demonstrates how changing global geopolitical relations, the strengthening of demands for indigenous people's rights, and increasingly diverse non-British immigration patterns moved the basis of majority settler forms of national identity towards varying multicultural and bicultural frames of belonging.

This book is essential reading for students of the political history of British settler states, within and across these area studies, and will be invaluable for citizenship specialists, especially with expertise in ethnic and indigenous studies, still debating whether the British World is being revived or is irretrievably lost."

—David Pearson, Adjunct Associate Professor, School of Social and Cultural Studies, Victoria University of Wellington

Redefining Citizenship in Australia, Canada, and Aotearoa New Zealand

Studies in Transnationalism

Jatinder Mann
Series Editor

Vol. 2

The Studies in Transnationalism series is part of the Peter Lang Humanities list.
Every volume is peer reviewed and meets
the highest quality standards for content and production.

PETER LANG
New York • Bern • Berlin
Brussels • Vienna • Oxford • Warsaw

Jatinder Mann

Redefining Citizenship in Australia, Canada, and Aotearoa New Zealand

PETER LANG

New York • Bern • Berlin

Brussels • Vienna • Oxford • Warsaw

Library of Congress Cataloging-in-Publication Data

Names: Mann, Jatinder, author.
Title: Redefining citizenship in Australia, Canada, and
Aotearoa New Zealand / Jatinder Mann.
Description: New York: Peter Lang, 2019.
Series: Studies in transnationalism, vol. 2
ISSN 2578-9317 (print) | ISSN 2578-9325 (online)
Includes bibliographical references and index.
Identifiers: LCCN 2018052792 | ISBN 978-1-4331-5108-8 (hardback: alk. paper)
ISBN 978-1-4331-5109-5 (ebook pdf) | ISBN 978-1-4331-5110-1 (epub)
ISBN 978-1-4331-5111-8 (mobi)
Subjects: LCSH: Citizenship—Australia—History—20th century.
Citizenship—Canada—History—20th century.
Citizenship—New Zealand—History—20th century.
Naturalization—Australia—History—20th century.
Naturalization—Canada—History—20th century.
Naturalization—New Zealand—History—20th century.
Indigenous peoples—Legal status, laws, etc.—Australia—History—20th century.
Indigenous peoples—Legal status, laws, etc.—Canada—History—20th century.
Indigenous peoples—Legal status, laws, etc.—New Zealand—History—20th century.
Classification: LCC JF801 .M338 2019 | DDC 323.6—dc23
LC record available at https://lccn.loc.gov/2018052792
DOI 10.3726/b15770

Bibliographic information published by **Die Deutsche Nationalbibliothek**.
Die Deutsche Nationalbibliothek lists this publication in the "Deutsche
Nationalbibliografie"; detailed bibliographic data are available
on the Internet at http://dnb.d-nb.de/.

The paper in this book meets the guidelines for permanence and durability
of the Committee on Production Guidelines for Book Longevity
of the Council of Library Resources.

© 2019 Peter Lang Publishing, Inc., New York
29 Broadway, 18th floor, New York, NY 10006
www.peterlang.com

Printed in the United States of America

This book is dedicated to John. Thank you so much for all your love, support, and encouragement. This is for you, handsome…

CONTENTS

ACKNOWLEDGMENTS

As with my first monograph, the writing of this book has been a journey that has taken place in different countries and continents, and I would like to thank those who have supported me throughout this venture. This book emerged out of my Banting Postdoctoral Fellowship research project at the University of Alberta (U of A) in Edmonton, Alberta, Canada. I would like to thank Peter Lang Publishing for agreeing to publish my second monograph. In particular, I express gratitude to Meagan Simpson for commissioning the manuscript, and Jennifer Beszley and Luke McCord for seeing it through to production. I would like to thank my Research Assistant, Ken Ng for his help with putting the index of the book together. Additionally, I express my gratitude to Hong Kong Baptist University (HKBU) for its generous subvention, which contributed to the publication of this monograph.

An article based on parts of Chapter 1 entitled "The End of the British World and the Redefinition of Citizenship in Australia, 1950s-1970s" was published in the *Chinese Journal of Australian Studies*. An article based on parts of Chapter 2 entitled "The End of the British World and the Redefinition of Citizenship in Canada, 1950s-1970s" was published in the *Asian Journal of Canadian Studies*. An article based on parts of Chapter 3 entitled "The End of the British World and the Redefinition of Citizenship in Aotearoa New

Zealand, 1950s–1970s" was published in *National Identities*. A scholarly book chapter based on parts of Chapter 2 entitled "The Redefinition of Citizenship in Canada, 1950s-1970s" was published in Jatinder Mann (ed.), *Citizenship in Transnational Perspective: Australia, Canada, and New Zealand* (New York: Palgrave Macmillan, 2017). I would like to thank the publishers of the journals and edited book for their permission to publish these sections of the book.

I owe thanks to many institutions and people for their assistance during the process leading to the completion of this manuscript. In particular, I acknowledge the U of A, the Australian National University (ANU), Carleton University, the Victoria University of Wellington (VUW), King's College London, and HKBU. I thank all my friends and colleagues in these institutions for their constant encouragement and support in the writing of this book. I would especially like to mention the School of Politics and International Relations at the ANU, the School of Indigenous and Canadian Studies at Carleton University, and the Stout Research Centre for New Zealand Studies at VUW, for providing me with a scholarly home and material support which enabled me to carry out the research for my three case studies.

I would also like to express my immense gratitude to Professor Janine Brodie for her considerable guidance, support, and feedback during my Banting Postdoctoral Fellowship at the U of A. Actually, the thanks even goes as far back as when I applied for a Banting Postdoctoral Fellowship (the most prestigious fellowship of its kind in Canada) and she kindly agreed to be my mentor/supervisor. My project benefitted immensely from having Janine as my mentor/supervisor, and I will forever be grateful for this.

I am thankful to the Social Sciences and Humanities Research Council (SSHRC) of Canada for awarding me a Banting Postdoctoral Fellowship, without which this book would not have been possible. I am also grateful to the Office of the Vice-President (Research) at the U of A for its extremely generous research support, which enabled me to carry out my research in Canberra, Australia, and Wellington, Aotearoa New Zealand. Thanks are also due to the International Council for Canadian Studies for awarding me the inaugural Avi Arensen Canadian Studies Postdoctoral Fellowship, which enabled me to conduct my research in Ottawa, Canada.

The staff members at Archives New Zealand Te Rua Mahara o te Kāwanatanga, Library and Archives Canada, the National Archives of Australia, the National Library of Australia, and the National Library of New Zealand Te Puna Mātauranga o Aotearoa were always very helpful. I would also like to thank the permission holders of the following personal papers and fonds for their kind permission to consult restricted parts of them: Al Grassby Papers, Sir Billy Snedden Papers, Lester B. Pearson Fonds, Pierre Elliott Trudeau Fonds, Jack Pickersgill Fonds, Richard Albert Bell Fonds, and the David Watt Ballantyne Papers.

Lastly, but certainly not least, I would like to thank my friends and family all across the world for your constant support and belief in me. It was not always easy writing this book, and I often had to dig deep, but your words of encouragement always helped. I hope to continue thanking you all for many more books to come.

Jatinder Mann
Hong Kong, March 2019

ABBREVIATIONS

ALP—Australian Labor Party
EEC—European Economic Community
FCAATSI—Federal Council for the Advancement of Aborigines and Torres
Strait Islanders
MP—Member of Parliament
UK—United Kingdom
UN—United Nations
US—United States

INTRODUCTION

Adopting a political and legal perspective, my book undertakes a transnational study that examines the demise of Britishness[1] on the conceptualisation of citizenship and the impact that this historic shift has had on Indigenous and other ethnic groups in Australia, Canada, and Aotearoa New Zealand. During the 1950s and 1970s an ethnically based citizenship was transformed into a civic-based one (based on rights and responsibilities). The major context in which this took place was the demise of British race patriotism in Australia, English-speaking Canada, and Aotearoa New Zealand. Although the timing of this shift varied, Aboriginal groups and non-British ethnic groups were now incorporated, or appeared to be incorporated, into ideas of citizenship in all three nations. The development of citizenship in this period has traditionally been associated with immigration in Australia, Canada, and Aotearoa New Zealand. However, the historical origins of citizenship practices in all three countries have yet to be fully analysed. This is what my book does. The differences between Australia and Aotearoa New Zealand on the one hand and Canada on the other will be particularly enlightening, as the latter contained a majority non-British population: French-Canadians and other long-standing European groups. Furthermore, the Māori population of Aotearoa New Zealand had long-standing political representation in the national parliament, which was not the case in Australia and Canada, which represents another fascinating dimension to the study. The overarching question addressed by my book is: Why and how did the end of the British World lead to the redefinition of citizenship in Australia, Canada, and Aotearoa New Zealand between the 1950s and 1970s in regard to other ethnic and Indigenous groups?

There has been no study of the redefinition of citizenship in terms of ethnicity and Indigeneity in Australia, Canada, and Aotearoa New Zealand during the 1950s and 1970s in the transnational British World perspective.[2] Although Heidi Bohaker and Franca Iacovetta[3] have examined migrants and First Nation groups in Canada between the 1950s and 1970s, they focused on citizenship programs (i.e., integration policy) rather than citizenship legislation, which is the subject of this book. What is more, they did not place developments with both groups in the context of the demise of Britishness, which is the most original aspect of my book. Anna Haebich,[4] although looking at both migrants and Aboriginal groups, focused on assimilation policy as she described it between the 1950s and 1970s, and did not place her study in the context of the decline of British race patriotism as the basis of national identity in Australia.[5]

Most literature on citizenship in Australia has tended to trace its development from Australians advancing from the status of being "subjects to citizens."[6] Specifically, the majority argue that the key turning point for Australians was the *British Nationality and Australian Citizenship Act* of 1948. But this was not the case. As I have shown in my article on "The Evolution of Commonwealth Citizenship," this Act was an attempt by Australia to preserve the common status of British subjects that Canada's unilateral action of introducing its own national citizenship had jeopardised. Therefore, the Australian Act actually affirmed Australia's Britishness.[7]

This book has many unique features. These include the transnational approach, which will enable the impact of a broad concept of national identity on the conceptualisation of citizenship in relation to other ethnic groups and Indigenous peoples to be explored through the experiences of three different countries. The comparisons that will be made between each will be important in themselves, but they will also bring unique characteristics or features of each country to the forefront.

My book consulted government archives, citizenship acts, naturalisation legislation, parliamentary debates, newspaper editorials, and speeches and personal papers of key figures in the period to chart the impact of the demise of Britishness on the definition of citizenship in terms of Aboriginal and other ethnic groups in Australia, Canada, and Aotearoa New Zealand. The specific archival sources I consulted included: Cabinet records, files of Foreign/External Affairs, and those of the Attorney-General Departments that deal with the formulation of legislation and its operation. The focus on these sources in all three national archives of the countries of my study enabled me to pursue a comparative examination of policy, which is one of the most unique features of the book. The book also engages with key secondary sources.[8]

Specifically, the book focuses on key points in the redefinition of citizenship during the period of my study in terms of other ethnic and Indigenous peoples. So, for Australia, I looked at the major citizenship legislation between the 1950s and 1970s; particularly the 1973 *Australian Citizenship Act*, which removed the status of British subject from Australian citizenship. Alongside studying the actual Act itself, I consulted government documents leading to its introduction;[9] key personal papers of political figures that were responsible for it, such as Minister for Immigration Al Grassby;[10] parliamentary debates regarding its passage; and newspaper editorials on the public reaction to the legislation. On the Indigenous side, the 1967 referendum on whether the Commonwealth government should be allowed to legislate for Aboriginal people (this had previously been the purview of state governments) and if they should be counted as a part of the national census was the key event during the 1950s and 1970s. As with the abovementioned 1973 *Australian Citizenship Act*, I studied the referendum itself; consulted government documents on the decision to hold it;[11] looked at the personal papers of key figures involved in its adoption, such as Prime Minister Harold Holt;[12] examined parliamentary debates regarding the referendum; and explored popular reaction to it, through newspaper editorials.

In the case of Canada, I focused on the major points in the redefinition of citizenship towards other ethnic and Indigenous groups between the 1950s and 1970s. The 1977 *Canadian Citizenship Act* was the most significant piece of legislation during this period in terms of other ethnic groups, as, similarly to the Australian Act above, it removed the status of British subject from Canadian citizenship. As with the Australian Act, I actually focused on the 1977 *Canadian Citizenship Act* itself; consulted government documents leading to its introduction;[13] studied the personal papers of key figures responsible for its framing, such as Minister for Manpower and Immigration Bud Cullen;[14] explored parliamentary debates regarding its adoption; and examined newspaper editorials for popular reaction to the proposals. On the Indigenous side, a particular highlight is the Diefenbaker government's move in 1960 to extend the franchise to all Aboriginal people in the country. As with the above 1977 *Canadian Citizenship Act*, I focused on the actual legislation itself; examined key government documents leading to its introduction,[15] as well as personal papers of key figures responsible for it, such as Minister of Citizenship Ellen Fairclough;[16] studied parliamentary debates surrounding its adoption; and explored popular reaction to the legislation through newspaper editorials.

The Aotearoa New Zealand case study is an interesting one, as unlike Australia and Canada, the Indigenous people in its territory had political representation in the national parliament from its establishment as a nation (although it was not proportionate to their numbers in the population). However, it did have a similar experience to the two countries in terms of its citizenship legislation towards other ethnic groups. The 1977 *British Nationality and New Zealand Citizenship Act* was the most important piece of legislation as it also removed the status of British subject from Aotearoa New Zealand citizenship. As with both the Australian and Canadian cases above, I focused on the actual legislation itself; consulted the government documents leading to its introduction;[17] explored the personal papers of key figures responsible for it; examined the parliamentary debates surrounding its adoption; and studied newspaper editorials for the popular reaction to the proposals.

In terms of structure, the book consists of three chapters on Australia, Canada, and Aotearoa New Zealand, and a fourth chapter on comparisons. Going into more detail, Chapter 1 on "Redefining Citizenship in Australia, 1950s–1970s" argues that in the 1950s, Australia very much identified itself as a British country and an integral part of a wider British World, which had the UK at its centre. However, by the 1970s, this British World had come to an end, as had Australia's self-identification as a British nation. During this period, citizenship in Australia was redefined in a significant way from being an ethnic (British)-based one to a more civic-founded one which was more inclusive of other ethnic groups and apparently Aborigines. This chapter argues that this redefinition of citizenship took place primarily in the context of this major shift in national identity. After having established the context of the end of the British World in Australia (with a focus on the UK's application for entry into the EEC and the British withdrawal from "East of Suez"), it explores the *Nationality and Citizenship Act* of 1955, the *Nationality and Citizenship Act* of 1960, the *Citizenship Act* of 1969, and the *Australian Citizenship Act* of 1973, to illustrate the way in which citizenship became more inclusive of other ethnic groups in the country. It then studies Aboriginal policy during the 1950s, the awarding of the right to vote to Aborigines in 1961, the

3. Heidi Bohaker and Franca Iacovetta, "Making Aboriginal People 'Immigrants Too'": A Comparison of Citizenship Programs for Newcomers and Indigenous Peoples in Postwar Canada, 1940s–1960s," *Canadian Historical Review* 90, no. 3 (September 2009), 427–61; David Pearson, "Theorizing Citizenship in British Settler Societies," *Ethnic and Racial Studies* 25, no. 6 (November 2002), 989–1012, looks at citizenship in Australia, Canada, and New Zealand, but he took a sociological perspective and adopted a theoretical approach.

4. Anna Haebich, *Spinning the Dream: Assimilation in Australia, 1950–1970* (North Fremantle, WA: Fremantle Press, c2007).

5. The most recent work on this is Jatinder Mann's *The Search for a New National Identity: The Rise of Multiculturalism in Canada and Australia, 1890s–1970s* (New York: Peter Lang, 2016). James Curran and Stuart Ward's *The Unknown Nation: Australia After Empire* (Parkville, Victoria: Melbourne University Press, 2010) also focuses on Australia's self-identification as a British nation. A comparable work on the demise of Britishness in English-speaking Canada is José Igartua's *The Other Quiet Revolution: National Identities in English Canada, 1945–1971* (Vancouver: UBC Press, 2007). There has not been any in-depth book-length work on the decline of Britishness in Aotearoa New Zealand. However, James Belich does explore it in a broader history of Aotearoa New Zealand in *Paradise Reforged. History of the New Zealanders from the 1880s to the Year 2000* (Auckland: Penguin Books, 2002). Stuart Ward also explored Aotearoa New Zealand's self-identification in a broader comparative chapter on Australia, Canada, and New Zealand: "The 'New Nationalism' in Australia, Canada and New Zealand": Civic Culture In the Wake of the British World" in *Britishness Abroad: Transnational Movements and Imperial Cultures*, edited by Kate Darian-Smith, Patricia Grimshaw, and Stuart Macintyre (Carlton, Victoria: Melbourne University Press, 2007).

6. This is literally the beginning of the title of Alistair Davidson's book, *From Subject to Citizen: Australian Citizenship in the Twentieth Century* (Cambridge: Cambridge University Press, 1997).

7. Jatinder Mann, "The Evolution of Commonwealth Citizenship, 1945–48 in Canada, Britain and Australia," *Commonwealth and Comparative Politics* 50, no. 3 (July 2012): 293–313.

8. I relied on the existing secondary literature to establish the context of the demise of Britishness in the three countries. The key sources in this regard are Jatinder Mann, "The Introduction of Multiculturalism in Canada and Australia, 1960s–1970s," *Nations and Nationalism* 18, no. 3 (July 2012); Jatinder Mann, "'Leavening British Traditions'": Integration Policy in Australia, 1962–1972," *Australian Journal of Politics and History* 59, issue 1 (March 2013); Jatinder Mann, "'Anglo-Conformity'": Assimilation Policy in Canada, 1890s–1950s," *International Journal of Canadian Studies* 50 (December 2014); Mann, *The Search for a New National Identity*; Curran and Ward, *The Unknown Nation*; Igartua, *The Other Quiet Revolution*; Neville Meaney, "'In History's Page': Identity and Myth" in *Australia's Empire*, edited by Deryck M. Schreuder and Stuart Ward, *The Oxford History of the British Empire Series*, general editor Wm. Roger Louis (Oxford: Oxford University Press, 2008); Ward, "The 'New Nationalism' in Australia, Canada and New Zealand"; James Curran, *The Power of Speech: Australian Prime Ministers Defining the National Image* (Carlton, Victoria: Melbourne University Press, 2006); Phil Buckner, ed., *Canada and the*

End of Empire (Vancouver: UBC Press, 2005); and Stuart Ward, *Australia and the British Embrace: The Demise of the British Ideal* (Carlton South, Victoria: Melbourne University Press, 2001).

9. National Archives of Australia (NAA), A5925 462/LEG: Legislation Committee—Cabinet Minute—Australian Citizenship Bill 1973.

10. National Library of Australia (NLA), MS 7798: Personal Papers of Al Grassby.

11. NAA, A406 E1967/30: 1967 Referendum constitution alteration—main file. NAA, A406 E1967/30 Part P: Referendum, 1967: Constitution alteration—Report on conduct of referendum.

12. NAA, M2684 116: [Personal papers of Prime Minister Holt] 1967 Referendum—"Yes" campaign, 1966–1967. NAA, M4299: [Personal Papers of Harold Holt].

13. Library and Archives Canada (LAC), RG19-F-2: Secretary of State—Citizenship Legislation, 1952–1976. LAC, RG3260-0-8-E: Department of Citizenship and Immigration Fonds, 1967–2012.

14. LAC, R11236-0-8-E: Jack "Bud" Cullen Fonds, 1969–1984.

15. LAC, RG26-A-2-A: Miscellaneous Re: Indian administration, 1942–1963. LAC, RG6-F-4: Indians—Indian conferences, general, 01/1959–06/1972.

16. LAC, R12805-0-0-E: Ellen Fairclough Fonds, 1951–2004.

17. Archives New Zealand (ANZ), R13024762: General—Naturalisation of Aliens and New Zealand Citizenship, 1972–1978. ANZ, R20761256: Commonwealth Affairs—Legislation and constitutional affairs—Nationality—NZ Citizenship: General [11/71–09/76], 1971–1976.

· 1 ·

REDEFINING CITIZENSHIP
IN AUSTRALIA, 1950s–1970s[1]

In the 1950s Australia very much identified itself as a British country and an integral part of a wider British World which had the UK at its centre. However, by the 1970s this British World had come to an end, as had Australia's self-identification as a British nation. During this period, citizenship in Australia was redefined in a significant way from being an ethnic (British)- based one to a more civic-founded one which was more inclusive of other ethnic groups and apparently Aborigines. This chapter will argue that this redefinition of citizenship took place primarily in the context of this major shift in national identity. After having established the context of the end of the British World in Australia (with a focus on the UK's application for entry into the EEC and the British withdrawal from "East of Suez") it will explore the *Nationality and Citizenship Acts* of 1955 and 1960, the *Citizenship Act* of 1969, and the *Australian Citizenship Act* of 1973 to illustrate the way in which citizenship became more inclusive of other ethnic groups in the country. It will then study Aboriginal policy during the 1950s, the awarding of the right to vote to Aborigines in 1961, the 1967 constitutional referendum, and the International Convention on the Elimination of All Forms of Racial Discrimination, between the 1960s and 1970s, to highlight how citizenship in Australia also appeared to incorporate Aborigines at this time.

Theoretical Background

Before exploring these several themes, it will be useful to briefly discuss the theoretical background to citizenship in Australia during the 1950s and 1970s—namely, the distinction between normative citizenship (citizenship as status) and substantive citizenship (citizenship as rights and obligations). T. H. Marshall formulated "citizenship" as a designation given to those who are full participants of a community. Through this he enlarged citizenship to incorporate civil rights, as well as political and social citizenship.[2] According to Wayne Hudson and John Kane, though, "What most Australians understand by citizenship is a mixture of legal and political citizenship….The history of legal and political citizenship in Australia, however, is problematic."[3] This relates to the fact that in the 1950s, citizenship in Australia was very much normative—it did not entail extensive rights and obligations. And to complicate things even more, British migrants could attain this status on much easier terms in comparison with non-British migrants. Aboriginal Australians, though possessing the "status" of Australian citizens, were deprived of rights which are usually associated with citizenship through a swathe of restrictive legislation—at both the federal and state levels. Helen Irving emphasised that "The political rights we most readily associate now with citizenship were… not what defined a citizen but what followed from being a citizen."[4] David Dutton argued that "The legal meaning of Australian citizenship has never been singularly defined, and must even now, be sought in the common law, and a multitude of Commonwealth and state statutes dealing with immigration, passports, the franchise, jury service, employment in the public service, and social security."[5] According to Sangeetha Pillai, "The commencement of the NCA 1948 signified the emergence of Australian statutory citizenship…. However, this did not symbolize a radical shift in notions of formal membership of the Australian community, but rather a relatively gradual evolution from previous statutes which had shaped such notions without using the language of citizenship."[6] Nevertheless, by the 1970s, citizenship in Australia was considerably more substantive compared with the 1950s, and all migrants were put on an equal basis in terms of attaining this citizenship. Ann-Mari Jordens neatly encapsulated this redefinition, "Over 30 years, the presence of large numbers of non-British migrants in Australia slowly eroded the conception of Australian citizenship from a status based on British ethnicity and culture to one based on equality of rights and responsibilities."[7] However, I will argue that a shift in national identity rather than increasing multi-ethnicity was the main reason for this redefinition. Jordens added that a "culturally normative conception of citizenship was clearly reflected in the definition of 'alien' embodied in the [1948] Act....A nation's understanding of itself is revealed by the categories of people it regards as foreign, alien and 'other'....From 1948 to 1987 Australia's citizenship legislation defined an alien as 'a person who does not have the status of British subject and is not an Irish citizen or a protected person.'"[8] Turning to Aborigines and citizenship, the most that one can really say about when Aboriginal groups became Australian citizens is that, primarily during the 1960s, Aboriginal groups gradually secured the substantive citizenship rights that up to that point had been withheld from them at the State and Commonwealth levels as State and Commonwealth statutes that limited their citizenship rights were slowly repealed.[9] Susan Dodds maintained that "In considering ways of thinking about Australian Aboriginal citizenship, the history of European engagement with indigenous Australians acts as a constant reminder of the gap between abstract idealisations of liberal democratic citizenship and the reality of colonial and post-colonial Australian social policy....Aboriginal and Torres Strait Islander peoples were not simply 'overlooked' in the process of nation building; their status as rights bearers was actively undermined."[10] Ann Curthoys stated that "In Australia there have been for a long time two distinct yet connected public and intellectual debates concerning the significance of descent, belonging and culture.... One revolves around the cleavage between indigenous and non-indigenous peoples, and especially the status of indigenous claims deriving from a history of colonization....The other debate centers on the immigrant, and his or her challenge to Australian society at large."[11] This chapter contributes to both of these debates.

Context of the End of the British World

Having established this theoretical background, the chapter will now turn to exploring the context of the end of the British World as the major reason for the redefinition of citizenship in Australia between the 1950s and 1970s. In the post-Second-World-War period, Australia was very much a British society and an integral part of a wider British World. The *British Nationality and Australian Citizenship Act* of 1948 is an excellent and very appropriate example of this. Although this Act established the concept of Australian citizenship for the very first time, it emphasised *British Nationality* over *Australian Citizen-*

ship. Furthermore, the status of British subject was preserved and white immigrants[12] from the British Commonwealth were given preferential treatment in terms of naturalisation.[13] The Suez Crisis of 1956[14] was a further demonstration of Australia's identification as an integral part of a wider British World. Throughout the episode the Australian government fully supported the UK's position of overturning President Nasser's decision to nationalise the Suez Canal. Australia offered unequivocal support for the UK, as it considered itself a British country. The UK was still the centre of a wider British World, and, therefore, backing the UK was still regarded as supporting the "mother-country."[15]

However, in the early 1960s the first signs that Australia's Britishness was beginning to wane started to emerge. The first application of the UK government for entry into the EEC in 1961 marked the beginning of the unraveling of the belief that Australia was part of a wider British World. It came as a psychological shock to the Australians, as they had previously received repeated assurances from the British that there was no question of them making a choice between Europe and the Commonwealth. However, the Australian government became increasingly concerned by the lack of communication from London during 1960 and 1961, when the UK was reconsidering its position towards the EEC. Despite repeated requests for information, the British refused to indicate which way they were thinking until a more solid agreement had been secured with the Six (this was the six original members of the EEC—France, Germany, Italy, Belgium, The Netherlands, and Luxembourg. The latter three were collectively known as Benelux).[16]

There were increasing rumours and speculation in early 1961 about a reversal of British policy. This led to the Australian government's sudden interest in European economic matters. Minister for Trade John McEwen announced to the Cabinet in February that although the entire picture was not clear, it appeared as if the UK was shifting closer and closer towards something along the lines of full membership of the EEC. The Australian Prime Minister Robert Menzies expressed the deep concerns of the Australian people about this eventuality. He specifically drew attention to the political and strategic effects that Britain's decision would have on the Commonwealth. If Britain were to join the EEC, how would it then consider Australia, Canada, and the rest of the Commonwealth?[17]

But unlike the UK, Australia did not have an alternative geographic grouping to redirect its interests to. Thus, the Australian government decided to use whatever means it could to ensure that British entry into the EEC would not lead to a fundamental shift in Australia's long-standing political and economic ties to the UK. Menzies' subsequent tough probing of the British government illustrated the level of Australia's concerns. The issue of Britain and Europe had initiated a re-evaluation of the very concept of "British interests," rather than being seen as just a temporary conflict of interest between Australia and Britain. Menzies increased the pressure by stating that the UK had a very hard choice between the Commonwealth and Europe. On 31 July 1961, British Prime Minister Harold Macmillan announced his government's decision to seek membership of the EEC.[18] Macmillan's EEC statement resulted in a diverse range of responses in Australia. The *Sydney Morning Herald* represented the general feeling, however, announcing that the British action was one of the most historic statements of the century.[19]

If the UK's application for membership of the EEC initiated the breakdown of Britishness in Australia, its resolve in 1967 to end its military role "East of Suez" was the culmination. This move was significant in itself as it illustrated the end of the UK's military world role. To commentators in both the UK and Australia it appeared that the decline of one of the last symbols of the Anglo-Australian relationship would result in the demise of Australia's long-standing British self-identification. This was due to British race patriotism in Australia being founded on the idea that Britons in Australia and the UK had a community of interest, which the British decision to withdraw from "East of Suez" acted blatantly against. But some time before the UK announced its move, there had been increasing problems in the British-Australian strategic relationship, which had led to Australia progressively becoming a part of the US sphere. Nevertheless, this had not affected Australia's Britannic identity in any significant way, as it had always (with a few noteworthy exceptions) preserved a differentiation between sentiment and interest, particularly when it came to foreign policy. Moreover, although the UK had not yet become a member of the EEC, its failed bid in 1961–63 had most definitely resulted in Australia questioning their future relationship and had led to initiatives to broaden Australian trade.[20]

As expected, there were Australian protests aimed at the British over their announcement. Alexander Downer, Australian High Commissioner in London, tried to persuade the British government that it would be a travesty of history if the UK were to be simply a European power. But largely, Downer's emotive reaction was not typical of most Australians' views in 1967, or indeed of those of the new Holt government. Although Foreign Minister Paul Hasluck did suggest to Prime Minister Harold Holt that connections of familial ties and common wartime experiences should be emphasised in communications with the UK, this was only a small component of the overarching Australian plan. Even the most ardent disciples of the British heritage had been compelled to accept the existence of this new world.[21]

Holt attempted to articulate a unique Australian identity based on both a British heritage and the European migrant cultures. In an Australia Day speech in 1967 he acknowledged: "Ours is not a long story as the history of many other nations is counted but in that time we have evolved our distinctive national identity and character [...] We have been assisted to do so by our heritage of British democracy and the cultures of European civilization." But he did not elaborate on what this apparently special Australian character and identity of the country entailed.[22]

The end of Britishness and the question of whether an Australian nationalism could be located to replace it coalesced in the late 1960s under Prime Minister John Gorton. Although Holt asked important questions, Gorton's public addresses on this subject were an illustration of the confusion and problems faced by national leaders in the late 1960s. Acknowledging that they could now develop a homegrown national identity, but at the same time wanting to hold onto the British connection, they found themselves on the horns of a dilemma. Hence, Gorton attempted to push an idea of "Australianism." In his opinion, the development of a sense of national pride represented a central goal for his government.[23]

The Whitlam government has often been associated with an unexpected emergence of a more autonomous and confident Australian nationalism; however, Gorton can be regarded as a predecessor of this drive, particularly in his arts policy initiatives. By establishing the Australian Council for the Arts, facilitating the re-emergence of the Australian film industry, and laying the basis for the introduction of an Australia Film and Television School, Gorton was linking himself and his government with an emerging faith in Australia's cultural uniqueness. While Holt had laid the foundation for a federal arts programme, Gorton took it up and supported it, not so much because of a newly discovered love of the arts, but instead due to his political search for a "new nationalism." Therefore, he promoted home-grown dance, music, opera, and above all, television and film. He had limited success in the achievement of this goal, however.[24]

The Sunday Australian captured the substance of the "new nationalism" in early 1972: "A splendid opportunity exists to build a multi-national society, rich and diverse in its origins but cohesive in its identity [...] Australia must be a country in which our people are concerned with a common purpose and a sharing of common identity."[25] This talk of Australia as a multi-national society but with a particular focus on national cohesion, along with somehow also possessing a clear idea of community and identity, combined the key concepts and contradictions of the "new nationalism." The decline of the idea that Australia was a part of a wider British World was helped by the long-drawn-out way in which the UK entered the EEC, which occurred in 1973, a dozen years after the original application. It was also assisted by the realisation by Australian leaders that the nation's trading future was in Asia, which for the majority of its past had been its psychological enemy. A white British Australian identity was no longer wanted and no longer appropriate as the nation attempted to come to terms with its presence in a changed world. In the early 1960s, then, the concept of Australia as a "British" country started to lose credibility and relevance. Later in the decade the "new nationalism," which emphasised a domestic Australian identity, arose as a possible replacement for Britishness. But this entire period was one of questioning and uncertainty. Thus, apart from an emphasis on national cohesion and uniquely Australian creative effort, there was not much substance to the "new nationalism."[26] This was the context in which nationality and citizenship legislation was amended during the 1960s and 1970s.

The *Nationality and Citizenship Act* of 1955

The *Nationality and Citizenship Act* of 1955 was the first notable reform of citizenship legislation in Australia (in that a new piece of legislation was actually introduced) since the inaugural *British Nationality and Australian Citizenship Act* of 1948. The slowly changing views on British nationality vis-à-vis Australian citizenship amongst certain sections of the Australian population in the 1950s were on display in a letter from a Sidney W. Smith to Prime Minister Robert Menzies on the occasion of the census:

> The collector forced me to put British. Now, Sir, my parents came to this country at a very early age with their British parents. I was born at Maitland N. S. Wales sixty-six years ago and am proud to call myself an Australian and I take it as an insult to be forced to cross it out by an Immigrant Census collector. Trusting you will see fit for this Commonwealth to have its own identity in future.[27]

Menzies queried the situation with Harold Holt, the Minister for Immigration; Secretary of the Department Sir Tasman Heyes produced a memorandum in which he outlined the legal position:

So far as our own law is concerned, it is set down, as you know, in the Nationality and Citizenship Act that certain persons are "Australian citizens" and "British subjects." (Certain others are "protected persons"—the natives of our trust territories.) Everyone who is an Australian citizen is a British subject. There is no provision in the Act enabling anyone to claim that he is of Australian "nationality."[28]

Although Heyes did qualify his remarks with "To sum up the answer to your questions seems to me to be that you are—(a) an Australian citizen and a British subject under Australian law; (b) of Australian nationality so far as international law is concerned."[29] With this information, the Prime Minister's Department could respond to Sidney W. Smith along the following lines:

The Nationality and Citizenship Act 1948/53 distinguishes between citizenship and nationality. Under that Act a person born in Australia is, with certain exceptions, an Australian citizen. By virtue of the Act, such a person is also a "British subject." It seems, under the circumstances, that you would not have been incorrect in showing your nationality as Australian. However, the form impliedly requested that in the case of British Commonwealth citizens their nationality should be shown as British.[30]

So, even the Commonwealth government was beginning to recognize that more and more Australians preferred referring to themselves as "Australian" citizens as opposed to "British" subjects.

Other issues in regard to Australian citizenship at the time included why there were not a higher number of immigrants applying for naturalization, and whether the legal conditions in relation to naturalization were too strict.[31] In August 1954 an ALP MP for Port Adelaide, Albert Thompson, took this even further, asking Holt "whether any consideration has been given to the high cost to New Australians of making an application for naturalization in connection with newspaper advertisements and the fee that is charged."[32] He added that "If not, can the matter be examined with the object of lessening the cost because of the necessity for having all people who are willing to confirm to the laws of the country naturalized?"[33] The Minister for Supply, Howard Beale, replied that he would have the issue investigated and provide Thompson with an answer.[34]

However, the broader issue of numbers of immigrants not seeking Australian citizenship was raised again the following month, this time by another Parliamentarian, Alan Bird, the ALP member for Batman: "It is apparent from the figures to which I have referred, that for some reason or other, many eligible persons are not keen to seek naturalization....I appeal to the Government to give urgent consideration to this matter, because it is essential that those eligible to apply should do so as quickly as possible."[35] He continued with "Does the Government think that the requirements of the Nationality and Citizenship

Act are too stringent? Does it consider that the fee which is charged is too high, and that the nature of the naturalization ceremony is a deterrent?"[36] Bird also raised the specific issue of the £5 payment for naturalization: "I also ask the Minister whether he thinks that the payment of the fee of £5 might deter some immigrants from seeking considering naturalization....A fee for naturalization was not charged until 1932, and since that time it has remained the same."[37]

In October 1954 Holt responded to this repeated pressure, stating that the issue "was considered by the recent Australian Citizenship Convention and the Commonwealth Immigration Advisory Council." He added that "certain recommendations relating to that and other matters have come to me and... those recommendations are now receiving my consideration with a view to their presentation in Cabinet."[38] The following month, Heyes wrote to his Minister arguing that:

> Our suggestion was that fees be abolished. I understand the proposal has now been made that all persons, British or alien, applying for Australian citizenship should pay a fee of £1. This would mean an increase (10/-) for British applicants and a reduction (£4) for aliens. I would not suggest that we strongly oppose such a policy of "non-discrimination" but merely offer the comment that we may be criticised for simultaneously changing fees to the disadvantage of British people but to the advantage of non-British migrants.[39]

Therefore, the reference to the "disadvantage of British people" demonstrated the continuing strength of Britishness in Australia at this time. Nonetheless, Holt took Heyes' advice and suggested to Cabinet that the £5 charge for naturalization be removed: "The fee of £5 represents a substantial deterrent to new settlers who might otherwise become Australian citizens....Apart from this aspect it is suggested that it is wrong in principle that fees should be charged for the conferment of the status of Australian citizen upon new settlers who have been found worthy of it in all other respects."[40]

The government finally introduced the *Nationality and Citizenship* Bill in April 1955. In introducing the bill, Holt maintained that "The House might be interested to know that the action now being taken is part of a more comprehensive approach designed to encourage the person who is qualified on all counts by residence to become a full citizen of Australia."[41]

The Leader of the ALP Opposition, Arthur Calwell, who was also the Minister for Immigration responsible for the original 1948 *British Nationality and Australian Citizenship Act*, expressed his general support for the bill:

> The requirement of a five-year period of residence proceeding naturalization has never been altered, and I hope that it will never be altered. Some people have said that

it would encourage New Australians to become naturalized if they were allowed to acquire citizenship within twelve months of their arrival in the country....Under the bill it is proposed to eliminate the requirement to advertise and also to lower the fee that is charged. These are steps in the right direction.[42]

So, the Cabinet had not decided to remove the naturalization fee altogether. Another Parliamentarian, Percy Clarey, the ALP member for Bendigo, commented that "At the same time, they will be able to appreciate more, not only the advantages of Australian citizenship but the responsibilities that are associated with it."[43] He added that:

> The second desirable feature of the bill is that it will make the conferring of citizenship a less formal matter than has been the case in the past. By the amendment of the principal act and by an endeavor to let the person who is becoming a naturalized Australian citizen see that the Australian people welcome him as a citizen, as a person with whom they will be living in the future, and as a person whom they trust to discharge the responsibilities of citizenship.[44]

The latter was a reference to the introduction of public citizenship ceremonies, a departure from the previous situation whereby new citizens only read out their citizenship pledge to a judge. Bird, who had been a long-time campaigner for reform of the nationality and citizenship legislation, suggested that:

> The Government should embark upon a vigorous press campaign to give plenty of publicity by means of advertisements and informative articles to the matter. The subject could also be covered in radio broadcasts, in addition, leaflets should be printed on a large scale in foreign languages to inform immigrants just how good things will be for them when they become Australian citizens.[45]

Thus, Bird's thinking was that through this advertising campaign drawing attention to the ways in which naturalisation had been made easier, migrants would be more willing to seek citizenship. Although the *Nationality and Citizenship Act* of 1955 did not introduce any groundbreaking changes to citizenship legislation, it showed that gradual change was taking place. Britishness in Australia would have to decline for more substantial changes to take place.

The *Nationality and Citizenship Act* of 1960

The *Nationality and Citizenship Act* of 1960 built on the previous changes in 1955. One of the main thrusts for change was agitation on the part of naturalised citizens on the distinctions that were made between them and natural-born British subjects when it came to the privileges of citizenship. In 1957 attention was drawn particularly to the fact that the "Minister may deprive of citizenship any person who within five years after naturalization is sentenced to imprisonment for 12 months or longer."[46] The following year the government responded to this criticism by conceding that the point was a fair one: "From the point of view of a new settler naturalization should give full citizenship rights available to native born Australians....The Minister tells us something of the support for the view that the present formal discrimination against naturalized or registered citizens should be discontinued."[47] In a memorandum produced by Minister for Immigration Athol Townley on the "Amendment of Nationality and Citizenship Act—Grounds for Depriving Naturalised Persons of Australian Citizenship," attention was drawn to the fact that equivalent Canadian legislation, although broadly similar to Australia's, did not contain a provision depriving a naturalised citizen of their citizenship if they were imprisoned within five years of being naturalised.[48] This continued a long-term trend of Australia, Canada, and Aotearoa New Zealand constantly comparing their nationality and citizenship legislation with each other, as they were based on the same model.

Townley acknowledged the concern expressed by some surrounding the deprivation of citizenship provisions in the current legislation, while at the same time trying to assuage this concern in a speech at the opening of the Citizenship Convention in 1958:

> A surprising variety of people during recent months have expressed some concern about what they believed to be discrimination between naturalized Australian citizens and natural-born Australian citizens as a result of certain provisions, particularly Section 21, of the Nationality and Citizenship Act. These provisions, as some of you know, can be used to deprive a naturalized citizen of his Australian citizenship under certain conditions, such as if he commits acts of disloyalty or certain crimes. In actual fact these provisions have almost never been invoked.[49]

The Australian government then proceeded to determine exactly what its Canadian counterpart had done in the recent revision of its own citizenship legislation, especially in regard to the distinctions between naturalised and natural-born citizens.[50] It received extracts from the parliamentary debates in the Canadian House of Commons surrounding the passage of the legislation at the end of 1958, specifically, a speech by Minister for Citizenship and Immigration Ellen L. Fairclough on the introduction of the bill from its High Commission in Ottawa:

Mrs. Fairclough: Mr. Speaker, the primary purpose of this bill is to remove certain discriminations which now exist against other than natural-born Canadian citizens in relation to loss of Canadian citizenship and, in addition, to make it clear that a person who does not take the oath of allegiance in good faith at the time of acquiring Canadian citizenship is liable to have his Canadian citizenship revoked, subject to the right of such person to a hearing before a commission of court as provided by the act. The bill also makes provision for obtaining a ruling from an independent tribunal if doubt exists as to whether a person has ceased to be a Canadian citizen under the act.[51]

Secretary of the Department of Immigration Sir Tasman Heyes replied to his counterpart in the Department of External Affairs in August 1960 that:

The debates in the House of Commons have been read with interest. What strikes us most forcibly here is not what was said, but what was apparently left unsaid, in regard to the continued existence of Section 18 of the Canadian Act, whereby naturalized Canadians (as distinct from "natural born" citizens) can apparently still lose citizenship through residence abroad….We shall be interested to learn of any intention of the Government to amend Section 18, or of any pressure which may develop for such amendment. It was considered here that removal of discrimination between naturalised and Australian born people inevitably entailed repeal of Section 20 of our Act, corresponding in principle to the Canadian Section 18.[52]

Heyes followed this up with a further request in August 1960 for the Australian High Commission in Ottawa to "ascertain where there has been any change in Canadian Citizenship law or if any change is contemplated."[53] The Department of External Affairs received a prompt reply the following month: "In reply to your memo number 271 of 1st September, 1960, no significant change has been made in the Canadian Citizenship Act, nor has there been any open political pressure of any magnitude for such change."[54]

So, the government decided to introduce a Nationality and Citizenship Bill in October 1960, but it did not deal with the main concerns expressed particularly by Dutch migrants about the discrimination against them and other naturalised citizens; instead, it focused on more practical matters of the naturalisation process. I would argue that this was a reflection of the continued strength of Britishness at this time, as it was still considered important to differentiate between naturalised and natural-born citizens:

Except in the details referred to below, the above Bill is in accordance with Cabinet Decision No. 938 dated 2 August, 1960, which authorised the introduction of a Bill to amend section 36 of the Nationality and Citizenship Act—(a) to provide that an applicant for citizenship should state to an officer the information in support of his application required by section 36, eliminating the present requirement of that section for the information to be contained in a statutory declaration, and (b) to abolish the present requirement of section 36 for an applicant to produce certificates of character from three Australian citizens.[55]

In an explanatory memorandum on the legislation, Minister for Immigration Alexander Downer outlined one of the main motivations behind the bill: "These amendments are designed to simplify the rather complex application procedure for Australian citizenship….This has been found to be beyond what could reasonably be expected from alien new settlers, and is proving a serious deterrent to many would-be applicants for naturalization."[56] He then drew particular attention to one of the current requirements that it was the intention of the legislation to change:

> Many migrants who wish to become Australian citizens are extremely diffident about asking Australian citizens to certify that they are persons of good repute, as they are now required to do so, knowing full well that in many instances the Australian citizens are not really in a position to vouch for them. Some new settlers are anxious not to impair their good relations with their Australian acquaintances, sometimes achieved only after careful cultivation, by a request which might embarrass their friends.[57]

Downer attempted to bring a personal touch to what was practical legislation in his second reading speech on the bill later that month:

> Thus, a somewhat cold, legal process will give way to what I hope will be always a friendly encounter between an applicant and a Departmental official. Without wishing to claim too much, I am hopeful that, if the House agrees to this simplification of procedure, the whole machinery of naturalization will become easier, more co-operative, and more attractive to the many thousands we are anxious to clothe with full citizenship rights.[58]

The reference to "full citizenship rights" should be particularly noted, as this was an important shift in political rhetoric on the issue. The continued prevalence of Britishness was apparent in Downer's comment on the proposed legislation being "an example of the Government's constant desire to bring more and more of our settlers from Europe and other lands into the all-embracing status of British subjects and Australian Citizens."[59] The legislation passed and came into law by December 1960. In a press statement by Downer that month he said application for naturalisation by migrants was now so simple that every eligible person could apply without difficulty. However, he appealed directly to those migrants that were eligible to apply for naturalisation but had not yet done so, "We want you to apply for Australian Citizenship….

But you must remember it is a worthwhile prize and you must be worthy of it."[60] He added that "It is the most valuable gift Australia can offer you....We have made it easier for you to seek it....Now I hope you will take advantage of the new and freer legislation."[61] The essence of the legislation then was encapsulated in some notes on the citizenship bill: "The purpose of this Bill, therefore, is to help migrants to become Australians in law without any real weakening of the conditions governing the grant of citizenship."[62] Hence, the legislation was not exactly groundbreaking. But it again illustrates the gradual change that was taking place on the issue. More substantive change would have to wait until the demise of Britishness, which was just about to begin with the UK's first application for entry into the EEC in 1961.

The *Citizenship Act* of 1969

The *Nationality and Citizenship Act* was changed in 1955, 1960, 1969, and 1973. As mentioned above, the 1955 and 1960 amendments were minimal, as views took another decade to begin to shift.[63] The significant changes in 1973 have rightly been given considerable attention by scholars. However, the 1969 changes were also important, and in some ways laid the foundation for the subsequent changes in 1973. Therefore, I will focus on them next.[64] In late 1967 the *West Australian* suggested amending Australian naturalisation ceremonies so that applicants would only be required to swear allegiance to the Queen of Australia. It justified this move in terms of the goal of increasing rates of naturalisation and highlighted that non-British migrants had no basis for cherishing British ties.[65] Commonwealth Director of Migration G. E. Hitchins wrote a letter early the following year to Peter Heydon, Secretary of the Department of Immigration, in which he recommended amending the Oath of Allegiance to remove the reference to the "Queen, her heirs and successors" and simply asking the applicant to declare their loyalty to "Australia and the Constitution" as well as contemplating whether the renunciation of former allegiance was really required and considering a reduction in the qualifying period for naturalisation to perhaps three years. He added that there was some opposition by certain migrants to swearing allegiance to the Queen, whereas they would not be against declaring loyalty to Australia.[66]

A Departmental Committee to review the *Nationality and Citizenship Act 1948–1967* also made some recommendations on amendments. In particular, with the aim of placing more importance on Australian citizenship, it recommended that the title of the Act be revised from *Nationality and Citizenship Act* to *Australian Citizenship Act*. This would follow Canada's Act. In addition, in furtherance of the Minister's opinion that more emphasis should be placed on "Australian Citizenship" than in the past, it suggested the inclusion of a new Section (similar to one in the *Canadian Citizenship Act*) allowing that when Australians were asked to state their national status, it would be acceptable to declare "Australian citizen."[67] In terms of practicalities, an Inter-Departmental Committee stated that the impact of this on other federal legislation could be handled with a clause in the Act itself, but State governments would need to introduce legislation individually to make sure that the basic description "Australian citizen" met their legislative provisions regarding British subjects.[68] In April 1968 Heydon drew the attention of the Minister for Immigration, Billy Snedden, to a new provision in the proposals for revision of the *Nationality and Citizenship Act* that he had under consideration which would allow Australians, when required to state their national status, to declare that they were an "Australian citizen," and that mention of "British subject" in other Commonwealth legislation would be considered to refer to both Australian citizen or British subject.[69] Furthermore, he suggested the following response to a question without notice by Ian Wilson, Liberal MP for Sturt, on the subject:

> I recognise, as the honorable member says, that misunderstandings can arise out of the use of the phrase "British" to describe the status of Australians, now that the phrase is used by the British Government, and indeed internationally, to mean people and things pertaining to the United Kingdom alone. This fact has not lacked the Government's attention as for example in the description of Australian passports as British passports which has now ended.[70]

But the following month Heydon qualified his remarks to Snedden in his comments on one of the Inter-Departmental Committee's main recommendations:

> The time may well come when our laws generally will cease to give such a privileged position to settlers from other Commonwealth countries—and will attach significance instead to the status of Australian citizens, the prerequisites for which will be common to all settlers; but while our laws remain as they are, our nationality legislation should be attuned to them.[71]

He added that the Committee's report stated that a British subject with resident status had all the key rights and obligations of citizenship, and in particular, he could not be deported after five years (crime-free) residence; to give them the right to apply for citizenship after five years did no more than give "de jure" acknowledgement of a current "de facto" context.[72]

The legal consequences of emphasising Australian *Citizenship* over *British Nationality* were discussed within the Attorney-General's Department in late 1968:

> I understand that the proposal that a section be inserted to the effect that whenever Australians are required to state their national status, it would be sufficient to state "Australian citizen" was taken from the Canadian Citizenship Act 1946 which has an equivalent section. While this Act declares Canadian citizens to be British subjects, it does not specifically provide for British nationality....It would seem to me that before the Attorney-General could make any public statement as to the proposed changes there must be some clarification of the Commonwealth's intention as regards nationality and Australian citizens being British subjects.[73]

This highlighted the differences between the initial citizenship legislation adopted by both Canada and Australia in the post-Second-World-War period, which related to Britishness operating in a bicultural society in the former and a predominantly monocultural one in the latter.[74]

The member for Hindmarsh, Clyde Cameron, expressed the ALP Opposition's view on the Liberal-National Coalition government's proposals in late 1968:

> The Opposition, generally speaking, and subject to a further examination of this proposal—we will not have an opportunity to examine it further until the Bill is introduced next year—is generally in accord with what is now proposed. However, I raise at once some doubt as to the advisability of giving to any person, not matter what the circumstances that may exist, the right to be naturalised after only 3 years in this country.[75]

This opposition to reducing the period that a non-British migrant had to wait before being naturalised is interesting, as the ALP position would change quite drastically in just a few years. Cameron added, though, that "I am pleased indeed that the Government proposes to drop this old Union Jack idea of calling ourselves British subjects....I do not like the word 'subject.'"[76] This, on the other hand, was a much more traditional ALP position.

Newspapers also reacted generally very positively to the proposals. According to the *Age*: "the decision...will, in effect, reduce from five to three years the time which alien immigrants of good character, and with a reasonable command of English, must wait before they become eligible for citizenship."[77] *The Melbourne Herald* maintained that "For many foreign-born migrants, the proposals announced last night for easing the conditions of naturalisation will be a practical form of welcome to Australia."[78] The *Sydney Morning Herald* argued that "Those who have willingly committed themselves to Australia are entitled to expect that everything will be done to remove unnecessary barriers against obtaining full citizenship rights....But the legislation continues to recognise the privileged position of migrants from Britain and Commonwealth countries over those from Europe."[79] *The Daily Telegraph* asserted that "A migrant who needs more than three years to decide to become a citizen is hardly worth having anyway—and putting those who do want citizenship into a kind of limbo for five years could be psychologically harmful."[80] *Il Globo*, an Italian-Australian publication, triumphantly declared that "Australian citizens will have to consider themselves above all 'Australian,' and 'British subjects' in a secondary sense only....Our paper has fought ceaselessly for years for such a justified reform."[81]

Minister for Immigration, Billy Snedden, highlighted in his second reading speech on the Bill that "The Bill...proposed some changes which are fundamental to our national status and the concept of Australian citizenship, as well as to the rules under which our citizenship may be acquired."[82] There was a diverse range of responses to the Bill in Parliament, although most approved of the general principle of the legislation. Wilson commented that "There is no doubt there is a growing sense of Australian nationality amongst the people of this country....I applaud the decision to give primacy to the expression 'Australian citizen.'"[83] Arthur Calwell criticised the reduction in the period of naturalisation for non-British migrants: "I think that our gift of naturalisation is so great and so valuable that it should not be lightly regarded....If is necessary to attract all sorts of good people to Australia from all countries I do not think that we should cheapen the value of our citizenship by making it available too easily to a lot of people who want it."[84]

The *Australian Citizenship Act* of 1973

The *Australian Citizenship Act* of 1973 was the next major reform of Australian Citizenship and Nationality legislation. As mentioned above, it built on the reforms of the *Citizenship Act* of 1969. One of the major elements the Bill introduced was a suggested new Oath (or Affirmation) of Allegiance: firstly, it removed the renunciation of allegiance which had been a source of considerable emotional turmoil for some migrants, and secondly, allegiance was now to be sworn to the Constitution of Australia—specific mention of the Queen was not made. The Bill also provided for a transitional period of two years (after the new Act commenced) during which:

> Commonwealth citizens, Irish citizens, and South African and Pakistani citizens already resident in Australia, will be able to become Australian citizens after one year's residence; and...aliens who have lived in Commonwealth countries or served under those countries' Governments may have such residence or service accepted as part of the new qualifying period of three years' residence for the grant of Australian citizenship.[85]

The Bill did not adjust the context in which citizens of Commonwealth countries, whether they became Australian citizens or not, carried on having the status of British or Commonwealth of Nations subjects and hence had benefits including the vote and ability to be employed in the public service under Parliamentary legislation.[86] Nevertheless, it was emphasised that the Bill would remove (after a transitional period) the past previous discrimination between citizens of Commonwealth nations and others, particularly by requiring the same period of residence for all, and providing everyone with the chance to attend citizenship ceremonies.[87]

In his second reading speech on the Bill, Minister for Immigration, Al Grassby, emphasised the main thrust of the legislation, which was to establish equality between all migrants:

> The guiding principles for the Government in the vitally important matter of the grant of Australian Citizenship is that there should not be discrimination between different groups of settlers seeking to join the family of the nation. Wherever they were born—whatever their nationality—whatever the colour of their complexion—they should all be able to become Australian citizens under just the same conditions....So it is that this Bill provides for all, regardless of origins, the same requirements as to residence, good character, knowledge of the language and of the rights and duties of citizenship, and intention to live here permanently.[88]

The Bill also stipulated that all those applying for citizenship, apart from children under sixteen, would need to take the Oath or Affirmation of Allegiance, with no regard to their previous nationality. This meant that migrants from all the thirty-one Commonwealth countries would now have the same chance as other migrants to participate in citizenship ceremonies appropriately marking the significant event of their becoming citizens.[89] Grassby also emphasised another notable change in the proposed legislation:

It is important to end the confusion which has been permitted to continue since the Citizenship Act of 1949 and the use of terminology which has given many Australians the mistaken impression that they are not only Australians citizens but also citizens of the United Kingdom of Great Britain and Northern Ireland. This has not been the case for twenty-four years yet the past Government permitted Australians to remain confused on this point.[90]

The Opposition, however, opposed all main features of the Bill. Philip Lynch, former Minister for Immigration and Deputy Leader of the Opposition, fired the opening salvo:

The Opposition rejects the major provisions of this Bill for a number of fundamental reasons. The legislation seeks to remove the position of preferment which British migrants have enjoyed since the inception of Australia's immigration program...our early arrivals with relatively limited exceptions, came almost solely...from the British Isles....The Government seems intent on ending that special relationship....I have...indicated that the Opposition is opposed to the proposal to delete all references to the Queen from the oath of allegiance taken by migrants at citizenship ceremonies. It is equally opposed to the Government's proposal to omit the renunciation of allegiance to another country.[91]

But Grassby did also receive support from his side of the house. Maxwell Oldmeadow, the member for Holt, rose to support the Bill and stated that he and his side of the house did not share the alarm expressed by Lynch. There were no disincentives to British migrants. He also drew attention to the fact that Grassby had stated that renunciation of former citizenship served no legal purpose, though his most salient comments were: "A nation which has come of age, which has confidence in its future and has successfully emerged from the shadows of colonialism neither requires nor will accept such a sacrifice.... Australian citizenship must always be preserved and solidified by its highest common factors."[92] The Opposition, however, was not finished: Alexander Forbes, the member for Barker, chimed in with a reference to British migrants: "Just who does the Minister for Immigration think he is kidding? Since when did people who are placed in a privileged position object because there was discrimination in their favour?"[93] He scathingly added, with a reference to non-British migrants, that "Citizenship is an act of identification with the adopted country and with the values and mores of its inhabitants....Persons who cannot accept these things have not sufficiently identified as to be ready for citizenship."[94]

But the government was not to be cowed on the Bill. The ALP member for Bowman, Leonard Keogh, made a lively riposte to Forbes:

> As the honourable member for Barker (Dr. Forbes) was making his speech this evening I expected him to break out at any time into a verse from "Rule Britannia." My colleague, the honourable member for Liley (Mr. Doyle) said to me when he walked into the chamber that he felt sure that he must have been in Rhodesia listening to Ian Smith....The Immigration policy of the Government seeks to rid the nation of the inconsistencies, inequalities and discrimination that we believe should no longer be allowed to exist when we are seeking to bring people from various countries and to welcome them as citizens in their own right in Australia.[95]

Therefore, Keogh criticised the Imperial hanging-on of the Opposition at the same time as stressing the positive moves the government was trying to make to remove the discrimination between different types of migrants. Grassby picked up on this theme in his reply to MPs' responses to his second reading speech:

> The Opposition has attempted tonight to turn back the tide of history. It has rejected the concept of Australian citizenship as the badge of a free, strong and independent people....How could any Minister responsible for immigration and citizenship go out to the million here and now and the tens of thousands still coming and draft them off like so many sheep and cattle, saying: "You go to the one year pen; you go to the 3-year pen; you go to the 5-year pen....Italians, Dutch, Germans, Greeks and Lebanese to the right and wait for 3 years; Tongans, Zambians, Canadians, British and Indians to the left and wait for one year if you are light enough and 5 years if you are not."[96]

Grassby pleaded to all members of Parliament to look at the citizenship legislation in a non-partisan way instead of on the level of petty party politics. The Bill simply recommended that all discrimination be removed from the conditions for the granting of Australian citizenship to migrants.[97]

In another speech on the *Australian Citizenship Bill of 1973*, Grassby attempted to draw links between the current citizenship legislation and its predecessor in 1969:

> The present leader of the Opposition when Minister for Immigration introduced a Citizenship Bill in 1969 which showed a progressive outlook by recognising the growing importance of the status of Australian citizen. That Bill specifically provided that an Australian when asked to state his nationality had only to say "I am an Australian citizen"....."What this Government now puts to this House in the present Australian Citizenship Bill is that it is time we progressed still further towards reality by ending the artificial discriminations in the present Act, in the matter of requirements for Australian citizenship."[98]

However, his call fell on deaf ears. Though the Bill passed the House of Representatives relatively easily due to the government's majority in that house, it faced a much tougher time in the Senate, where the Opposition held the balance of power. Grassby was forced to accept some amendments to his legislation, in particular, migrants having the choice to swear allegiance to the Australian Constitution *or* to the Queen.

So, I have shown above how the end of the British World led to a redefinition of citizenship in Australia between the 1950s and 1970s in relation to other ethnic groups. The chapter will now turn to Aborigines and the redefinition of citizenship in Australia between the 1950s and 1970s.

Aboriginal Policy During the 1950s

The *West Australian* newspaper outlined the Commonwealth government's policy on Aborigines in early 1950:

> The policy of the Federal Government in the administration of native affairs is to try to raise the status of the aborigines to enable them to take their place as members of the community with full citizenship rights. It includes the pursuit of a positive plan of education for children and adults, social service benefits, health services and conditions of employment.[99]

In May 1950 the Minister for Territories, Paul Hasluck, announced that the "Commonwealth Government, exercising a national responsibility for the welfare of the whole Australian people, should cooperate with State Governments in measures for the social advancement as well as the protection of aboriginal races throughout the country."[100] He put this broad intention into concrete form the following year by recommending in a memorandum for Cabinet that "The Commonwealth Government invite State Governments to be represented at a Conference, to be held in Canberra in August, 1951, of Federal and State Ministers responsible for native welfare, and that the Department of Territories prepare the agenda and supporting proposals for circulation to the State Governments beforehand."[101] A further key suggestion was that:

> A proposal be placed before this conference to establish an Australian Council of Native Welfare, composed of the Federal and State Ministers and the permanent heads of Departments charged with native welfare;….and that the Council communicate its decisions in the form of recommendations to the Government or Governments responsible for executive actions.[102]

In terms of practicalities, he recommended that "the principle of special financial contribution by the Commonwealth for funds necessary for the advancement of native welfare be accepted." He added that "the Treasurer, in consultation with the Minister for Territories, be asked to consider the means by which proposals for expenditure in accordance with this principle can best be handled and any consequential proposals which should be submitted to the States."[103]

At the actual conference in September 1951 the following significant statement was made on the citizenship status of Aborigines:

> The Commonwealth and States, having assimilation as the objective of native welfare measures, desire to see all persons born in Australia enjoying full citizenship. It is also desirable that there should be uniformity throughout Australia in the enjoyment of the privileges of citizenship, and any limits which may be set on these privileges....There are at the present time in Australia many persons of aboriginal or part-aboriginal blood who are prepared for and capable of accepting the full responsibilities of citizenship. In the future, as the measures for the advancement of native welfare show results, the number of persons so qualified will increase.[104]

So, citizenship rights would be extended to Aborigines as and when they reached a certain level of "development." Several initiatives took place in regard to Aborigines and citizenship over the course of the decade. At the beginning of 1954 *The Courier-Mail* reported that "The remaining semi-hostile aborigines in Queensland will be asked to fill in a questionnaire for the new Commonwealth-wide Census." It added that "the Queensland Federal Electoral Officer (Mr. E. S. Olsen) said that Torres Strait Islanders would be included also....Every possible attempt will be made to seek further data on our natives, if they are willing to co-operate."[105] The State Returned Serviceman's League in Queensland also publicly declared its support for full citizenship rights for all Aboriginal ex-servicemen. The view expressed was that if an Aboriginal person was good enough to serve his country then he deserved to be given full citizenship rights as well.[106] The *West Australian* drew attention to plans by the Trade Union movement to include Aborigines in their ranks: "The way is now open for Northern Territory aborigines to become unionists....The Amalgamated Engineering Union at a conference with the Administrator (Mr. Wise) and Administration officials agreed to admit natives and to lower education standards for apprentices."[107] Therefore, there was a growing cross-section of Australian society that was vocalising its support for Aborigines to be awarded citizenship rights just like other Australians.

A few years later, in 1957, the General Secretary of the Australian Workers Union, T. Dougherty, expressed his support for an improvement in the conditions of Aborigines to Lady Jessie Street, who was affiliated with the Anti-Slavery League of the UK, and who in many ways had dedicated her life to improving the status and conditions of Aborigines:

> I am sure the children of Australia's oldest inhabitants do not know that many of them who are working on pastoral properties are entitled to award rates and conditions and, of course, the main exploiters of them in this country, the big pastoralists, will not go to the trouble to inform them of their rights....The A.W.U. will continue to do anything possible to improve the wage standards and conditions of all aborigines, as its officials and members, along with all other decent thinking people throughout the Commonwealth, believe that the injustices and shocking treatment, which has been the lot of the Aborigines and has been a blot on Australia's history for far too long, SHOULD BE REMOVED AS QUICKLY AS POSSIBLE.[108]

So, there was growing pressure upon the Commonwealth government in the 1950s from a range of sources to improve the situation of Aborigines across the country so that they could exercise the full rights of Australian citizenship. However, one argument that the government made repeatedly was that it did not have power to legislate for Aborigines outside of the Northern Territory. There was then agitation for this constitutional arrangement to be changed. In response to one particular exhortation by Mr. Joske in May 1957, Hasluck gave the following reply:

> Most of the practical work which can be done to advance the welfare of the native people has to be done in the States by State Departments, such as the Department of Education, Department of Lands, Department of Agriculture, Department of Health, the Housing Commission, The Department of Justice, the Child Welfare Department, and so on. Even if the powers were transferred to the Commonwealth, it would still be necessary for the Commonwealth to use State instrumentalities in any practical efforts it made to assist the aborigines.[109]

Lady Jessie Street attempted to counter Hasluck's argument by approaching Don Dunstan, then a member of the South Australian Legislative Assembly (and future Premier of the state) that same month: "I am inclined to think that if we can get the different States to amend their laws concerning aboriginals to bring them in line with the status and conditions of aboriginals in the Northern Territory, we will establish uniformity of treatment of aborigines and pave the way for the Commonwealth amendment of the Constitution."[110]

Pressure continued to be applied upon the Commonwealth government, as illustrated by a letter sent to Hasluck at the end of 1957 by W. W. Greenridge, Director of the Anti-Slavery and Aborigines Protection Society:

> The Conference of Federal and State Ministers on Native Welfare, held in Canberra in 1951, agreed that the common goal throughout Australia, should be to give the aborigines the same opportunities, rights, privileges and status as Australians of European race. In pursuance of that decision the Native Welfare Ordinance was passed, which purported to give them citizenship, but it contains a provision enabling their citizenship to be suspended by declaring them "wards."[111]

Aside from this notable criticism, Greenridge also made several other recommendations, drawing on a comprehensive study undertaken by Street:

> Lady Street has suggested that the aborigines should be taught the basic principles of democracy by making it possible for them to elect representatives to the Native Welfare Councils. We support that recommendation. She noticed that…at cattle and sheep stations Child Endowment for aborigine children was paid to the Managers of the stations instead of to the parents of the child. We feel that steps should be taken to acquaint the aborigines of their rights and to assist them in enforcing them, and that Child Endowment should be paid to the persons entitled to it.[112]

The Society attempted to keep Hasluck on side by saying that they had been "encouraged to make these suggestions to you by your sympathetic replies to previous communications, and we hope that you will not interpret our remarks as criticism.…We only desire to co-operate with you in improving the lot of the aborigine, and are well aware of what you have done to ameliorate their lot already."[113] Tim Rowse argued that Hasluck once maintained that Indigenous Australians had always been citizens. Instead, he asserted, they were citizens to whom additional laws, some supportive, many damaging, had been applied. Hasluck did not regard initiatives to improve the conditions of Aborigines as the granting of "citizenship" to Indigenous people. Reformers, he maintained, should stop calling for Indigenous Australians to be "granted" citizenship.[114]

Awarding of the Right to Vote to Aborigines in 1961

There was considerable pressure on the government from various lobby groups to give Aborigines the vote for the federal franchise. One of the most vocal lobbyists was Lady Jessie Street. In a letter to Prime Minister Robert Menzies in early 1960 she placed the refusal of the Australian government to give Aborigines the vote in a broader international context:

> Canada is giving their Indians the vote; I enclose a copy of the Canadian Bill.…It seems that the Governments of Australia, South Africa, the U.S.A. and Portugal

are the only ones who have not changed their attitude and still deny political rights to their coloured people....In view of these developments I am writing to ask you to consider reviewing our Australian policy towards our Aborigines. I believe that all adult Aborigines should be given full political rights....I feel most humiliated that Australia should be regarded as so backward in her treatment of her native people.[115]

President of the Western Australian Native Welfare Council, E. C. Gare, also wrote to Menzies in late 1960, adding to the pressure with some very effective constitutional arguments:

My Council has requested me to submit for the consideration of your Cabinet, a proposal that an amendment be made to the Commonwealth Electoral Act for the purpose of allowing Australian Aborigines to enrol and vote for the Federal Parliament....As the Commonwealth Government is prohibited from making *Special* laws for the people of the Aborigine race it would seem that that race should come within the jurisdiction of all laws common to other Australians and there should be no discrimination against Aborigines in any way by special law. If this argument holds, it is unconstitutional to exclude aborigines from voting for Commonwealth Parliament.[116]

Acting Secretary of the Department of Territories, J. E. Willoughby, wrote to the Secretary of the Prime Minister's Department in early 1961 about Gare's letter:

The legality of the proposals by the Chairman of the Western Australia Native Welfare Council is for decision by the Attorney-General's Department. It would seem however, that a more positive approach, and one more in keeping with the present development of aborigines throughout Australia, could be made by the State adopting common standards in relation to definition, exemption and control.[117]

However, Alexander Downer, in his capacity as Acting Prime Minister, only conceded to Gare that there appeared to be no constitutional impediment to the revision of the *Commonwealth Electoral Act* that he suggested.[118]

Gare, though, followed up his letter with a further one to Menzies in April 1961 in which he maintained that "the Commonwealth has a duty to see that all persons born in Australia are full and free citizens of the Commonwealth and entitled to vote for Commonwealth elections irrespective of any State law as to State Electoral enrolment." And he hoped that "early action can be taken to amend the Commonwealth Electoral Act so as to remove this injustice against Aborigines."[119] Downer replied to him again in his capacity as Acting Prime Minister a few months later:

As previously stated, I am advised that the Constitution places no bar on the Commonwealth Parliament allowing the enrolment and voting of aborigines. Whilst I would not agree that the provisions of the Commonwealth Electoral Act which at present prevent certain aborigines from voting are contrary to section 51 (xxvii.) of the Constitution, I would agree that there is nothing in section 51 (xxvii.) to prevent the Commonwealth from extending the Commonwealth franchise to all aborigines, if it should be desired to do this as a matter of policy.[120]

In actual fact, at the instigation of the Minister for the Interior, the government had already agreed that a select committee be appointed to look into and report back on whether the right to registration and the franchise currently awarded by the *Commonwealth Electoral Act 1918–1953* on individuals mentioned in section 39 of that legislation should be expanded with or without conditions, restrictions, or qualifications to all aboriginal groups of Australia; aboriginal groups of Australia grouped in specific categories, and if so, what categories; and if so, the adjustments, if any, that should be made to the clauses of that legislation regarding registration or the franchise.[121] The Committee gathered evidence and deliberated for several months. The constitutional expert, K. H. Bailey, corresponded with the committee towards the end of 1961. One of his most significant comments related to Section 51 (xxvi.) of the constitution:

> The words "other than the aboriginal race in any State" contained in Section 51 (xxvi.) often give rise to misunderstanding because they are read as constituting a limitation upon the powers of the Parliament to make laws generally. The true position is, however, that they constitute a limitation only upon the power to make "special" laws with respect to "the people of any race"—that is, upon the power contained in section 51 (xxvi.) itself.[122]

The *Report of the Select Committee on Voting Rights of Aborigines* was subsequently tabled in Parliament on 19 October 1961. The major recommendations were that the Commonwealth Electoral Act should be revised to allow for: all aborigines of voting age to be awarded the franchise; registration should be voluntary but exercising the franchise should be compulsory for aborigines who were registered; early administrative action should take place to make registration and exercising the franchise compulsory for aborigines in New South Wales and Queensland as these aborigines had long been a part of the Australian community; and Aborigines who were entitled to be registered and to exercise the franchise should be informed of their right.[123]

Press reaction to the report was generally extremely positive, with *The Canberra Times* remarking that "Few Parliamentary reports have had more human warmth than that of the Select Committee on Voting Rights for Aborigines which has recommended that the right to vote at all Commonwealth elections be accorded to all Aboriginal and Torres Strait Islander subjects of the Queen."[124] The *Sydney Morning Herald* hoped "that the Federal Government will accept the committee's view and, in due course, legislate accordingly."[125] The *Age* added that Aborigines "Unlike women…have no suffragette movement to press their case, but joint committee of the House of Representatives has surveyed their case with a calm, unprejudiced eye, and recommended without qualifications they should enjoy the same voting rights as white Australians."[126] The *West Australian* related the report to the situation in Western Australia: "Though the committee was confined to consideration of the franchise, its conclusions in reaching unanimous finding that all aborigines and Torres Strait Islanders be given the right to a Federal vote carry the conviction that all natives should have full citizenship."[127]

Increasing overseas interest in the plight of the Aborigines was communicated in a telegram from the Department of External Affairs to all posts at the beginning of 1962:

> Overseas interest in the Aborigines is still small, but it has increased during the past year, and could rapidly increase still further, particularly in countries whose policies are greatly influenced by racial discrimination. As the number of colonial dependencies diminishes, the scope of anti-colonist attacks will become increasingly restricted, and political agitators in Asia, Africa and Latin America are likely to indulge instead in emotional criticism of other countries' domestic policies, especially where these appear to involve discrimination by white people against coloured people.[128]

Thus, overseas interest in the Australian government's policies towards its Aborigines was becoming a growing concern.

The Cabinet considered the Report of the *Select Committee on Voting Rights of Aborigines* and agreed that the *Electoral Act* should be revised to: give Aborigines and Torres Strait Islanders of voting age the right to register and exercise the franchise; make exercising the franchise after registering, but not registering itself, compulsory for them; and make the exercise of pressure or undue influence, in relation to registration, an offence on top of the current offence in relation to exercising the franchise.[129] In April 1962 the *West Australian* emphasised the significance of the legislative changes based on this decision: "The Bill to extend Federal voting rights to all Australian aborigines is a landmark in post-Federation history.…It can now be only a matter of time before natives in all parts of Australia are given the right to vote at State as well as Federal elections."[130] But the following month Lady Jessie Street took a contrary, much more critical view:

> Gestures are being made of appointing Select Committees, amending laws and regulations…to give the appearance of removing discriminations against aborigines, but the basis of these discriminations, sections 127[131] and 51 (xxvi) remains. While

aborigines have not the constitutional status and rights of full citizens they will be victims of discrimination.[132]

Repeal and amendment of these sections was the basis of the 1967 referendum.

The 1967 Referendum

There is some considerable historiographical debate surrounding the significance of the 1967 referendum. The referendum ultimately sought to repeal Section 127 of the constitution and repeal the words "other than the Aboriginal race in any State" from Section 51 (xxvi). According to Rowse, "The common narration of the 1967 referendum is to exaggerate its benefits, declaring it to be the moment when Aborigines attained 'citizenship'....This is strictly speaking, a misconception."[133] Nevertheless, he does concede that the amendment of the Constitution in the 1967 referendum is regularly reflected upon by Aborigines of a younger generation as the point at which Aboriginal people were "granted citizenship."[134] Bain Attwood and Andrew Markus went even further and maintained that "The 1967 referendum to alter Australia's Constitution is now seen as an event that marked a major turning point in Aboriginal-European relations in Australia."[135] Terry Widders and Greg Noble argued, though, that "The supposed coming into political existence of indigenous people through the 1967 referendum, as it had been mythologised in white history, has by no means been a democratic panacea, and nor has it been seen as such by indigenous people."[136] Christine Flether contrarily asserted that "The 1967 constitutional referendum was the turning point in Aboriginal affairs—a watershed in their cultural and political freedoms."[137] And Michael Dodson stated that "The 1967 referendum, at least in principle, lifted many of the formal and overt forms of discrimination....Citizenship provided a ticket of entry into the political system."[138] My own opinion is that though its practical effect is certainly debatable, its symbolic value was extremely important.

Government moves towards considering constitutional amendments regarding Aborigines began in early 1965 with a Cabinet Submission by the Attorney-General, Billy Snedden:

> There would assuredly be international approbation of any move to repeal section 127, as it savours of racial discrimination. Its repeal could remove a possible source of misconstruction in the international field....I think also that the average elector would feel that either the Commonwealth should have the power in sec-

tion 51 (xxvi) in relation to all races, including people of the aboriginal race or ought not to have the power at all; and I believe the failure to include a proposal to delete the underlined parts might well prejudice the success of a referendum that wants the repeal of section 127.[139]

However, the Cabinet only agreed to the abolition of Section 127 of the Constitution being put to referendum simultaneously as the question of the nexus.[140,141]

This led to pressure being applied on the government by New South Wales State Secretary of FCAATSI, Faith Bandler, on 30 April 1965. FCAATSI was the leading organisation calling for constitutional amendments regarding Aborigines,[142] and Bandler was a particularly passionate and conscientious advocate of the organisation:

A Referendum to amend the Commonwealth Constitution will be held later this year and the Government has already agreed to include in this the repeal of Section 127 which discriminates against Aborigines by excluding them from the census. However there is another section of the Constitution which also discriminates against Aborigines and the Government is still hesitant as to whether or not to include repeal of Section 51 Clause xxvi in the forthcoming Referendum.[143]

Snedden attempted to secure Cabinet agreement to have the words "other than the aboriginal race in any State" removed from the Constitution again on 23 August 1965,[144] but the Cabinet once again refused to support this.[145] A few months later, the *Sydney Morning Herald* questioned whether the proposed referendum went far enough as "it will still leave the Commonwealth Government without any direct responsibility for Aboriginal advancement outside the Northern Territory, and it will still leave power of 'discrimination' in the hands of the various States."[146] Mrs. L. Lippmann, Convenor of the Legislative Reform Committee of FCAATSI, commented in a letter to Snedden early the following year that it appeared likely that proposals for the inclusion of the amendment of Section 51, Placitum xxvi of the Constitution would be put before Parliament. And she emphasised the importance of this initiative, which would enable FCAATSI and other organisations working for the advancement of Aborigines to vociferously campaign for the referendum proposals.[147] Her enthusiasm was most likely due to Menzies' successor as Prime Minister, Harold Holt, taking office just a few weeks earlier. He was considered more receptive to including the second proposal on Section 51 (xxvi), and consequently announced a few weeks later that the government had decided not to hold the proposed referendum (which included only the one proposal) that year.[148]

It was left to the new Attorney-General, Nigel Bowen, to raise the issue again at the beginning of 1967. He argued in a Cabinet Submission that:

> The Government announce that it will hold a referendum to seek legislative power for the Commonwealth with respect to aborigines by omitting the words "other than the aboriginal race in any State" from section 51(xxvi.) and, if the referendum is successful, will hold discussion with the States to formulate a joint policy whereby the States will be responsible for administration, but the Commonwealth will have a role of policy participation.[149]

The Cabinet finally agreed to this course of action the following month.[150] Holt announced the government's intention to include two proposals concerning Aborigines in a constitutional referendum very soon after: "Our intention, Mr. Speaker, is to put through the necessary legislation relating to these proposals as soon as practicable….I expect it to be introduced in this House within the next week or two….We proposed to have the measures passed by the two Houses as expeditiously as possible."[151] The Leader of the Opposition, Gough Whitlam, expressed the Opposition's support for both measures.[152] The *Sydney Morning Herald* explained the government's shift in position as a reaction to the persuasive arguments made by William Wentworth, a government backbencher who had introduced a Private Members Bill along similar lines the previous year.[153]

FCAATSI immediately swung into action. It published several information pamphlets to promote a "Yes" vote for the two Aboriginal proposals in the upcoming referendum.[154] It is no exaggeration to say that FCAATSI's extensive campaigning was the reason for the success of the Aboriginal proposals in the referendum on 27 May 1967. An illustration of this is an expose on Bandler in *The Australian Women's Weekly* in May 1967. She maintained that "A Yes vote will mean that the Aboriginal people can come under Commonwealth law….Aborigines are the only Australians who live under six separate laws, one for each State….The eyes of the world are on Australia and her handling of black Australians….Not only Asia is watching but Africa and the whole Western world."[155] The general press reaction to the Aboriginal referendum proposals was overwhelmingly positive.[156] A few days before the referendum Bandler drew attention to the public confusion on the Aboriginal issue in the *Sydney Morning Herald*. She pointed out that many Australians thought a "Yes" victory on the Aboriginal question in the referendum would give Aborigines the vote—whereas in actual fact they already had this. Bandler laid the blame for this confusion firmly at the doorsteps of the federal government and political parties, as they had not played much of a role at all in the campaign. She suggested that perhaps the government thought the Aborigines question would assist it in also securing support on the nexus question. Bandler showed this through the fact that the fifteen-page pamphlet which the Commonwealth government handed out to all voters included only two and a half pages on the Aborigines question.[157]

In the actual event there was an overwhelming majority in support of the constitutional amendments in regard to Aborigines—over 90 per cent (the biggest Yes vote in the history of federal plebiscites)—whereas the nexus proposal failed dismally.[158] Nevertheless, The *Sydney Morning Herald* pointed out that it was depressing that the largest No vote was recorded in parts of Australia where the question had real impact—in other words, in places where there were Aborigines to resent and to be prejudiced about: "The No vote was worst in the three States—Western Australia, South Australia and Queensland—that have been most criticised for their treatment of the remaining Aboriginal population."[159]

After the 1967 referendum the federal government was reluctant to act on its new authority to legislate for Aborigines.[160] The federal government set up an Office of Aboriginal Affairs after the 1967 referendum, but there was little substantive change until the new government in 1972.[161] Hence, Attwood and Markus concluded "that the government's belated decision to conduct the referendum was a rather uninterested, even cynical, one that had little if anything to do with any program of change in Aboriginal affairs, and much more to do with maintaining the status quo, shoring up the government's position at home, and bolstering Australia's image abroad."[162] But as well as allowing the Whitlam government in 1972 to enter the policy field, the successful referendum also put pressure on the subsequent Fraser government to stand up to the Queensland and Western Australia state governments. In this sense, its practical impact was important in the longer term.

International Convention on the Elimination of All Forms of Racial Discrimination, 1960s–1970s

A recurrent theme in terms of Aboriginal policy during the 1960s and 1970s was whether Australia would sign and subsequently ratify the International Convention on the Elimination of All Forms of Racial Discrimination. A survey was undertaken by an Inter-Departmental Committee on Racial Discrimination to determine which parts of Australia's existing legislation contravened the convention as it currently stood. The results of the survey were outlined in April 1964: "The survey has disclosed that there are still remaining a number of discriminatory provisions, but in most cases these provisions are being reviewed by the Departments concerned." In making recommendations, the Committee took into account "the pressures for the removal of racial discrimination that have developed, both within Australia and internationally, and Australia's vulnerability on this issue from an international viewpoint." One of the key recommendations of the Committee was that "action be taken for the removal, wherever practicable, of discrimination on grounds of race in Commonwealth Acts and Regulations, Ordinance of the mainland Territories and practices thereunder."[163]

The main obstacles to Australia's signing of the convention were highlighted in a memorandum later that year:

> There is some legislation in external territories which could be described as discriminatory; the Commonwealth imposes restrictions on the right of Aborigines to leave Australia; Aborigines do not everywhere have the same political rights as "other" Australians; and it is apparent that Aborigines working in the pastoral industries often receive lower remuneration than other pastoral workers.[164]

The following year the Attorney-General's Department stressed to the Prime Minister's Department the importance of the issue of racial discrimination in current international times: "The question of racial discrimination, in present world circumstances, is a particularly important one and it is essential that the Australian government should be able to speak authoritatively in this matter in relation to the substantive articles of the Convention." However, it drew attention to one of the main problems that Australia faced in this regard: "At present, the Commonwealth Government cannot speak with full knowledge of the situation in Australia because many of the provisions of the draft convention concern matters which fall within the jurisdiction of the States."[165] This was an issue that came up repeatedly when the subject was discussed.

The damage that discrimination, real or even perceived, could do to Australia's international reputation was eluded to later in the year: "Any stories emanating from Australia which suggest that racial discrimination existed— either in law or in fact—were regarded as noteworthy in other countries and could conceivably form the basis for a campaign should the Communists or others decide deliberately to provoke difficulties for us."[166] An example of this was the perception that was given in a publication actually produced by the Australian government about its Aboriginal population:

The opening paragraph of "Aborigines in the Community" reads as follows: "The Commonwealth Constitution declares that the responsibility for aborigines within State boundaries was a matter for the sovereign States and excluded them from the census." This bold statement would not mean much to non-Australians who are not well acquainted with the Federal relationship between the Commonwealth Government of Australia and the State Governments. All that the external reader would learn from this sentence would be that Australian aborigines were excluded from the official Australian census and the only impression which this could leave would be that in Australia aborigines were regarded as not fully equal with other Australian citizens.[167]

This all contributed to Australia ultimately supporting the adoption of the Convention at the end of 1965, despite having some reservations on certain aspects of it.[168]

When it came to Australia actually signing the Convention, it was certainly influenced by what Aotearoa New Zealand and Canada were doing, as they all also had Indigenous populations. Australia's High Commission in Wellington commented in April 1966 that:

Speaking generally, I do not think New Zealand has anything to fear from any scrutiny of race relations in this country....It would be idle to deny that there are isolated incidents of discrimination, but they are, in my opinion, of little importance....This being so, there should be no reason why New Zealand should not be a party to suitable convention on racial discrimination.[169]

And word was received from the Australian High Commission in Ottawa a few months later that Canada had signed the Convention, subject to ratification:

The Secretary of State for External Affairs, the Honourable Paul Martin, today announced the signature by Canada, subject to ratification, of the International Convention on the Elimination of all Forms of Racial Discrimination, which was approved by the twentieth session of the United Nations General Assembly in a resolution adopted unanimously on December 21, 1965. The Convention binds states which ratify it to condemn racial discrimination and to ensure the adequate protection of racial groups or individuals belonging to these groups.[170]

Similar to its Australian counterpart, the Canadian government made the argument that it could only ratify the Convention after consultation with the provinces, as a lot of legislation that would need to be amended to conform to the convention came under their jurisdiction.

So, a strong recommendation was subsequently made within the Department of External Affairs for Australia to also become a signatory to the Convention. It was highlighted that Aotearoa New Zealand's Mission to the UN had strongly recommended that the Aotearoa New Zealand government do the same, and Canada had already done so.[171] It was pointed out that "Our Permanent Representative to the United Nations in New York favours early signature by Australia." In particular, in September 1966 he had maintained that:

> In view of the critical comment on Australia by Africans and perhaps others which is likely to arise from reference to the recent ICJ decision on the South West African issues, it would be helpful if the Australian delegation to the coming General Assembly were in a position to make a statement, perhaps in the Minister's speech, announcing the intention of the Government to sign the convention.[172]

It was also emphasised that "The Australian Government is in general agreement with the purposes of the Convention and has always made clear its firm opposition to all manifestations of racial prejudice." The government had also, especially in recent times, "actively pursued a policy aimed at removing archaic legislation involving discrimination."[173] The submission specifically recommended that:

> Australia should sign the International Convention on the Elimination of Racial Discrimination during the 21st Session of the United Nations General Assembly; that an appropriate occasion be taken at the discretion of the Australian delegation to the General Assembly to announce this decision; that State Governments be informed of this decision and that ratification would be dependent on consultations with them.[174]

Australia finally signed the convention in late 1966.[175]

The issue of racial discrimination garnered particular international attention in the early 1970s with South Africa's policy of apartheid:

> It is important, therefore, that we should emphasise that the policies of apartheid racial discrimination and limited franchise being followed by certain governments in southern Africa find no support in Australia. On the contrary, the Government's policy is one of promoting an integrated Australian society looking towards political and racial equality for all, of supporting self-determination on the basis of majority rule, say for the people of Papua New Guinea, and of co-operating with the United Nations towards that end.[176]

The Whitlam Government which came to power in 1972 took up the issue of racial discrimination with particular vigour. An excellent demonstration of this was its intention to finally ratify the Convention in early 1973:

> On the occasion of the International Day for the Elimination of Racial Discrimination, the Prime Minister and Minister for Foreign Affairs, Mr. Whitlam, has reaffirmed that the government was resolved to ratify the International Convention

on the Elimination of All Forms of Racial Discrimination as soon as the necessary legislative and other measures could be completed.[177]

Furthermore, Whitlam said that the government had signaled its intention to introduce legislation to allow Australia to enact the convention, and this would be introduced very soon. Moreover, he added that the government's plan to enact the convention on the elimination of racial discrimination followed initial moves adopted by Australia since last December. In addition, "Mr. Whitlam said that in order to pave the way for ratification he had sought the cooperation of the premiers of Queensland and Western Australia in giving high priority to the removal of the remaining minor pieces of discriminatory legislation in those states."[178]

So, the whole issue of the adoption of the International Convention on the Elimination of All Forms of Racial Discrimination illustrated the impact of international pressure on the Australian government to remove discrimination in its legislation. However, I would still argue that it was more willing to act on this pressure as Australia's national identity had shifted away from Britishness to a "new nationalism."

This chapter has shown how the end of the British World and its replacement with a "new nationalism" led to a redefinition of citizenship in Australia between the 1950s and 1970s. The UK's first application for entry into the EEC in 1961 and the announcement of its military withdrawal from "East of Suez" in 1967 were particular highlights which signaled the end of the British self-identification of Australia. Through focusing on the *Nationality and Citizenship Acts* of 1955 and 1960, the *Citizenship Act* of 1969, and the *Australian Citizenship Act* of 1973, the chapter has demonstrated how non-British migrants were gradually put on a much more equal basis to their British counterparts in being able to attain Australian citizenship and exercise the benefits of Australian citizenship, such as employment in the Public Service. It has also illustrated how Aboriginal policy during the 1950s, the awarding of the right to vote for Aborigines in 1961, the 1967 Referendum, and the International Convention on the Elimination of All Forms of Racial Discrimination during the 1960s and 1970s, collectively led to the removal of the constitutional discriminations against Aborigines and actually allowed them to exercise the rights of Australian citizenship which they had theoretically held since 1948. I will now turn to exploring the end of the British World and the redefinition of citizenship in Canada, in terms of both other ethnic groups and Indigenous peoples.

Notes

1. The research for this chapter was conducted while I was a Visiting Fellow in the School of Politics and International Relations (SPIR) at the Australian National University. I am grateful to SPIR for all its support, both material and intellectual.

2. Kim Rubenstein, *Australian Citizenship Law in Context* (Pyrmont, NSW: Lawbook, 2002), 10.

3. Wayne Hudson and John Kane, "Rethinking Australian Citizenship," in *Rethinking Australian Citizenship*, ed. Wayne Hudson and John Kane (Cambridge: Cambridge University Press, 2000), 2.

4. Helen Irving, *To Constitute a Nation: A Cultural History of Australia's Constitution* (Cambridge: Cambridge University Press, 1997), 158.

5. David Dutton, *Citizenship in Australia: A Guide to Commonwealth Government Records* (Canberra: National Archives of Australia, 1999), 17.

6. Sangeetha Pillai, "The Rights and Responsibilities of Australian Citizenship: A Legislative Analysis," *Melbourne University Law Review* 37, no. 3 (January 2014), 736–85.

7. Ann-Mari Jordens, *Alien to Citizen: Settling Migrants in Australia, 1945–75* (St. Leonards, NSW: Allen & Unwin, 1997), 189. However, there was still protection for British subjects who were on the electoral roll as late as 1983 to remain on the roll, even if they were not citizens.

8. Ann-Mari Jordens, *Promoting Australian Citizenship, 1949–71* (Canberra: Administration, Compliance and Governability Program, 1991), 1.

9. John Chesterman and Brian Galligan, "Indigenous Rights and Australian Citizenship," in *Individual, Community, Nation: Fifty Years of Australian Citizenship*, ed. Kim Rubenstein (Melbourne: Australian Scholarly, 2000), 67.

10. Susan Dodds, "Citizenship, Justice and Indigenous Group-Specific Rights-Citizenship and Indigenous Australia," *Citizenship Studies* 2, no. 1 (1998), 106.

11. Ann Curthoys, "An Uneasy Conversation: The Multicultural and the Indigenous," in *Race, Colour and Identity in Australia and New Zealand*, eds. John Docker and Gerhard Fischer (Sydney: UNSW Press, 2000), 21.

12. The White Australia Policy which had been established in 1901 and was primarily aimed at preventing Asian immigration to Australia was very much alive and well at this time.

13. For more on the *British Nationality and Australian Citizenship Act of 1948* see Mann, "The Evolution of Commonwealth Citizenship, 1945–48 in Canada, Britain and Australia," 293–313.

14. This was a crisis precipitated by the nationalisation of the Suez Canal by Egyptian President Gamal Abdul Nasser in July 1956, which in turn led to the UK and France, who had substantial commercial interests in the canal, entering into a clandestine agreement with Israel to invade Egypt in October 1956, thus giving the two powers the opportunity to in turn send troops into the canal zone on the pretext of "separating the warring parties."

15. For more on the prevalence of Britishness in Australia at this time see Jatinder Mann, *The Search for a New National Identity*, Chapter 4. It should be emphasised, however, that Australia's Britishness was not a sign of inferiority, rather, Australian Britons saw themselves as superior to those in the "mother-country." It was argued that the extreme Australian

climate, the exigencies of colonial life, and a better diet had produced a stronger and fitter British population in the Antipodes.

16. Ward, *Australia and the British Embrace*, 69, 70.

17. *Ibid.*, 71, 79.

18. *Ibid.*, 81, 85, 86, 88.

19. *Sydney Morning Herald (SMH)*, August 2, 1961, cited in Ward, *Australia and the British Embrace*, 89.

20. Mann, "'Leavening British Traditions,'" 49.

21. *Ibid.*, 49–50.

22. *Ibid.*, 50.

23. *Ibid.*, 53.

24. *Ibid.*

25. NLA, MS 6690/Series 12/Box 40/File 22: Immigration Advisory Council, Extract from *Sunday Australian*, 13 February 1972, "Pride and Prejudice," 8.

26. Mann, "'Leavening British Traditions,'" 54, 55, 62.

27. NAA, A432 1961/3191, Sidney W. Smith to Prime Minister R. G. Menzies, 8 July 1954.

28. NAA A432 1961/3191, Memorandum by T. H. E. Heyes, Secretary, Department of Immigration for the Minister—"Question of How Australians May Describe Their National Status," July 1954, 1.

29. *Ibid.*, 3.

30. NAA, A432 1961/3191, A. S. Brown, Secretary, Prime Minister's Department to S. W. Smith, 23 August 1954.

31. Australian Parliamentary Debates, *House of Representatives (H of R)*, vol. 4, 1954, 18 August 1954, Governor-General's Speech, 383.

32. Australian Parliamentary Debates, *H of R*, vol. 4, 1954, 24 August 1954, Albert Thompson, 532.

33. *Ibid.*

34. *Ibid.*, Howard Beale, 532.

35. Australian Parliamentary Debates, *H of R*, vol. 4, 1954, 14 September 1954, Alan Bird, 1218.

36. *Ibid.*

37. *Ibid.*, 1218–19.

38. Australian Parliamentary Debates, *H of R*, vol. 5, 1954, 27 October 1954, Harold Holt, 2356.

39. NAA A446 1965/45441, T. H. E. Heyes, Secretary, Department of Immigration to The Minister for Immigration, 10 November 1954, 1.

40. NAA A446 1965/45441, Cabinet Submission 163 by H. E. Holt, Minister for Immigration, 5.

41. Australian Parliamentary Debates, *H of R*, vol. 6, 1954–55, 21 April 1955, Harold Holt, 105.

42. Australian Parliamentary Debates, *H of R*, vol. 6, 1954–55, 21 April 1955, Arthur Calwell, 106, 107.

43. Australian Parliamentary Debates, *H of R*, vol. 6, 1954–55, 21 April 1955, Percy Clarey, 114.

44. *Ibid.*, 115.

45. Australian Parliamentary Debates, H *of R*, vol. 6, 1954–55, 21 April 1955, Alan Bird, 129.

46. NAA A463 1957/2783, Outward Cablegram from Department of External Affairs to Australian Embassy, The Hague, 18 July 1957.

47. NAA A5840 507, Notes on Cabinet Submission No. 981—Grounds for Depriving Naturalised Persons of Australian Citizenship, 17 January 1958, 1.

48. NAA A5840 507, Memorandum by Athol Townley, Minister for Immigration on "Amendment of Nationality and Citizenship Act—Grounds for Depriving Naturalised Persons of Australian Citizenship (including Appendices).

49. NAA A463 1957/3309, Speech at Opening of Citizenship Convention by Athol Townley, Minister for Immigration, 21 January 1958, 29.

50. NAA A446 1965/46671, T. H. E. Heyes, Secretary, Department of Immigration to The Secretary, Department of External Affairs, 7 November 1958.

51. NAA A446 1965/46671, R. P. Thompson, Second Secretary, Australian High Commission, Ottawa to The Secretary, Department of External Affairs (including copy of statement by Hon. Ellen L. Fairclough, Minister for Citizenship and Immigration), 12 December 1958, 8.

52. NAA A446 1965/46671, T. H. E. Heyes, Secretary, Department of Immigration to The Secretary, Department of External Affairs, 15 January 1959, 12.

53. NAA A446 1965/46671, T. H. E. Heyes, Secretary, Department of Immigration to The Secretary, Department of External Affairs, 23 August 1960, 22.

54. NAA A446 1965/46671, R. P. Thompson, Second Secretary, Australian High Commission, Ottawa to The Secretary, Department of External Affairs, 7 September 1960, 1.

55. NAA A432 1960/1196, Nationality and Citizenship Bill 1960—Memorandum by Parliamentary Draftsman, 17 October 1960, 1.

56. NAA A432 1960/1196, Memorandum for Cabinet by A. R. Downer—Proposed amendments to Nationality and Citizenship Act, 1.

57. *Ibid.*, 2.

58. *Ibid.*, 3.

59. *Ibid.*, 4.

60. NAA A446 1965/45472, Press Statement by the Minister for Immigration (The Hon. A. R. Downer M. P.)—Citizenship applications simplified, Canberra, 18 December 1960, 1.

61. *Ibid.*, 2.

62. NAA A446 1965/45472, Notes on Citizenship Bill.

63. Davidson, *From Subject to Citizen*, 88.

64. Some of the changes in the *Citizenship Act of 1969* were most certainly inspired by amendments to Canadian legislation a few years earlier—this is not surprising, as the original *British Nationality and Australian Citizenship Act of 1948* was modeled on the *Canadian Citizenship Act of 1946*. The idea of citizens of other Commonwealth countries swearing an oath of allegiance to the Queen of Canada was a case in point.
NAA, A446 1965/46671: Cable from Department of External Relations (following from Ottawa) to Department of Immigration, 26 January 1967, 126.

65. NAA, A446 1957/66699: Extract from *West Australian*, "Seeking More Citizens," 11 December 1967.

66. NAA, A446 1957/66699: G. E. Hitchins, Commonwealth Director of Migration to Peter Heydon, Secretary, Department of Immigration, 28 February 1968, 1.
67. NAA, A446 1967/72349: Departmental Committee to Review the Nationality and Citizenship Act 1948–1967—Possible Amendments Discussed, and Recommendations of Amendments, 1, 3–4.
68. NAA, A446 1967/72349: Nationality and Citizenship Act 1948–1967—Inter-Departmental Discussions, 1–2.
69. NAA A446 1967/72349, P. R. Heydon, Secretary, Department of Immigration to The Minister for Immigration (including draft of proposed answer to question without notice by Mr. Ian Wilson MP), April 1968, 239.
70. Ibid., 1.
71. NAA, A446, 1967/72349: Heydon to The Minister for Immigration, May 1968, 2–3.
72. Ibid.
73. NAA, A432 1968/3377: A. C. C. Menzies, Senior Assistant Secretary (Advisings) to The Secretary, Attorney-General's Department, 18 October 1968, 2.
74. It also again illustrated the impact of revisions to Canadian citizenship legislation on the Australian situation. In fact the Australian Department of Immigration thanked the Canadian High Commission in Canberra for providing information on the revisions to the Canadian Citizenship regulations the following month.
NAA, A446 1965/46671: G. A. Cole, for Secretary, Department of Immigration to A. R. Menzies, High Commissioner for Canada, 1 November 1968.
75. Australian Parliamentary Debates, H of R, Vol. 61, 12 November 1968, Clyde Cameron, 2730.
76. Ibid.
77. NAA, A446 1978/75530: Extract from Age—"Rewarding the triers," 14 November 1968.
78. NAA, A446 1978/75530: Extract from Melbourne Herald—"Short Cut Citizens," 13 November 1968.
79. NAA, A446 1978/75530: Extract from SMH—"Becoming a citizen," 14 November 1968.
80. NAA, A446 1978/75530: Extract from Daily Telegraph—"Migrants," 14 November 1968.
81. NAA, A446 1978/75530: Extract from Il Globo—"Thanks to Minister Snedden—Australian Citizens to be 'less British,'" 19 November 1968, 2.
82. NAA, A446 1969/70341: Citizenship Bill, 1969—Second Reading Speech by the Hon. B. M. Snedden, Minister for Immigration, 2.
83. Australian Parliamentary Debates, H of R, Vol. 63, 1 May 1969, Ian Wilson, 1597, 1598.
84. Australian Parliamentary Debates, H of R, Vol. 63, 13 May 1969, Arthur Calwell, 1602.
The provisions of the Citizenship Act of 1969 relating to an Australian Citizen having the status of a British subject rather than being a British subject were not proclaimed until 20 February 1973. This was because many State laws referred to people who were British subjects, it was essential therefore that each State should amend its laws before the federal provisions could be enacted. South Australia was the last to do this and thus the remaining provisions of the Act could be proclaimed.
NAA, A446 1978/75531: Citizenship Circular 1/73 by H. J. Grant (for Secretary), 9 February 1973, 1–2.
85. NAA, A446/75532: Citizenship Circular 4/73 by G. E. Hitchins (for Secretary) on "Australian Citizenship Bill 1973," 12 April 1973, 2.

86. *Ibid.*
87. NLA, MS 7798/Series 3/Box 40: Papers of Al Grassby—Notes on "Discrimination in Citizenship Legislation and Policy of Previous Government."
88. NAA, A446/75532: Second Reading Speech on Citizenship Bill 1973 by the Hon. A. J. Grassby, Minister for Immigration, 1, 2.
89. *Ibid.*, 4–5.
90. *Ibid.*, 5–6.
91. Australian Parliamentary Debates, *H of R*, Vol. 83, 9 May 1973, Phillip Lynch, 1899, 1900, 1901.
92. Australian Parliamentary Debates, *H of R*, Vol. 83, 9 May 1973, Maxwell Oldmeadow, 1902, 1903.
93. Australian Parliamentary Debates, *H of R*, Vol. 83, 9 May 1973, Alexander Forbes, 1908.
94. *Ibid.*
95. Australian Parliamentary Debates, *H of R*, Vol. 83, 9 May 1973, Leonard Keogh, 1911, 1913.
96. Australian Parliamentary Debates, *H of R*, Vol. 83, 9 May 1973, Al Grassby, 1925, 1926.
97. *Ibid.*, 1926.
98. NLA, MS 7798/Series 3/Box 40: Speech by Minister for Immigration, The Honourable A. J. Grassby on Australian Citizenship Bill 1973, 2.
99. "Citizenship Rights: Federal Policy On Native Affairs," *The West Australian*, 2 February 1950, 22.
100. "Aborigines' Voice," *The West Australian*, 16 June 1950, 2.
101. NLA, MS 5274/Series III/Box 33/Folder 10: Memorandum for Cabinet by P. M. C. Hasluck, Minister for Territories on "Native Welfare Council," 28 May 1951, 2.
102. *Ibid.*, 2.
103. *Ibid.*, 3.
104. NLA MS 5274/Series III/Box 32/Folder 2, Commonwealth and States Conference on Native Welfare, Canberra, 3–4 September 1951—Statement on Citizenship Status, 1.
105. "Aborigines in Census," *The Courier-Mail*, 20 January 1954, 9.
106. "RSL Backs Aborigines," *The Courier-Mail*, 14 June 1954, 3.
107. "Aborigine May Now be in Union," *The West Australian*, 28 December 1954, 8.
108. NLA, MS 2683/Series 10/Box 28/Folder 23, Message received from Mr. T. Dougherty, General Secretary, Australian Workers Union, 29 April 1957.
109. NLA, MS 4695/Series 1/Folder 5275, The Rt. Hon. The Minister for Territories, Paul Hasluck, to Mr Joske, 2 May 1957.
110. NLA, MS 2683/Series 10/Box 27/Folder 3, Jessie M. Street to Mr. D. Dunstan, M.L.A., S.A., 22 May 1957.
111. NLA, MS 2683/Series 10/Box 27/Folder 4: W. W. Greenridge, Director, Anti-Slavery and Aborigines Protection Society to Paul Hasluck, Minister for Territories, 17 December 1957, 1.
112. *Ibid.*, 1, 2.
113. *Ibid.*, 2.
114. Tim Rowse, "Indigenous Citizenship," in *Rethinking Australian Citizenship*, eds. Wayne Hudson and John Kane (Cambridge: Cambridge University Press, 2000), 88, 89.

115. NLA, MS 2683/Series 10/Box 27/File 7: Jessie Street to Robert Menzies, Prime Minister of Australia, 9 March 1960, 1, 2.
116. NAA, A463 1966/793: E. C. Gare, President, W. A. Native Welfare Council Inc. to Robert Menzies, 22 November 1960, 1.
This was a reference to Section 51 (xxvi) of the constitution, which stated that the Commonwealth had the right to make special laws for all races, other than the Aboriginal race in any State.
117. NAA A463 1966/793, J. E. Willoughby, Acting Secretary, Department of Territories to The Secretary, Prime Minister's Department, 10 January 1961, 2.
118. NAA, A432 1960/3289 PART 2: Alexander Downer, Acting Prime Minister to Gare.
119. NAA, A463 1966/793: Gare to Menzies, 8 April 1961.
120. NAA, A432 1960/3289 PART 2: Downer to Gare, 4 July 1961, 1.
121. NAA, A463 1966/793: Background Note on "Select Committee on Voting Rights of Aborigines" by Mr. J. McCusker, 8 August 1961, 2–3.
122. NAA A432 1960/3289 PART 2, K. H. Bailey to The Secretary, Select Committee on Voting Rights of Aboriginals, 6 October 1961, 1.
123. NAA, A463 1966/793: Outward Cablegram from Department of External Affairs to All Posts, 19 October 1961.
124. NAA, A1838 557/1 PART 2: Australia and Foreign Affairs—Digest of Press Opinion on report of Parliamentary Committee on voting rights for aborigines, 25 October 1961, 3.
125. *Ibid.*, 4.
126. *Ibid.*, 1.
127. *Ibid.*, 3.
128. NAA, A1838 557/2 PART 3: Savingram from Department of External Affairs to All Posts, 12 January 1962, 2.
129. NAA, A4940 C3496: Cabinet Minute—Decision No. 52, 13 February 1962.
130. "Natives' Voting Rights," *West Australian*, 20 March 1962, 6.
Western Australia and the Northern Territory did indeed give Aborigines the State or Territory votes that same year.
131. This referred to the section of the Australian constitution, which declared that Aborigines should not be counted in the census.
132. NLA, MS 2683/Series 10/Box 28/ Folder 16: Comments on Report from the Select Committee of Voting Rights of Aborigines by Jessie M. G. Street, April 1962, 4.
Margaret Thornton, who argued that "Enfranchisement certainly did not guarantee instantaneous admission to the community of equals," supported this.
Margaret Thornton, "Legal Citizenship," in *Rethinking Australian Citizenship*, eds. Wayne Hudson and John Kane (Cambridge: Cambridge University Press, 2000), 118.
133. Tim Rowse, "Diversity in Indigenous Citizenship," *Communal/Plural* 2 (1993): 49.
134. Rowse, "Indigenous Citizenship," 92.
135. Bain Attwood and Andrew Markus, "Representation Matters: The 1967 Referendum and Citizenship," in *Citizenship and Indigenous Australians: Changing Conceptions and Possibilities*, eds. Nicolas Peterson and Will Sanders (Cambridge: Cambridge University Press, 1998), 118.
136. Terry Widders and Greg Noble, "On the Dreaming Track to the Republic: Indigenous People and the Ambivalence of Citizenship," *Communal/Plural* 2 (1993): 106.

137. Christine Fletcher, "Living Together but not Neighbours: Cultural Imperialism in Australia," in *Indigenous Peoples' Rights in Australia, Canada & New Zealand*, ed. Paul Havemann (Auckland: Oxford University Press, 1999), 336.

138. Michael Dodson, "First Fleets and Citizenship: The Citizenship Status of Indigenous Peoples in Post-Colonial Australia," in *Citizenship in Australia: Democracy, Law and Society*, ed. S. Rufus Davis (Carlton, Victoria: Constitutional Centenary Foundation, 1996), 215.

139. NAA, A5840 507: Submission No. 660—Constitutional Amendments: Sections 24 to 27, 51 (xxvi.), 127 by B. M. Snedden, Attorney-General, 22 February 1965, 12, 14.

140. The nexus referred to the constitutional arrangement in which there had to be roughly double the number of Senators in the House of Representatives in the Australian Parliament.

141. NAA, A5840 507: Cabinet Minute—Decision No. 841, 7 April 1965.

142. Murray Goot and Tim Rowse, explore the Impact of FCAATSI's Campaign Efforts on Australian Public Opinion in *Divided Nation: Indigenous Affairs and the Imagined Public* (Carlton, Victoria: Melbourne University Press, 2007), 55–59.

143. NLA, 2683 Series 10/Box 27/File 9: Letter from Mrs. Faith Bandler, N.S.W. State Secretary, The Federal Council for Advancement of Aborigines and Torres Strait Islanders (FCAATSI), 30 April 1965.

144. NAA, A5827 VOLUME 31: Cabinet Submission No. 1009—Constitutional Amendments: Sections 24–27, 127 and 51 (xxvi.) by B. M. Snedden, Attorney-General, 23 August 1965, 5.

145. NAA, A5827 VOLUME 31: Cabinet Minute—Decision No. 1175—Submission No. 1009—Constitutional Amendments: Sections 24–27, 127 and 51 (xxvi.), 30 August 1965, 2.

146. "Does Referendum Go Far Enough," *SMH*, 17 November 1965, 2.

147. NAA, A432 1967/3321 PART 1: Mrs. L. Lippmann, Convenor, Legislative Reform Committee, The Federal Council for Advancement of Aborigines' and Torres Strait Islanders (FCAATSI) to B. M. Snedden, Attorney-General, 2 February 1966.

148. NAA, A432 1967/3321 PART 1: Referendum—Statement by the Prime Minister, Mr. Harold Holt, 15 February 1966, 1.

149. NAA, A406 E1967/30: Cabinet Submission on "Constitutional Amendment: Aborigines" by Nigel Bowen, Attorney-General, January 1967, 8.

150. NAA, A5840 79: Cabinet Minute—Decision No. 79, 22 February 1967.

151. Australian Parliamentary Debates, *H of R*, Vol. 54, 23 February 1967, Harold Holt, 115.

152. Australian Parliamentary Debates, *H of R*, Vol. 54, 1 March 1967, Gough Whitlam, 264.

153. "Aborigines," *SMH*, 28 February 1967, 2.

154. NLA, MS 8256/Series II/Sub-Series II/Box 175: "YES" vote—Information (1)—Referendum—Federal Council for the Advancement of Aborigines and Torres Strait Islanders, 31 March 1967, 1, 2.

NLA, MS 8256/Series II/Sub-Series II/Box 175: "YES" vote—Information (3)—Referendum—Federal Council for the Advancement of Aborigines and Torres Strait Islanders, 31 March 1967, 1, 2.

NLA, MS 8256/Series II/Sub-Series II/Box 175: Vote "YES" on both questions—Referendum Day—Voting is Compulsory, 27 May 1967.

155. NLA, MS 8256/Series 11/Sub-Series II/Box 175: Says a friend of the Aborigines: "Let's tell the world there's only one Australia, and his color doesn't matter at all" by Kay Keavney, *Australian Women's Weekly*, 10 May 1967.

156. "Appeal For Yes Vote To Realise 'Dream,'" *SMH*, 13 May 1967, 9.
"Holt Puts Yes Cases," *SMH*, 16 May 1967, 1.
"The Yes Case," *Age*, 17 May 1967, 5.
"A Good Look at the Aborigines," *SMH*, 17 May 1967, 6.
"The Final Week," *SMH*, 22 May 1967, 2.
"Holt, Whitlam end 'Yes' Case," *Canberra Times*, 25 May 1967, 12.
"YES Vital to Help Aborigines," *Age*, 26 May 1967, 3.
"No. 2: Aborigines," *SMH*, 26 May 1967, 4.
"Shoulder to the Wheel," *Age*, 26 May 1967, 5.

157. "Public Confusion Evident on Aboriginal Issue," *SMH*, 24 May 1967, 4.

158. "Record Yes on Second Issue," *SMH*, 29 May 1967, 1.

159. "The referendum," *SMH*, 29 May 1967, 2.

160. John Chesterman and Brian Galligan, *Citizens Without Rights: Aborigines and Australian Citizenship* (Cambridge: Cambridge University Press, 1997), 186.

161. Christopher Cunneen and Terry Libesman, *Indigenous People and the Law in Australia* (Sydney: Butterworths, 1995), 42.

162. Attwood and Markus, "Representation Matters," 125.

163. NAA A1838 557/5 PART 1, M. R. Booker, First Assistant Secretary to the Minister, 24 April 1964, 1.

164. NAA A1838 929/5/6 PART 1, Memorandum on "The Draft International Convention on the Elimination of all forms of Racial Discrimination," 1–2.

165. NAA A1838 929/5/6 PART 1, H. A. Doyle, for the Secretary, Attorney-General's Department to The Secretary, Prime Minister's Department, 12 July 1965.

166. NAA A1838 557/2 PART 4, Minute by H. Neil Truscott, Head, Information and Cultural Relations Branch on "Foreign Affairs Committee" for The Secretary, Department of External Affairs, 7 September 1965, 2.

167. NAA A1838 557/2 PART 4, Patrick Shaw, Permanent Representative, Australian Mission to the United Nations to The Secretary, Department of External Affairs, 6 October 1965.

168. NAA A1838 929/5/6 PART 4, Outward Cablegram from Department of External Affairs to Australian Embassy, Saigon, 16 December 1965, 1.

169. NAA, A1838 929/5/6 PART 5, D. J. Horne, Counsellor, Australian High Commission, Wellington to The Secretary, Department of External Affairs (including copy of letter from Mr. J. M. McEwen, Secretary of Maori Affairs, 13 April 1966), 21 April 1966, 1.

170. NAA A1838 929/5/6 PART 5, C. A. Ransome, Third Secretary, Australian High Commission, Ottawa to The Secretary, Department of External Affairs (including copy of press release by Department of External Affairs, Canada, 24 August 1966), 26 August 1966, 30.

171. NAA A1838 929/5/6 PART 5, M. R. Booker, First Assistant Secretary to the Acting Minister, 2.

172. *Ibid.*, 2–3.

173. *Ibid.*, 4.

174. *Ibid.*
175. NAA 1838 929/5/6 PART 7, J. McEwen, Acting Prime Minister to Mr. T. W. Roper, National Abschol Director, National Union of Australian University, 21 January 1969.
176. NAA A1838 555/10/9 PART 2, Circular Memorandum by R. A. Woolcott, Assistant Secretary, Department of Foreign Affairs (including excerpt from House of Representatives, 20 April 1972), 27 April 1972.
177. NAA A1838 555/10/9 PART 2, Outward Cablegram from Department of Foreign Affairs, 20 March 1973.
178. *Ibid.*

· 2 ·

REDEFINING CITIZENSHIP
IN CANADA, 1950s–1970s[1]

In the 1950s, English-speaking Canada very much identified itself as a British country and an integral part of a wider British World which had the UK at its centre. Canada's bicultural nature, with the French-Canadians, complicated this self-identity. However, by the 1970s, this British World had come to an end, as had Canada's self-identification as a British nation. During this period, citizenship in Canada was redefined in a significant way from being an ethnic (British)-based one to a more civic-founded one which was more inclusive of other ethnic groups and apparently Indigenous peoples. This chapter will argue that this redefinition of citizenship took place primarily in the context of this major shift in national identity. After having established the context of the end of the British World in Canada (with a focus on the Suez Crisis of 1956 and the UK's application for entry into the EEC) it will explore the *Canadian Citizenship Acts* of 1957, 1962, 1967, and 1977 to illustrate how citizenship became more inclusive of other ethnic groups in the country. It will then study the amendments of the *Elections Act* in 1950 and the *Indian Act* in 1955; the awarding of the right to vote for First Nations (I will use the contemporary term "First Nations" in this chapter to describe Indigenous groups who were historically referred to as "Indians." However, any quotes from historical sources will of course employ the term used at the time) in 1960; and the 1969 White Paper to highlight how citizenship in Canada also appeared to incorporate Indigenous groups at this time.

Theoretical Background

Before studying these several key points, it is prudent to spend some time on the theoretical context to citizenship in Canada during the 1950s and 1970s—primarily, the difference between normative citizenship (citizenship as status) as opposed to substantive citizenship (citizenship as rights and obligations). According to Christina Gabriel, "Conceptualizations of citizenship are generally characterized by issues of inclusion and exclusion, rights and duties, and full participation....The nature of each of these issues, however... is historically specific, shifting, and the object of political debate."[2] Post-war ideas of citizenship have been heavily influenced by T. H. Marshall's theory of citizenship rights.[3] Marshall maintained that "Citizenship is a status bestowed on those who are full members of a community....All who possess the status are equal with respect to the rights and duties with which the status is bestowed."[4] However, although not everyone who has citizenship shares equitably in the social, political, and economic benefits of their society, it does bestow specific crucial rights.[5] Will Kymlicka and Norman Wayne argued that "Citizenship is not just a certain status, defined by a set of rights and responsibilities....It is also an identity, an expression of one's membership in a political community."[6] Jane Jenson asserted that "Citizenship involves much more than the recognition provided by a passport....It has come to mean the attribution to citizens of a range of rights, including civil rights that protect individuals and groups from state interference; political rights of democratic participation; and substantive social and economic rights which recognize society's responsibility for all its members."[7] Due to shifting outlooks and the large numbers of non-British migrants in the 1950s and 1960s, the difference in the way that British subjects and aliens were treated started to be criticised by the latter. The idea that citizenship is a privilege and not a right was also increasingly questioned by non-British migrants.[8] Canadian citizens, however, continued to be British subjects until 1977, when Canadian citizenship was acknowledged as a right in relation to a series of new initiatives incorporated in changes to the *Citizenship Act*. Gary Caldwell asserted that a major transformation of the 1947 Citizenship Act in 1977 resulted in significant shifts, the most important of which was the lowering of the probation term from five to three years, and the allowing of double citizenship. From then onwards, someone could become a Canadian citizen while keeping American or French citizenship, for example.[9] According to Linda Cardinal and Marie-Joie Brady, "The new Citizenship Act constituted a framework that served to denounce the discriminatory practices that had defined the linkages between the British Crown and its many subjects such as Aboriginal peoples, British citizens, French Canadians, or immigrants....Until the first half of the twentieth century, Aboriginal peoples living in reserves had the status of minors."[10] Darlene Johnston maintained that "Citizenship....The very word conjures up notions of freedom and autonomy, the right to participate, a sense of belonging....The Western political tradition regards the evolution of citizenship as its crowning achievement....However, for the First Nations over whom Canada asserts jurisdiction, the experience of Canadian citizenship has been somewhat less ennobling."[11] Kenneth Carty and Peter Ward argued that "In postwar Canada, newly ascendant liberal views on race and ethnic relations challenged traditional biases in electoral law, and, in response, governments dismantled these barriers one by one....But not until 1960 was universal suffrage, the proclaimed goal of popular democracy, truly achieved."[12] But Alan Cairns was even critical of this milestone, as he asserted that "In Canada, the extension of the franchise to status Indians in 1960 was a response more to the multiracial and multicultural nature of the new Commonwealth than to pressures from Indian peoples, many of whom viewed this 'gift' as an instrument of assimilation."[13] Hamar Foster maintained that Prime Minister Elliott Trudeau's 1969 White Paper proposed disestablishing the Department of Indian Affairs and Northern Development, the repeal of the *Indian Act*, and the stock provision of services through mainstream provincial institutions. Indigenous groups did not really trust the provinces, and the recommendations—regardless that the majority of those who were affected by them also wanted to see the end of the *Indian Act*—were thus nearly unanimously opposed.[14] Broadening it out, according to Augie Fleras and Jean Leonard Elliott, state initiative reactions to Indigenous demands are contrasting. In one way, political discussion in Canada is increasingly leaning towards acknowledgment of the First Peoples as a "distinct society" with specific rights and claims against the government on a level above citizenship. State officials seem prepared theoretically to recognise the basis of Indigenous national demands, if only to avoid a conflict in the legitimacy of the nation or to avoid international condemnation.[15] Joyce Green maintained that for Indigenous peoples, states are fundamentally agents of oppression, maintaining an imposed and illegitimate

sovereignty against Indigenous peoples through a colonial settler order legiti-
mated by racist myths and policy. The kinder, gentler colonialism of equitable
inclusion in state citizenship is definitively incorporation into, not liberation
from, the settler state.[16]

Context of the End of the British World

Having laid this theoretical foundation, the chapter will now turn to studying the context of the end of the British World as the key cause for the
redefinition of citizenship in Canada between the 1950s and 1970s. After
the Second World War, English-speaking Canada very much still saw itself
as an integral part of a wider British World. As stated above, this Britannic
identity was complicated by the presence of a competing founding European group: the French-Canadians.[17] The *Canadian Citizenship Act* of 1947 is
an excellent example of the bicultural nature of Canada at the time. The
legislation enshrined the concept of Canadian citizenship for the very first
time, but it also maintained the status of British subject, and British subjects
from other parts of the Commonwealth were given privileged positions in
comparison with non-British subjects in terms of naturalisation.[18] However,
English-speaking Canada's Britishness began to unravel with the Suez Crisis
of 1956. According to Jose Igartua, "The Suez incident became a litmus test
of Canada's sense of place on the international scene, of Canadian values,
and of national unity….It provoked both defenders and opponents of the
Canadian position at the United Nations into arguments based on varying
conceptions of what Canada was as a country, and what it should be."[19]
The Liberal government did not support the Anglo-French action. Though
Prime Minister Louis St. Laurent saw Nasser as a dictator, he believed that
to respond to aggression with aggression, except under the auspices of the
UN, would lead to an estrangement in relations with neutral nations such
as India, and would offer the Soviet Union an excuse to interfere even more
in the Middle East.[20] The US was also firmly opposed to the Anglo-French
action, partly for the same reason. This consequently also influenced the
Canadian government's position, as Canada was a core ally of the Amer-
icans in the context of the Cold War and the threat of communism.[21] In
contrast, John Diefenbaker, the Progressive Conservative spokesman on external affairs (and future prime minister), expressed his party's position of
being solidly behind the UK on the issue. He called on the St. Laurent gov-

ernment to support the UK in criticising Nasser's action as the abrogation of an international contract.[22]

After the British and French had invaded Egypt, the position of the Canadian government shifted from lack of support for the Anglo-French action to open criticism and condemnation of it. But the Progressive Conservative Shadow Minister for Foreign Affairs, Howard Green, scathingly maintained that "The United States would have far more admiration for Canada...if this government stopped being the United States chore boy....Now this government, by its action in the Suez Crisis, has made this month of November, 1956, the most disgraceful period for Canada in the history of this nation."[23] The Progressive Conservatives hence argued that the Liberal government was taking such a firm line against the Anglo-French action in Suez because it was keen to be seen as following the US position. They instead believed that Canada should support the UK one hundred per cent. The Progressive Conservatives' anti-American tone was obvious. This would later be exemplified by the personal animosity between Diefenbaker, when he became prime minister, and President John F. Kennedy.

The English-language press, usually loyal to Britain, was now divided. A survey of the twenty-six English-language dailies displayed a fifty-fifty split between those who agreed with the government and those who supported the Anglo-French intervention.[24]

The positions of the two parties were polarised even further when Canada took a leading role in the UN Emergency Force (which the US sponsored) into Egypt, which signalled an embarrassing retreat for the UK and France, and symbolised to the whole world that they were no longer global superpowers.[25] To the Progressive Conservatives it appeared to be yet another instance of the Liberal government's readiness to follow American policy, but once they themselves were in power they came to realise that the ties with the "mother-country" were not as strong as they once were.[26]

In the context of concerns over US dominance in Canada, the UK's decision to seek membership of the EEC in 1961 was a deathblow to British race patriotism in English-speaking Canada. British Prime Minister Harold Macmillan's European ambitions were in no way the first disagreement between the UK and Canadian governments in terms of their own interests. However, it represented a clash of interests in a completely different league from those that had affected the harmony of the Commonwealth in the past. As Andrea Benvenuti and Stuart Ward made clear "The prospect of

British adoption of a European common tariff, and the long-term political implications of European unity, raised fundamental questions about the material and ideological foundations of a 'Greater Britain.'"[27] The Macmillan government's justification for directing its energies to Europe has been well studied.[28] The decision to seek membership of the EEC essentially came down to a belief that the UK's future outside of Europe would involve an ever-declining world position, both economically and politically. Most importantly, Macmillan believed it necessary to publicly maintain the façade that the UK would never ascend to the EEC under conditions that were detrimental to the economic interests of the Commonwealth. Hence, before proclaiming any formal decision to seek membership, the Macmillan government believed it necessary to make some moves towards "consulting" Commonwealth governments. Unsurprisingly, Secretary of State for the Colonies and Commonwealth Relations, Duncan Sandys, met with a cool reaction in Ottawa, and evidently failed to persuade the Diefenbaker government. Regardless of his reassurances that the UK cabinet had not yet made a firm decision to seek membership of the EEC, the Canadian ministers got the overall impression that the UK had in fact already decided to open negotiations.[29]

Canadian irritation with British methods arose more clearly a few months later at the Commonwealth Economic Conference in Accra, when Canada's Finance Minister, Donald Fleming, and Trade Minister, George Hees, directly attacked the UK's promises to the Commonwealth, made openly over several years, which they argued were plainly set to be broken.[30]

The Liberal opposition, headed by Lester Pearson, accused the government of leading the criticism of the UK, and announced their unqualified backing for the UK's EEC membership application. Fleming was made to openly refute the view that Canada had acted in an aggressive way against the UK.[31] He justified his government's reaction to the EEC question in an address at Winnipeg: "Like all families, we have had our differences; like all human associations ours is not a perfect one, but by and large our aims have been common, and where they have diverged we have brought our differences to the conference table and discussed them as members of a family."[32] The language used by Fleming illustrates how Britishness still had some resonance in English-speaking Canadian society.

Diefenbaker agreed not to attack the British government publicly; he did, however, take the chance to express his worries to Macmillan privately. One such opportunity arose when Macmillan visited Ottawa in April 1962.

During his visit, Diefenbaker emphasised the impact of trade preferences "in maintaining the cohesion of the Commonwealth" in its entirety, and for Canada, specifically, "as a means of staving off United States domination." The political economic shift in Canada to a continental economy had begun in a large way after 1945. Diefenbaker stressed that the Canadian government "was keenly concerned with the preservation of the Commonwealth and feared that its future would be endangered by the political implications of United Kingdom entry."[33] Benvenuti and Ward argued that "These comments reveal the extent of Canadian anxieties concerning the less tangible aspects of British entry into Europe—the unravelling of the British world raised acute awareness of the 'other quiet revolution,' and posed difficult questions about Canada's sense of place and purpose in the post-imperial world."[34]

"It was our purpose to develop national symbols which would give us pride and confidence and belief in Canada."[35] Prime Minister Lester Pearson's comment on the adoption of the new Maple Leaf Flag in 1965 encapsulates the essence of the "new nationalism" during this period. It emerged as something to fill the supposed void left by the demise of Britishness in English-speaking Canada. The "new nationalism" involved the construction of local symbols of identity to replace those of British race patriotism. In this respect, an earlier antecedent was the establishment in 1957 of the Canada Council for the Arts, which aimed at supporting uniquely Canadian cultural endeavours.

Pearson elaborated upon what the "new nationalism" meant in a speech in 1963 around Dominion Day, which was the predecessor to Canada Day: "A nation is more than its parts...there is a Canada above its regions... there is an unhyphenated Canadianism above what is English-Canadian or French-Canadian or any other of the cultures that have contributed to our nation."[36] This is a remarkable statement by Pearson. The emphasis on an "unhyphenated Canadianism" reflected his desire for "one nation" and national cohesion.

Biculturalism was also a prime feature of the "new nationalism" in Canada. Pearson emphasised the bicultural nature of Canada in an address he gave to the Canadian French Language Weekly Newspapers' Association in August 1963. He maintained that Canada was wealthy and lucky in more ways than one, especially as it was the benefactor and reserve of two magnificent cultures.[37] He pressed the issue by pointing out that the two groups were inseparable, as hundreds of thousands of English-speaking Canadians lived in Québec and nearly a million French-Canadians resided outside Québec.[38]

Nevertheless, things were certainly starting to change, as was demonstrated by Pearson's remarks at the Third Freedom Festival in Toronto in May the following year, when he observed that "How infinitely poorer Canada would have been—how very much harder it would be to meet our challenges today—without the enriching differences represented in the people and cultures here tonight!"[39]

At the same time that the "new nationalism" was developed under Pearson, the Quiet Revolution was progressing in Québec (this was the mass modernisation of the province of Québec economically, politically, and socially), and its consequences were becoming more apparent. *Citizen*, a government journal aimed at migrants, devoted an entire full-length article to it at the close of 1964. It quoted Leon Balcer, Deputy Leader of the Progressive Conservative Party and its Québec lieutenant, who described the Quiet Revolution as an awakening of Québec. A young generation of French Canadians were breaking into the areas of business, finance, industry, and science. Norbert Prefontaine, executive director of the Canadian Centenary Council, went even further, describing it as a "coming of age."[40]

When asked by a journalist at *Le Devoir* whether people were exaggerating when they discussed the Quiet Revolution in Québec, Rene Levesque, the Liberal Minister of Natural Resources in Québec (and future premier), replied: "There is no exaggeration, and indeed we have not yet finished measuring the significance of the recent changes in Québec....What is the result? A nation awake, in full swing, fed up with being seen as a museum, as 'the quaint old province of Québec,' a nation bend on advancing, rising: no longer just content to endure."[41] The references to Québec as a *nation* are particularly telling. French-Canadians during this period began to see Québec as their nation and Canada as their state, although some separatists were now also beginning to envisage Québec as their state.

Pearson responded to this growing nationalism in Québec by stressing a Canadian identity that incorporated French-Canadians. He stated in April 1965: "We must become increasingly proud of the composition and character of our people—the French part, the English part, and the *third force*[42] (these were Canadians of neither British nor French origin)....I don't believe that the Anglo-Saxon element in our society need be subordinated or minimized, because Canada is now a multiracial society."[43] This was a ground-breaking statement, as it was the first time that any Canadian leader had described their country as a multiracial society. This was the background in which citizenship legislation was amended between the 1950s and 1970s.

The *Canadian Citizenship Act* of 1957

The *Canadian Citizenship Act* of 1957 was the first major amendment of Canadian citizenship legislation since its inception in 1947. In July 1955 Minister of Citizenship and Immigration, Jack Pickersgill, outlined the main changes to the legislation to the Cabinet:

> It would include a clarification of the sections dealing with courts, and a provision to prevent persons employed outside of Canada by Canadian firms, or wives of diplomats and trade commissioners, who wished to become Canadian citizens, from being penalized because of their inability to meet the full residence requirements.[44]

However, it was highlighted during the Cabinet discussion that the suggestion on terms of residence included wives but not single women. It was argued that it should be applicable to all. The Cabinet subsequently "approved in principle the proposed amendments to the *Citizenship Act*, as recommended by the Minister of Citizenship and Immigration, and agreed that a draft measure be prepared accordingly." It was added, taking into account the point that had been made during the Cabinet discussion, that "amendments to the residence requirements governing persons employed outside of Canada, and others, would apply to both sexes."[45]

At the beginning of the following year it was suggested that the debate at the time of the adoption of the first *Citizenship Act* in the House of Commons should be consulted to determine if there was any mention as to the justification for treating natural born and naturalised individuals differently in this specific situation.[46] Pickersgill replied the subsequent month and stated that:

> There was nothing in the Parliamentary debate, at the time provision was made in the new Canadian Citizenship Act authorising the Minister to allow native-born Canadians to resume citizenship, which had a bearing on the amendment he now had in mind. He had considered the matter further and recommended that an appropriate amendment be made in the measure in the Senate.[47]

The Cabinet concurred that the bill to amend the *Canadian Citizenship Act*, which was currently in the Senate, be further changed to give the Minister of Citizenship and Immigration enough flexibility to allow individuals naturalised before 1947 who had forfeited Canadian citizenship to continue their citizenship without unnecessary delay on coming to live in Canada permanently.[48]

In April 1958 the significance placed on citizenship was highlighted in a draft Citizenship Day message written by the Department of Citizenship and

Immigration for Prime Minister Diefenbaker: "Citizenship Day is a timely reminder to all Canadians to pause and reflect upon the significance and duties
of citizenship. For citizenship is a great deal more than a political or legal concept. It is a moral concept, an ideal of justice and duty, a social virtue which
embodies the emotional feeling of patriotism, love of one's country."[49]

Even after the amended *Canadian Citizenship Act* was passed in 1957, the
distinction between natural born and naturalised citizens continued to be
raised in government. In a memorandum to Cabinet in May 1958, Acting
Minister of Citizenship and Immigration, Davie Fulton, pointed out that:

> Section 18 of the Canadian Citizenship Act provides that a Canadian citizen who
> resides abroad for a period of ten consecutive years ceases to be a Canadian citizen
> upon the expiration of such period. This provision does not apply to a natural-born
> Canadian citizen or to one who has served overseas in the Armed Forces of Canada
> etc....There is thereby created a distinction between the natural-born and the natu-
> ralised Canadian citizen.[50]

There had previously been a strong feeling that those who gained Canadian
citizenship should do so because of an intention to reside in Canada, and that
subsequent voluntary time overseas for up to ten years is enough to assume
that the individual had some other motivation or that their citizenship is not
of any use to them anymore and has thus ended by such time away. Contrarily,
there was an increasing feeling that this discrimination between the natural-
born and the naturalised was wrong, that the occasions of citizenship should
be the same for all, and that once obtained, Canadian citizenship should be
ended only by the adoption of the nationality or citizenship of another country.[51]

It was emphasised, though, that there were individuals that on becoming
Canadian citizens kept the citizenship or nationality of another nation due to
the law of that nation. As long as such an individual was a law-abiding Canadian, they should not suffer. A policy decision was thus needed as to whether this prejudice should be eliminated completely or kept in amended form.
If kept, there were some adjustments of administrative minutia that should
be implemented in any case, and in order to prevent statelessness it should
also be allowed that citizenship was not ended in these situations unless the
individual in question was, or henceforth became, a citizen or a national of
another nation.[52]

Fulton appeared to be more influenced by the argument about discrimination, as he recommended that:

Section 18 be amended in such terms as to make it clear that (subject to Section 19, *infra*) a Canadian citizen (other than a woman who acquires the citizenship or nationality of another country by marriage) loses his or her citizenship only by becoming a citizen or national of another country or by returning to and residing for ten years in a country of which such person is a national or citizen.[53]

It was also illustrated that there was a list of measures which led to distinctions between naturalised and natural-born citizens. It was noteworthy that some of these distinctions had been indirectly supported by some of Fulton's own party. The cases for and against were obvious, but one or two would be highlighted, as a policy decision was needed. The case for keeping these distinctions was that citizenship was a privilege that Canada only gave to those who were ready, and that those whose subsequent actions implied that they were not now, or then, appropriate individuals to become citizens, should be required to have their citizenship withdrawn; also, that though the citizenship of the natural-born could not be taken away, this was not discriminatory treatment as they had obtained Canadian citizenship by no intentional act of their own; instead, the naturalised had requested to become citizens, being aware of the existence of specific outlined provisions, acting against which could lead to a loss of Canadian citizenship. The case against keeping these measures was that although their existence might be justified, the reality was that two groups of citizens were being created. It was further highlighted that where Canadian law allowed for penalties for the actions encompassed in these measures, the treatment of all should be equal under the law and the naturalised should not be punished above and beyond the natural-born by having their citizenship taken away, a penalty that the natural-born were exempt from.[54]

Hence, in relation to Section 19 (referred to above), Fulton recommended that its first subsection be removed and the required changes adopted to allow the following:

To provide that a person who is not a Canadian citizen and who makes application for that purpose shall satisfy the Court which deals with the application or the Minister, as the case may be that he intends if granted Canadian citizenship to bear true allegiance to the Crown and to support democratic government, institutions or processes, as they are understood in Canada....To retain the provisions of subsection 19 (1) (a), but to make the revocation dependent upon notification to such person that his citizenship will be revoked unless he returned to Canada to stand trial...to authorise the Governor in Council after due inquiry having been made by the Revocation Commission established under the Canadian Citizenship Act or by a Superior Court of a Province to revoke the Citizenship of a person, other than a natural-born Canadian citizen, if he is satisfied that said person did not intend when granted Canadian Citizenship to support democratic government, institutions or processes, as they are understood in Canada.[55]

Later that same month it was stated that:

> The Cabinet Committee on Legislation had considered a memorandum submitted by the Acting Minister of Citizenship and Immigration recommending that certain amendments be made to the Canadian Citizenship Act to change the conditions governing the acquisition and revocation of Canadian citizenship. This would be accomplished by amending section 18 of the act to make it clear that a Canadian citizen loses his citizenship only by becoming a citizen or national of another country or by returning to and residing ten years in a country of which such person is a national or citizen.[56]

The Cabinet concurred that a bill be produced to revise the *Canadian Citizenship Act*, as suggested by Fulton.[57] The concern expressed above about the distinctions between natural-born and naturalised Canadian citizens occurred precisely at the same time as English-speaking Canada's self-identification as a British nation began to wane, as exemplified by the Suez Crisis of 1956. This is no coincidence. It was because of this context of the shift in national identity that citizenship legislation began to be amended to be more inclusive of other ethnic groups. However, as the above also shows, this was just the beginning of the process, and change would be gradual.

The *Canadian Citizenship Act* of 1962

The *Canadian Citizenship Act* of 1962 was the next major reform of citizenship legislation. Although its predecessor had made some notable changes, particularly in regard to the distinctions between natural-born and naturalised Canadian citizens, some differences between the two remained. This was outlined in a statement regarding amendment to the *Canadian Citizenship Act* in July 1960:

> Prior to September 6, 1958, the Canadian Citizenship Act in subsection (1) of Section 19 contained six broad clauses which provided for the revocation of Canadian citizenship of persons other than natural-born Canadian citizens. Because it was felt that these provisions discriminated unfairly against persons naturalized in Canada, the Bill amending the Canadian Citizenship Act provided that five of these six provisions be deleted from the Act. Of the original six it retained only that which provided for the revocation of Canadian citizenship by a person who had obtained a certificate of naturalization or Canadian citizenship by false representation or fraud or by concealment of material circumstances.[58]

However, the Bill also added one new cause for revocation. This stipulated that where an individual other than a natural-born Canadian citizen was accused of treason under the Criminal Code or with an offence under the *Official Secrets Act*, they did not lose their citizenship unless they failed, or refused, to come back to Canada of their own volition to appear before a preliminary investigation into the offence or at the trial. A positive consequence of the limiting of the series of measures for revocation had been to reduce the situations of statelessness. Moreover, another revision was made to Section 19 that allowed for the Minister of Citizenship and Immigration, if they had any doubt whether someone had stopped being a Canadian citizen, to forward the matter to a Court or Commission for a decision. In this manner, the minister could have adjudication from an independent body to resolve any uncertainty that may have been present.[59]

The following year the link between the newly adopted Bill of Rights and citizenship was illustrated by the Deputy Minister of Citizenship and Immigration, George F. Davidson, to Secretary to the Prime Minister, Claude Gauthier:

> Citizenship Day is of special significance being a day set apart for Canadians to unite in public ceremonies emphasizing the meaning of Canadian citizenship....This will be the first Citizenship Day since the dignity and worth of the human person and the right of every Canadian to fundamental freedoms has been declared in a national Bill of Rights. The Bill of Rights is a declaration of moral, spiritual and legal values, and gives to every Canadian the right to equality under law and denies discrimination against any person by reason of race, origin, colour, religion or sex. May each of us be able to say with pride on Citizenship Day, and on every day throughout the year: "I am Canadian, a free Canadian, free to speak, without fear, free to worship God in my own way, free to stand for what I think right, free to oppose what I believe wrong, free to choose those who shall govern my country. This heritage of freedom I pledge to uphold for myself and all mankind."[60]

In July 1961 *The Toronto Star* reported that former Liberal immigration minister Jack Pickersgill had moved an amendment to Prime Minister Diefenbaker's Bill of Rights that would allow naturalised Canadians equal rights as native-born citizens. The amendment, presented as a private bill, was given first reading. It took its place at the end of an extensive list of other private bills, and the likelihood of it being passed that session was slim. Pickersgill stated that it was motivated by the case involving a German-Canadian who was considered an expert on the history of art. The man was a naturalised Canadian, his wife was Canadian, and all his children were born in Canada. Due to the highly specialised expertise he had, he had to look for work abroad. He desired to keep his Canadian citizenship, but he would lose it automatically under Canadian law if he remained outside the country for a decade. Only naturalised Canadians who were in the employ of the government or worked for a Canadian firm could keep their citizenship after more than a decade. Pickersgill's amendment would make sure that naturalised Canadians could keep their Canadian citizenship as long as they did not take up the citizenship of another country.[61] Although the private bill had little chance of success, the fact that it was even introduced showed that attitudes towards the still-existing distinctions between natural-born and naturalised citizens were becoming an increasing concern.

The Canadian Council of National Groups—an association representing several different Canadian ethnic groups—also expressed this concern. In a memorandum to members of parliament, Michael Lucas, Executive Secretary of the council, argued that: "A tragic and contradictory situation exists between the provisions of the Canadian Bill of Rights and the deeds of political discrimination against radical thought or activity." Lucas added that the council had recommended and urged "That the Act and regulations be amended to comply with the Canadian Bill of Rights and including the provision that there shall be no discrimination against applicants for citizenship because of their exercise of free speech, free assembly and association, and freedom of the press."[62] But the council's most significant recommendation was:

> That the fundamental right to citizenship, subject only to the applicant meeting requirements as to minimum age and residence, etc. and the applicant being clear of any court record of a serious criminal offence, shall be specifically incorporated into the Canadian Bill of Rights and declared to be a constitutional right by making such a Bill of Rights part of the proposed Canadian Constitution.[63]

Internal government discussions on the continued discrimination between natural-born and naturalised citizens were on display in early 1964 in a memorandum by the Deputy Minister for Citizenship and Immigration, C. M. Isbister, to the Minister for Citizenship and Immigration, René Tremblay, which also referred to Pickersgill's earlier attempt to rectify this.[64]

In early 1964 Parliamentary Secretary to the Minister of Citizenship and Immigration Hubert Badanai expressed his support to his minister for the amendments to the Citizenship Act announced by the Prime Minister giving naturalised Canadians equal rights and privileges as natural-born Canadians. However, Badanai also drew attention to another area of Canadian citizenship which he believed deserved serious consideration:

> I would like to suggest a change in the procedure of the hearing of applications from married women of naturalized Canadian citizens, who cannot comply with language requirements. There are several hundred wives of Canadian citizens who, by reason

of age, or by living in isolated places, have not been able to master the English or the French language and indeed are unlikely to ever learn sufficiently to qualify, under our present regulations, when they appear before a judge for examination for citizenship. I would therefore propose that a citizenship court recommend the grant of a certificate of citizenship to an applicant who is the wife of a Canadian citizen even though she is unable to speak the English or the French language.[65]

This issue was most likely a personal one for Badanai, as he had migrated to Canada from Italy at the age of 18.

In a memorandum to Cabinet, Minister for Citizenship and Immigration, John R. Nicholson, outlined the current citizenship situation:

At present applicants must have an *adequate* knowledge of the responsibilities and privileges of Canadian citizenship and also an adequate knowledge of either English or French, although 20 years of residence in Canada is an alternative to the language requirement. Everyone, whatever his circumstances, must qualify under the adequate knowledge of responsibilities provision....The naturalised Canadian is subject to automatic loss of citizenship after residing abroad for 10 years, although some exceptions are provided.[66]

The government's commitment to make it easier for wives of naturalised Canadians to become citizens was displayed in notes on proposed amendments to the *Canadian Citizenship Act*:

Here is found the basis and intent of the present draft of amending legislation which includes several additional changes designed to remove other provisions which sometimes appeared to discriminate against legal residents of Canada who desire to be Canadians but who, due to extenuating circumstances, have experienced great difficulty in mastering English or French to a satisfactory degree.[67]

So, the above shows that there was a continuing gentle shift towards removing the distinctions between naturalised and natural-born citizens. This gradual change took place at the same time as English-speaking Canada's Britannic identity was in decline, expedited by the UK's application for entry into the EEC in the early 1960s; a "New Nationalism" was embraced as a replacement. I argue that this shift in national identity resulted in growing concern about discrimination against naturalised citizens.

The *Canadian Citizenship* Act of 1967

As illustrated above, the *Canadian Citizenship Act* was amended in 1957 and 1962. However, major reforms were not introduced until 1967 and then 1977. The 1977 reforms have quite rightly been given the majority of the attention, but the 1967 reforms very much laid the foundation for the subsequent Act, and so I will explore this first. In May 1964 the Cabinet approved amendments to the *Canadian Citizenship Act* which were primarily aimed at removing the discrimination between natural-born and naturalised Canadians and making it simpler for a person who was married to a Canadian citizen to acquire Canadian citizenship.[68] However, progress was slow, as the Cabinet was still discussing the changes nearly a year later. The changes were specifically aimed at removing Section 18 of the Act, which provided for the loss of Canadian citizenship by a naturalised Canadian who lived outside of Canada for more than a decade. The Cabinet Committee on Legislation had argued that new Canadians who went back to their country of origin—especially if it were a Communist nation—soon after being awarded citizenship might take the right offered by the deletion of Section 18. But the Minister of Citizenship and Immigration, John R. Nicholson, suggested that, considering its long-standing pledge, the government should agree to remove Section 18 of the *Citizenship Act*. The Cabinet ultimately agreed to this.[69] However, it was not until the end of 1965 that the *Victoria Daily Times* commented that the Citizenship and Immigration Acts would be getting a major revamp at the next session of Parliament.[70] The cause of the delay was apparently the heavy parliamentary backlog.[71]

In July 1966 the government was presented with the question of whether it was possible to swear allegiance to the Canadian state as opposed to the Crown when someone became a Canadian citizen. In the opinion of Legal Adviser to the Registrar of Canadian Citizenship, R. E. Williams, this was a "constitutional matter, and it would not I think, be possible to swear allegiance in Canada to the State." He added that the "Government never acts in its own name—only and always in the name of the Crown. Hence, we do not resort to the fiction of the state as doing or taking actions, as for example, is done in Republican Countries." He hit his point home with "There is therefore, no state as separate and apart from the Crown....It is appropriate therefore that the oath of allegiance—as acknowledging sovereignty, swearing fealty and relying upon protection, should be taken to the Queen as Head of the State."[72]

In October 1966 Clerk of the Court of Canadian Citizenship, J. R. Templeton, expressed his astonishment that there was no reference to "Canadian Citizens" in a questionnaire produced by the city of Ottawa. He thought it surprising "that your questionnaire asks residents of Ottawa whether they are

British subjects or Aliens and there is absolutely no reference to Canadian Citizens anywhere in the questionnaire." He emphasised his point with "it seems strange to me that there is no place on the form in question to indicate that you are a Canadian Citizen, particularly in view of the fact that the Canadian Citizenship Act came into effect on January 1st, 1947, that this is the eve of Centennial Year and especially because Ottawa is the capital of our country."[73] Thus, the prevalence of the status of British subject, especially at a provincial or municipal level, was still very evident. However, the criticism of this by Templeton illustrates that there was growing pressure to place more importance on Canadian citizenship. But the federal government did not feel that it should make the usage of the term "British Subject" a huge issue with the provincial governments at this point, as the situation was slowly improving by itself.[74]

In a memorandum to Cabinet in late 1966, the Secretary of State, Judy LaMarsh, outlined the status of the revision of the *Canadian Citizenship Act*:

> At the opening of the last three sessions of Parliament the Government has announced its intention to introduce amendments to the Canadian Citizenship Act to ensure full equality of rights for all Canadian citizens wherever they were born....In the intervening time a number of additional suggestions for amendment have been made, some of which have been approved by the Cabinet, and incorporated in a draft bill which has not yet been placed before Ministers. It would be desirable to rewrite the Citizenship Act completely but the legislative programme is so full that even if a revision could be prepared quickly, which is doubtful, it could not be introduced for some time.[75]

Hence, the revision process was taking a long time and LaMarsh could not even give an indication of when the final draft bill would be introduced, which perhaps indicates that it was not considered a top priority.

However, at the end of the year, Dr. K. M. Banreti-Fuchs, a naturalised Canadian, put pressure on Jean Marchand, Minister of Manpower and Immigration, to remove the inequality between natural-born and naturalised Canadians in the current *Canadian Citizenship Act*. Specifically, the provision whereby naturalised Canadians lost their citizenship if they lived outside Canada for over a decade. Dr. Banreti-Fuchs enquired "whether any concrete steps are being taken by your Department to correct the present state of affairs regarding our Citizenship Act."[76] LaMarsh replied that when the Parliamentary timetable permitted, she intended to "introduce amendments to the Canadian Citizenship Act which, amongst other things, will remove the element of discrimination concerning loss of citizenship to which you have referred."[77]

This was finally done in early 1967. But some members of the Cabinet expressed their concern that the proposal would lead to a debate on the Commonwealth and the privileged status of British subjects in citizenship issues. LaMarsh's response was that those sections of the draft bill relating to these matters should simply be deleted.[78] The Cabinet approved this the following day.[79] So, because Britishness had unravelled in English-speaking Canada by this point, the continued preferential treatment awarded to British subjects was a potentially contentious issue.

There was a lively debate when the bill finally reached Parliament in May 1967. Unsurprisingly, the debate first centred on the continued privileges of British subjects in the legislation. A French-Canadian Liberal MP, Auguste Choquette, pointed out that "According to the Citizenship Act those who are born in Canada are also British subjects, and I say this with apologies to the hon. member for York-Humber (Mr. Cowan)....Since Elizabeth II is Queen of Canada would the hon. member recommend that the status of British subjects for Canadian citizens be eliminated?"[80] He received a riposte from Richard Bell, the Progressive Conservative member for Carleton: "Indeed, I certainly would not....It is one of my great prides that in addition to being a Canadian citizen, which is my first love, I am also a British subject."[81] This was a long-standing view held by many English-speaking Canadians. However, Choquette received support from another English-speaking Canadian, the Liberal member for York-Scarborough, Robert Stanbury:

> The argument is put forward very often that naturally a person coming from a British country, with British parliamentary traditions, is more familiar with our democratic processes and our history and therefore should have rights superior to those afforded immigrants from other countries. But I would suggest that there is no longer any logic to this argument [this was due to the end of the British connection and bicultural considerations]....I think the least we could do in amending the citizenship act is recognize this kind of discrimination, ensuring for instance that the stress placed upon a person being a British subject does not accentuate the discrimination against others which is already inherent in our laws.[82]

This shows that attitudes were changing, even amongst English-speaking Canadians. Despite these continued distinctions, the Citizenship Bill passed the House of Commons and the Senate and received royal assent to become the *Canadian Citizenship Act* of 1967. I will now turn to examining the *Canadian Citizenship Act* of 1977.

The *Canadian Citizenship Act* of 1977

This Act finally removed the remaining privileges that British subjects had over other migrants to Canada. Similar to its predecessor, the *Canadian Citizenship Act* of 1977 had a very long legislative process. At the beginning of 1974 the Cabinet agreed that the draft Citizenship Bill, initially prepared for introduction in 1972, be forwarded to the Department for Justice for revision. Secretary of State, J. Hugh Faulkner, would revise the oath included in the draft Bill to incorporate references to both the Queen and to Canada, and would forward the finished product to caucus for its deliberation.[83] Faulkner would also confer with caucus regarding the issue of plural nationality. An announcement of the introduction of the Bill should be incorporated in the Speech from the Throne for the next session of Parliament.[84] Some months later the President of the Privy Council and the Government Leader in the House of Commons highlighted that the Bill would remove special treatment for British subjects. The Cabinet agreed to consider the draft Bill, entitled "An Act Respecting Citizenship," dated 24 April 1974, at a subsequent date.[85]

The Bill finally reached Parliament at the end of 1975—again, the delay seems to imply that it was not a high priority for the government—although it would later claim that this was due to a detailed consultation process with various representative ethnic group organisations. The Progressive Conservative member for Provencher, Jake Epp, maintained that the current Citizenship Bill should place more emphasis on the obligations of citizenship for new prospective citizens, alongside the rights that they would have. He thought this was particularly important as Canada was receiving considerable immigration from countries that did not have strong democratic traditions. Epp believed that it would be for the mutual benefit of all if Canada instructed them not only about economic adjustment, language, and social adjustment, but also about their responsibilities in their new nation.[86]

The New Democratic Party member for Greenwood, Francis Andrew Brewin, expressed his pleasure at the removal of the requirements for citizenship to show that they were of good character:

> I am…pleased to note that the requirements for citizenship do not include the provision of the old act, that the applicant must be of good character. Instead, there seems to be substituted the necessity of showing an adequate knowledge of Canada, of the responsibilities and privileges of citizenship and a "substantial knowledge of Canada."[87]

He ended with a broader point about the importance of Canadian citizenship, both for Canada and the new prospective citizen: "Canadian citizenship is of great importance. It is an essential element in our democratic system. It is a matter of special pride to those who have made their homes and plan to live their lives in Canada and are anxious to assume the responsibilities of full citizenship and exercise the full privileges of that status."[88]

However, the Liberal member for Davenport, Chas L. Caccia, was critical of the new knowledge of Canada provisions in the proposed act. He did not believe that reciting the knowledge of the names of capitals or rivers would be a particularly stimulating and interesting experience for new prospective citizens. Thus, Caccia asserted that knowledge of Canadian geography and official languages should not be emphasised as a qualification of citizenship, as many Canadians knew there were very good citizens in the far north, in the Arctic region, who likely did not speak a word of French or English, nevertheless they were Canadian citizens.[89] This view was most likely partly due to the fact that Caccia was of Italian descent and represented a Toronto riding that had the largest proportion of people descended from Southern Europe, including recent immigrants who were probably unable to become Canadian citizens due to these requirements.

The Progressive Conservative member for Perth-Wilmot, Bill Jarvis, was much more critical of the Bill, particularly the time it had taken to reach the house:

> I hope later in my remarks to be a little more charitable, but at the outset may I say it is my opinion that this bill has been gathering dust in the citizenship branch for years and all through the twenty-ninth parliament. It is absolutely ridiculous that we are sitting here in the closing days of 1975 debating whether an 18 year old can apply for citizenship....The bill received first reading in October, 1974. Seven months later we got around to having the second reading debate. Now, well along in 1975, we are just getting into the third day of debate on this very important piece of legislation.[90]

But Jarvis' more substantive comments related to the change in the status of British subjects. He asserted that this was a major change. Jarvis was not so much concerned with the change in status itself; rather, he was extremely critical of the "rotten job," as he put it, that the government had done in announcing the changes to British subjects. He said that he had never heard of a so-called advertising campaign by the government or any public pronouncements by the Secretary of State informing British subjects of their change in status or their change in voting rights.[91]

The Liberal member for York East, David Michael Collenette, countered that "Members of the official opposition cast aspersions on this party as being against the British connection, but many of us were born there and many of us were elected in constituencies where large numbers of the people came from Britain....British citizens should be aware that they are not in danger of losing their rights."[92]

However, the opposition was not yet finished, with the Progressive Conservative member for Granville-Carleton, Walter Baker, strongly criticising the change in status of British subjects in the new bill:

> I think it is correct to say that, by virtue of this bill, we are to treat those who are not British, and not members of the Commonwealth of Nations, in the same way as we treat British subjects...the minister implied that we were wrong to treat the British subject differently. But I suggest there was good reason for treating him differently.... We must bear in mind that many people who come to this country have enjoyed the British parliamentary system, British justice, and other protections of the law as a matter of traditions. An advantage is enjoyed by the citizen from Great Britain, a Commonwealth country...in terms of the necessity of absorbing new traditions.[93]

This illustrates that even though English-speaking Canada's self-identification as a British nation had declined in the 1950s and 1960s, it was a gradual process, and remnants still remained, even as late as the 1970s.

The Liberal member for Kamloops-Cariboo, Len Marchand, offered a contrary view to Baker on the change in status of British subjects:

> A bone of contention over the years regarding citizenship has been the term "British subject"....I always felt uneasy about the term because in no way did I feel like I was a British subject. I can understand how people coming from many other lands must feel. To me the term "British subject" connotes that a person comes from Britain.... There will no longer be a privileged status for anyone. People wishing to become Canadian citizens will be treated the same regardless of where they came from....This is a very progressive change and I welcome it.[94]

This had been a long-standing view held by many French-Canadian parliamentarians since the inception of the *Canadian Citizenship Act* in 1947. The difference now, though, was that a large number of English-speaking Canadian parliamentarians shared that position.

In July 1976 Faulkner announced the passage of the *Canadian Citizenship Act* the previous week. He acknowledged that the act had a long process of discussion and development, adding that his office had consulted numerous ethno-cultural organisations, both during the drafting of the Bill and when it was passing through parliament.[95] More detail was given in a news release the following month:

> The Secretary of State, J. Hugh Faulkner, stated that "This new Act will make the acquisition of citizenship a more logical, equitable and consistent process and I envisage that it will encourage many resident across the country to become official members of our great Canadian family." Under the new Act, applicants for naturalization are treated alike, regardless of...country of origin and citizenship now becomes a right, provided certain conditions are met.[96]

The *Canadian Citizenship Act* of 1977 was a ground-breaking piece of legislation, as it finally removed all inequalities, especially in terms of ethnicity, that had existed for such a long time in previous citizenship legislation. So, I have shown above how the context of the end of the British World in Canada led to the redefinition of citizenship in relation to other ethnic groups. I will now turn to exploring how this context led to apparent shifts in how Indigenous peoples in Canada were regarded when it came to citizenship.

Amendment of the *Elections Act* in 1950

Major reforms to the *Elections Act* took place in 1950. One of the notable changes was that First Nation people had the franchise extended to them if they lived off reservations. However, those living on reservations could only exercise their right to vote if they gave up their "Indian status" (primarily, not having to pay tax on any income produced on the reserve) under the *Indian Act*. This was known as "enfranchisement." In April 1950 the reactions of First Nations to this change were discussed in a memorandum by the Director of the Indian Affairs Branch for the Deputy Minister, Department of Citizenship and Immigration: "Many Indians apparently fear that if given the privilege of voting it would lead to the diminution of treaty rights and other special benefits which they enjoy at the present time....The franchise is taken by some as being synonymous with 'enfranchisement,' as used in the Indian Act."[97] The following month, two very contrary views on extending the franchise to First Nations were expressed. The Liberal MP for Coast-Capilano in British Columbia, James Sinclair, asserted that "The Provincial Government did this just before the last election and, from all accounts, the step proved to be a wise one....As far as my riding is concerned, I will be very glad to see the federal franchise extended to the Indians."[98] In direct contrast, the Minister of Trade and Commerce, Clarence Decatur Howe, maintained that "I shudder

at having to deal with 2,142 Indian voters in the Port Arthur constituency....
These votes will all be for sale and they are sufficient to turn any election....I
continue to be opposed to Indians having a vote."[99]

That same month Minister of Citizenship and Immigration, Walter Harris, outlined the current situation in relation to First Nations and the Elections Act to Prime Minister Louis St. Laurent:

> Every Indian person ordinarily resident on an Indian Reservation who did not serve
> in the military, naval or air forces of Canada in the war of 1914–1918 or in the War
> began on the 10th day of September, 1939 [was not entitled to vote]....It has been
> the opinion of Indian Affairs that the above provision does not bar from voting the
> Indian on the Reservation who is not in receipt of an annuity or other benefit under
> a treaty. About half the Indians in Canada would, therefore, be qualified....Further,
> Indians who are off the Reservations may vote whether in receipt of treaty money or
> not, and in the election of last year all the Indians in Yukon Mackenzie were entitled
> to vote because there are no Reservations in that Riding. Quite a few did vote, even
> though they might be in receipt of treaty money.[100]

At the end of May 1950 Harris highlighted:

> That there might be some difficulty in limiting voting privileges to those Indians
> who would voluntarily relinquish any taxation exemptions on personal property and
> income since this might tend to give the impression that the exemption was a right,
> whereas in reality it was merely a statutory provision and was not in any way related
> to treaty rights and obligations. As a matter of general principle it was felt that voting
> privileges should eventually be extended to all Indians. There were many difficulties
> to be overcome, however, not the least of which was the reluctance of a large segment
> of the Indian population being granted the voting franchise on condition that the
> taxation exemption be relinquished.[101]

However, the view that First Nation people should even be given the right
to vote on the federal level was not unanimously held. That same month, the
Liberal member for Athabasca, Joseph Mivelle Dechene, expressed his strong
opposition to Harris:

> Logically, the granting of the franchise would simply mean the beginning of the com-
> plete liberation of the Indian tribes from all their treaties' obligations and of course
> also relieving the Federal Government of theirs in that regard. Knowing the Indians
> as I do, they are far from being prepared for this role of citizenship. As a matter of fact,
> in the Province of Alberta we had to undertake the rehabilitation of the majority of
> the half-breeds in north part of the province because it was found that they had not
> succeeded in being assimilated and they actually had become a group of outcasts and
> pariahs almost comparable to the untouchables in India.[102]

In June 1950 Harris announced that since the removal of the bill to amend the *Indian Act* before prorogation of the last session of Parliament, First Nations and other concerned groups had been offered the chance to express their opinions on the suggested changes. It was then proposed that several further revisions be made to the bill before re-introduction during the upcoming session. One of the more significant new revisions concerned:

> Deletion of section 42 which provided for compulsory surrender of Indian reserves situated wholly or partly within the boundaries of a municipality. This procedure appeared to be contrary to the spirit of Indian treaties since it was understood that titles to the reserves would remain in the Crown, in trust for the Indians in perpetuity, and that such reserves would not be subject to alienation except under powers of expropriation for public purposes, which would apply to the lands of any other owners regardless of race.[103]

After deliberation, the Cabinet approved generally the suggested additional revisions to the *Indian Act* as proposed by the Minister of Citizenship and Immigration and concurred that the bill to amend the *Indian Act* be changed appropriately.[104]

The parliamentary debates surrounding the amendment of the *Elections Act* that same month were extremely lively, to say the least. Secretary of State, Frederick Gordon Bradley, outlined that:

> Section 1(1) is for the purpose of extending the franchise to Eskimos by removing them from the exemption in paragraph C. Section 1(2) of the bill amends paragraph (f) so as to bring the text in line with a later section in the bill and to afford to Indians the opportunity to acquire the vote by waiving their right to exemption from taxation on personal property.[105]

However, the Progressive Conservative member for Vancouver Quadra, Howard Green, asked Bradley to explain why the act was not revised to "give the vote to the Indians of Canada....In the bill there is a section giving the vote to Eskimos, but there is still a restriction against the Indians....My understanding is that the Indian does not have a vote unless he signs a waiver of exemption from taxation." Green added that he believed that "the time has come to give the vote to Indians in Canada....They have proved that they are well qualified to have that right in British Columbia; and if they are eligible to vote in a provincial election they should also be allowed to vote in a federal election."[106] Bradley responded to Green's criticisms:

> One of the bases for granting the franchise is that the holder of it shall be subject to the ordinary taxation laws of the land. That is a principle that goes a way back,

that there shall be no taxation without representation [a reference to the American Revolution no doubt]....It would be a curious situation if these people had the full franchise in Canada and yet were exempt from personal property taxes.[107]

But the independent member for Comox-Alberni, John Gibson, continued the attack on the bill:

I resent, and I am sure the Indians will also, the fact that these people are being placed in a different category from the Eskimo. I think it is an admitted fact that the Indian population is considerably advanced over the Eskimo population....I realize that perhaps that [not having to pay taxation on income earned on reserves] will have to be eliminated at some point, but I do not think it is right to give the Indian a vote only if he waives that exemption which is his by long usage. We are setting up about five different classes of Indians in connection with voting.[108]

The Progressive Conservative member for Carleton, George Drew, supported Gibson's position, arguing that "In this particular case you are imposing certain conditions in regard to the Indian which it seems to me are not keeping with our attempt to make a responsible citizen....I think every step should be taken to give the Indians full rights of citizenship and make them feel that they are citizens of this country in every way."[109] Drew was in turn supported by the Progressive Conservative member for Simcoe North, Julian Ferguson:

This in 1950; we are holding up the torch of democracy, yet we say that men and women who were the original citizens of this country may not have a voice in its government by means of the ballot. If an Indian served his country, he is given the privilege of voting; otherwise he is not....Let us take a step forward in this year 1950 and give every citizen of this country the right to voice his opinion of the government by marking his ballot. Do not ostracize and set apart one group of citizens of whom we should all be proud.[110]

But Bradley was not without his supporters either. The Liberal member for Skeena, Edward Applewhaite, maintained that "it seems to me this discussion has not been altogether fair to the committee or to the minister who introduced it." He added that "if you are going to throw the vote to anybody just like that, they will treat it with the same degree of respect and consideration with which, unfortunately, it is treated by a great many of us."[111] It is noteworthy that First Nations were being held to a higher standard than non-Indigenous people when it came to citizenship. The Co-operative Commonwealth Federation member for Rosetown-Biggar, Major James Coldwell, argued that "Whatever may be said about the matter, I think there is a principle involved....That principle is that the inhabitants of this country, no matter of what colour, race or creed, should have the right to vote."[112]

In late 1950 the President of the Native Brotherhood of British Columbia, Chief William Scow, wrote to Harris to express the opposition of his association to the proposed changes to the *Elections Act*:

> Whereas in the proposed amendment to the Dominion Elections Act it is provided that before obtaining the franchise all Indians belonging to Indian Bands in the province must waive certain rights in order to be qualified to vote and whereas this discrimination against Native Indians is viewed by Indian people as reflection upon their status and as an indication that the Parliament of Canada considers them to be inferior to other Canadians therefore be it resolved that this great convention of Native Indians representing all of the Indians in the province of British Columbia demand that as a symbol of equality by treatment and in recognition that their status is not inferior to their brother Canadians the franchise be granted to them in Dominion elections without any reservations or conditions of any kind.[113]

Harris replied to him that "the amendment to the Elections Act of last June was not intended as a reflection upon the status of the Indians, but was intended as an improvement in their status."[114]

Amendment of the *Indian Act* in 1955

The *Indian Act*, which governed relations between the Canadian federal government and First Nations, was amended in a notable way in 1955. It was a response to the revisions made five years earlier, in 1950, which was the first time that the act had been amended in a major way since its inception. Minister of Citizenship and Immigration, Walter Harris, illustrated this to the cabinet in late 1953:

> The Minister of Citizenship and Immigration said that, to implement an undertaking he had made at the time the Indian Act revision came into effect, he would shortly receive representatives of the main Indian groups in Canada for the purpose of reviewing the provisions of the Act in the light of experience since its coming into effect.[115]

The Legal Advisor of the Department of Citizenship and Immigration expressed his opinion on some of the questions raised by certain First Nation representatives on the relation of the *Indian Act* to pre-existing treaties:

> Mr. Andrew Paull, President, North American Indian Brotherhood, Vancouver, B.C., raised the question as to whether some sections of the Indian Act were valid

as they appear to be in conflict with alleged rights set out in treaties. Mr. Paull is of the opinion that where there is a conflict as between any treaty and any provision of the Indian Act, the provision in the treaty must prevail over that of the Statute. This question arose in the case of Rex vs Syliboy. Briefly this case dealt with the treaty of 1752 made between Governor Hopson and certain of the Mic Mac Indians of Nova Scotia. It was determined in this case that this so called treaty was not in reality a treaty.[116]

So, it is quite clear that the federal government did not view this argument favourably.

A second conference was held in Ottawa (the first taking place two years earlier) between government officials and First Nation representatives. As in 1951, the goal of the conference was to talk about the features of the *Indian Act*, together with possible revisions to it in the light of experience since it was adopted. Most of the discussion was focused on the administration of the Act instead of specific revisions to it: "It was again evident from the discussion that the problems of Indian communities varied from reserve to reserve and region to region and these differences accounted for the variety of viewpoints expressed towards particular sections of the Act." It was stressed, though, that "the unanimous view of those present, however, that the present Act had been beneficial to all Indians."[117]

In late 1954 James Brown wrote to the Minister of Citizenship and Immigration, Jack Pickersgill, suggesting that following the decision of the Ontario government to give its First Nation population the right to vote in provincial elections, "the Federal Government really ought to do something about the same question at an early date and hesitancy to do so might have results which would last over a good number of years."[118] In a memorandum to Pickersgill in late 1954 the Deputy Minister of Citizenship and Immigration, Laval Fortier, maintained that "it could be argued that the Indians, being the original inhabitants of this country, could be given the privilege to vote notwithstanding the fact that they are exempt of certain taxes on the income earned on the reserves." He added that "They are paying many other taxes, like any other citizens who do not have a sufficient income for taxation under the Income Tax Act."[119]

In a reply to Brown that same month, Pickersgill outlined the two major problems, as he saw them, with giving First Nations the right to vote in federal elections, and potential electoral consequences:

It seems to me that the two main difficulties about extending the franchise, generally, to Indians are (1) the nomadic character of many of the Northern Indians; and (2) the question of whether the vote should be given to people who have a perpetual exemption from certain taxes. The C.C.F. [Co-operative Commonwealth Federation] have been very assiduous in courting the Indians, and I suspect the effort of giving them a vote, for some considerable time, would be help the C.C.F. On the other hand, there is no doubt that eventually we want the Indians to be completely emancipated and enfranchised and just to be ordinary citizens.[120]

Towards the end of 1954 Pickersgill was reported as saying in the *London Free Press* that he "would like to see the day when there are no more reserves in Canada." "The day will come," he said, "when common citizenship is so attractive to Indians that they will abolish reserves and there will be no more distinct states among our people."[121] This was a prevailing belief at the time: that the distinctions between First Nations and other Canadian citizens should be broken down, so as to make them the same.

At the beginning of 1955 the Secretary of the Indian Association of Alberta, John Laurie, wrote to Pickersgill expressing the strongest opposition of the association to news reports that James Brown, MP, had sponsored a private members bill calling for voting rights to be extended to all First Nations living on reserves. He argued that "we regard such a matter as an infringement upon Treaty rights….The Treaties were certainly bi-lateral agreements between the representatives of the Crown and the Chiefs of the various bands in this province." He hit his point home with:

> The terms of the present Indian Act provide that any Treaty Indian residing on a reserve may, by his own initiative either 1. Apply for and usually receive enfranchisement (as the expense of all rights as an Indian); 2. Sign documents which will permit him to become eligible to vote in federal elections (as do Indian veterans) except that by so doing he renders himself liable to certain forms of taxation. As far as Alberta Indians are concerned, this is their stand: "we shall view any enforced change in Treaty status only as a complete violation of Treaty Rights."[122]

So, there was very strong opposition from certain First Nation representatives to any suggestion of giving them the right to vote without their permission, at the cost of very hard-fought rights.

At the beginning of 1955 Pickersgill sent a very matter-of-fact reply to Laurie; his tone certainly comes across as condescending and patronising:

> This will acknowledge your letter of January 10, in which you refer to a private bill sponsored by Mr. James Brown, M.P., to extend the franchise to all Indians residing on reserves. I believe what you have in mind is the notice of a proposed resolution presented to the House on January 7 by Mr. James Brown, the member for Brantford, Ontario. The proposed resolution reads as follows:

That in the opinion of this House, the government should consider the advisability of introducing legislation to amend the Canada Elections Act, so as to extend the franchise to every Indian, as defined in the Indian Act, who is ordinarily resident on a reserve.[123]

Pickersgill added that:

As you know, in 1950 Indians living on reserves were granted the right to vote in Federal elections in accordance with the provisions of the Canada Elections Act. I was, therefore, particularly interested in your view to the effect that extension of voting rights to Indians on reserves would be an infringement of treaty rights. I have had the various treaties covering the Indians of Alberta examined, and I am informed that there is no reference to voting rights in any of them. I gather from your letter, however, that you are under the impression that exercise of the franchise would alter the Indian status of Indians under treaty. This is not the case.[124]

In July 1955 Pickersgill announced to the cabinet that he intended to launch legislation in the next session of Parliament "to introduce a measure at the next session of Parliament to clarify and to add to the powers contained in a number of sections of the Indian Act....One of the main features of the legislation would be amendments to the liquor provisions to allow Indians on a reserve to decide by referendum whether they favoured temperance or not."[125] On the question of the franchise, in late 1955 Pickersgill told the cabinet that he would be meeting representatives of First Nations in the foreseeable future and would make use of the occasion to talk about the issue of awarding them the franchise. He did not believe that legislation should be adopted at the current time for that purpose.[126]

In the opening address at a First Nation conference organised in Ottawa in December 1955, Pickersgill initially praised the work of the leadership of the Indian Councils: "I think it is quite marvellous to observe the high sense of responsibility shown by those chiefs and councillors the Indians have elected themselves to look after their affairs, and there is nothing I welcome more than the new and great responsibilities that every year these band councils are taking."[127] However, he then entered into some very disturbing territory:

There was a time, of course, I do not need to remind any of you, there was a time four hundred years ago when your ancestors were the only people in this country, when you had the country to yourselves to run any way you liked. Now that situation is never going to happen again because, I am afraid, there are too many of us other Canadians and there is no possibility of your scalping us all and getting rid of us.[128]

If the comment was meant as a joke, it was in extremely poor taste. I am confident that it would not have been received well by his audience.

Awarding of the Right to Vote to First Nations in 1960

In the early 1960s pressure from the UN and decolonisation movements contributed towards the federal government addressing the issue of the federal franchise and First Nations. There was considerable internal discussion within the Department of Citizenship and Immigration about the awarding of the right to vote to First Nations in late 1959. Reports from agencies on the ground indicated that there was a high level of interest in voting amongst some First Nations, and relative indifference in others. In general, the consensus was that First Nations initially regarded the right to vote with suspicion. But they had largely become politically more conscious after they were awarded the franchise in provincial elections, and this had resulted in their having a closer affinity with their fellow residents in the areas in which they resided.[129] Director of the Department of Citizenship and Immigration, H. M. Jones, in a memorandum to the Deputy Minister, agreed completely with the idea that First Nations should be awarded an unrestricted right to vote. Those living on reserves had certainly not come forward in large numbers to receive the right to the franchise under the terms imposed by the existing legislation. Under the revisions to the *Indian Act* (which, from its first inception in 1876, regulated the lives of First Nations living on reserves in the country) in 1950, First Nations living on reserves could be awarded the right to vote only if they become "enfranchised"—which was essentially giving up their status as First Nations living on reserves. This was achieved through them executing a waiver of exemption from taxation on money earned on reserves. Jones then outlined the steps that would be required to achieve this end, which were primarily amendments to the *Indian Act* and the *Canada Elections Act*.[130] A few days later, Minister for Citizenship and Immigration, Ellen Fairclough, in a letter to the Minister of Justice, Davie Fulton, announced her intention to introduce legislation to award the federal franchise to First Nations along the lines that Jones had suggested.[131]

In a memorandum to cabinet on the subject in November 1959, Fairclough made a persuasive case for the change:

> The present legislation has created an anomalous situation: some of the most primitive Indians in Canada in the James Bay area of Québec and Ontario and also in the

Yukon and Northwest Territories have the right to vote because they do not live on reserves and, in fact, voted in the last federal election. On the other hand, the most educated Indians in the southern parts of the provinces because they live on reserves and have never felt they should execute a waiver of exemption from taxation, are not eligible to vote. It is considered that the present restrictions should be removed and the Indians given the same privileges with respect to voting as other Canadian citizens.[132]

Thus, the changes to the *Indian Act* in 1950 had not led to a large number of First Nations living on reserves deciding to become "enfranchised" and thereby being awarded the federal vote. The Cabinet approved the minister's recommendations the following month.[133]

There was also popular pressure for the government to act. In a brief submitted by the Primate of all Canada on behalf of the Anglican Church of Canada to the Joint Committee of the Senate and House of Commons on Indian Affairs[134] in January 1960, it was "urged that the federal vote be granted to all Indians residing on reserves without prejudice to their status."[135] However, the Aboriginal Native Rights Regional Committee of the Interior Tribes of British Columbia argued in its brief that "If we are to have the Federal vote at the expense of losing our aboriginal rights, we flatly refuse." They added that "we would appreciate a system of voting similar to the Maoris of New Zealand, where all the Indians of Canada would vote for an Indian or Indian representatives in Parliament."[136] First Nations were concerned that they would lose rights guaranteed to them by the *Indian Act* and the long-standing treaties that some of them had with the Crown[137] (which predated the *Indian Act*) if they were awarded the federal franchise.

In April 1960 the Senate finally approved the awarding of the federal franchise to First Nations. However, the *Saskatoon Star-Phoenix* drew attention to critical remarks by Liberal Senator Thomas A. Crerar of Manitoba, who said that passage of the legislation would lead to inequality and anomalies: "If the Indian is to become a full citizen he must accept all the responsibilities and not receive these favors[138]....We are setting up a discrimination between citizens and that is not what we want to do."[139] Hence, there was not unanimous agreement that the proposed changes were a positive thing.

There was so much concern amongst certain First Nations that the proposed changes would lead to a loss of the rights they had under the *Indian Act* and their own treaties with the Crown that some bands sought legal advice on their impact. There was particular worry over military conscription during wartime.[140] However, the Department of Citizenship and Immigration emphasised that "There is no compulsory feature in the legislation....It merely extends to the Indians the right to vote if they wish to do so." In the past, other legislation such as making the Family Allowances and Old Age Pensions payable to First Nations had engendered similar fears, but they had proven to be groundless.[141]

The *Globe and Mail* offered a First Nation perspective on the proposed changes through a First Nation person writing an editorial in the newspaper in which he asserted that "Many Indians in Canada look towards the granting of the Federal vote with suspicion, scepticism, distrust, and fear." The main cause of this, according to the author, was the continued existence of Section 112 of the *Indian Act*, which allowed the Minister of Indian Affairs to force a First Nation person, even an entire band or tribe, to be ejected from a First Nation Reserve.[142] The *Regina Leader-Post* also maintained that there would be extreme reluctance by First Nations to vote, as they were worried that by so doing they would lose rights guaranteed to them by the *Indian Act*. The newspaper argued that a written assurance by Prime Minister Diefenbaker detailing that this would not be the case would go a long way towards allaying their fears.[143]

In May 1960 Fairclough wrote to those First Nation individuals who had executed a waiver of exemption from taxation in order to be able to exercise the federal franchise informing them that under the new legislation they were no longer bound by the waiver. They were exempt again from taxation on income earned on reserves as well as being able to vote in federal elections.[144] Nevertheless, there was still some considerable anxiety expressed by various First Nation group representatives that their people would lose rights guaranteed by the *Indian Act* if they exercised the federal franchise and that voting would be compulsory.[145] Fairclough did her best to assuage these concerns in individual replies.[146] But she realised that a general statement on the subject would be more effective and so she released a press release the following month:

> Dominion Day 1960 marks another step forward in the progress of Canada's Indians. On July 1 all Indians aged 21 and over will gain the right to vote in federal elections....Parliament approved amendments to the Indian Act and the Canada Elections Act to permit the inclusion of Indian people on federal voters' lists....Indians will lose none of their rights or privileges by voting in federal elections. Repeated reassurances to this effect have been given in the House of Commons by the Prime Minister and by the Superintendent General of Indian Affairs, Mrs. Fairclough.[147]

This statement seemed to finally put concerns by First Nation representatives to rest, although the anxiousness of First Nations was completely understandable, as in the previous reform of the *Indian Act* in 1950 First Nations people had to become "enfranchised" in order to vote in federal elections.

The 1969 White Paper

The next major development in citizenship and Indigenous groups in Canada was the 1969 White Paper, which proposed making First Nations "equal" citizens with their "fellow Canadians" by, amongst other things, removing the special legal status of "Indians," repealing the *Indian Act*, passing on responsibility for First Nations to the provinces, and appointing a commissioner to deal with land rights which would negate the long-standing treaties that many First Nations had with the Crown. The White Paper was a consequence of the Hawthorne Report of 1966, which investigated the status of Indigenous people in the country and argued that a combination of long-standing government policies, particularly the Residential School System, had resulted in them becoming "Citizens Minus." It also made a list of recommendations to reverse this situation and instead make Indigenous peoples in Canada "Citizens Plus" due to their particular socio-economic circumstances. First Nations had been consulted before the White Paper was announced regarding revising the *Indian Act*, but the proposals went much further and actually called for the *Indian Act* to be abandoned altogether, which was not acceptable to a majority of, if not all, First Nations. Proposals were introduced at the beginning of 1968 to revise the *Indian Act*:

> The proposed legislation would remove from the present Act many features which were considered by the Indians of Canada to be undesirable, and would provide such important elements for the social and economic development of the Indian people as a development fund, the ability of Indian bands to incorporate, and improved education, and on the whole would open the way for Indians to become more independent and better able to participate in services provided by provincial governments.[148]

The Cabinet approved in principle the proposals of the Minister of Indian Affairs and Northern Development, Jean Chrétien. Specifically, it agreed that:

> Discussions be authorised on these changes with the provinces, the territories, and representatives of the Indian people...a report of these discussions be made to the Cabinet before drafting of the legislation is completed and introduced in the next session of Parliament...during these discussions the Indian people be advised that the Bill itself would be referred to them after first reading so that they could make addi-

tional comments directly to a Parliamentary Committee…and the Bill be referred to a Parliamentary Committee after second reading.[149]

However, a few months later, Chrétien suggested that discussion with First Nations regarding revision of the *Indian Act* should be postponed for a period of two months until after the upcoming federal election. First Nations themselves had apparently asked for the delay.[150]

In September 1968 Minister without Portfolio Robert Andras, who was assigned special responsibility for developing new policies on Indigenous people, gave a very frank address to the National Annual Conference of the Indian-Eskimo Association of Canada in Toronto:

> We still have not plugged the Indian point of view into the policy decision-making process. A consultation program on the revisions to the Indian Act has started, but as I have repeatedly said across this country, one cannot expect true and meaningful consultations to flow unless the prerequisites for communication are present; a feeling of mutual trust and respect; a willingness to admit past errors and the availability of similar resources to *both* parties to the exchange.[151]

Therefore, Andras was conceding here that the government had not acted in good faith when it came to genuine consultation with First Nations. This difference in opinion in the Cabinet between Chrétien and Andras was picked up on by the *Globe and Mail* the following month. The newspaper argued that "A major internal reorganisation of the much-criticised Indian Affairs and Northern Development Department, has infuriated one Cabinet minister, created strains in the Trudeau Cabinet and unleashed loud protests amongst Indian leaders."[152] It is no overstatement to say that the White Paper of 1969 produced metaphorical fireworks across the country.

One of these protests was an excellent speech in late 1968 by Harold Cardinal, a First Nation representative of the Indian Association of Alberta (and part of a group of university educated and politically savvy First Nation leaders at the time): "Where has the commitment for consultation gone when policy changes can be made that ignore the needs and the will of the Indian people?…The Indian Association of Alberta urges the Federal government to halt the Departmental re-structuring immediately pending consultation with Indian leaders."[153] He also offered solid suggestions for the start of a meaningful shift in First Nation/Government relations:

> The Canadian Government will have to commit itself morally, philosophically and legislatively to honouring *fully* its agreements under Treaties signed with Indians…. Let the Prime Minister give his Minister without Portfolio the authority and respon-

sibility to work directly with the member organizations of the National Indian Brotherhood in developing new policies for the Federal Government and the authority to implement the proposals that come out of this arrangement.[154]

Thus, Cardinal's emphasis was on greater consultation with First Nations by the government so as to produce better policy, which made obvious sense, as they were the ones who would be affected by any policies introduced by the government.

Chrétien attempted to explain his motivation in revising the *Indian Act* in early 1969:

> Increasing numbers of Indians in Canada were asking for equal citizenship in terms of rights and responsibilities and were indicating that they did not feel at home in Canadian institutions under present circumstances. The problem was made increasingly difficult by the fact that although everything the federal government was now doing for the Indian people fell within provincial jurisdiction and responsibility, several of the provinces were reluctant to extend to Indians such services as education, welfare roads, municipal government, health, housing and regional development.[155]

The Cabinet agreed that Chrétien prepare a memorandum outlining a "policy of full non-discriminatory participation in Canadian society for Indian people, together with the means by which such a policy might best be implemented."[156]

Chrétien subsequently outlined the specific steps the government would take to put the policy in practice:

> Propose to Parliament that the Indian Act be repealed and take such legislative steps as may be necessary to enable Indians to control Indian lands and to acquire title to them....Propose to the governments of the provinces that they take over the same responsibility for Indians that they have for other citizens in their provinces....Make substantial funds available for Indian economic development as an interim measure....Wind up that that part of the Department of Indian Affairs and Northern Development which deals with Indian affairs.[157]

In a further memorandum to Cabinet in October 1969 it was asserted that "the provinces appeared to agree with the policy but wanted the federal government to get the approval of the Indians before their public concurrence was sought, some provinces were insisting that they would not meet the federal government unless Indians were present at the negotiating table."[158] But the impact of Indigenous opposition to the proposals was evident as it was maintained that "Indian groups would want to prepare counter-proposals to the government's statement and should be encouraged to do so" and that "neither the Indians nor the provinces should be pressed, at this time, to agree publicly with the federal proposal; there would be need for three-way consultations (Canada, provinces, and Indians) later."[159]

A sign of how much things had changed was given in mid-1970 when Chrétien announced to Cabinet that the Indian Association of Alberta, with the support of the National Indian Brotherhood, would be making a presentation in which they would assert that they did not agree with the policy proposed by the government. He added that he would be telling the First Nation representatives that he was pleased that they had looked at the policy outlined by the government and that all of their recommendations would be examined by the government and then discussed with them.[160] So, the fierce backlash by First Nations to the proposed White Paper of 1969 (which supposedly had the lofty aim of making First Nations equal with other Canadian citizens) highlighted to the government that First Nations were "Citizens Plus"[161] due to the treaties that existed between many of them and the Crown which predated the existence of the state of Canada and/or the fact that they were the First Nations that inhabited what later became Canada and should be treated as such. So, many First Nations saw the White Paper as an attempt by the federal government to abandon its responsibilities through delegation to the provinces and abrogate its treaty obligations. The whole thrust of the White Paper reflected Prime Minister Pierre Elliott Trudeau's hostility to group rights. The strong reaction of First Nations to the proposals actually provided the impetus to the modern Indigenous rights movement in Canada. And it should be emphasised that the concept of "Citizens Plus" was contested, as there were, and still are, First Nations in Canada—the Mohawk Nation in Québec being a prominent example—that do not necessarily consider themselves Canadian citizens, but citizens of their own nations.

In conclusion, this chapter has illustrated how the end of the British World led to a redefinition of citizenship in Canada between the 1950s and 1970s. The key highlights of the unravelling of Britishness in Canada were the Suez Crisis of 1956 and the UK's decision to apply for membership of the EEC in 1961. This resulted in a shift away from a British-centred citizenship to one that was more inclusive of other ethnic groups and apparently Indigenous peoples. The *Canadian Citizenship Acts* of 1957, 1962, 1967, and 1977 demonstrated the gradual shift in terms of greater inclusivity towards other ethnic groups, as especially with the final Act, the last distinctions between British subjects and other migrants were removed from Canadian citizenship legislation. And on the Indigenous side, the amendment of the *Elections Act* in 1950 and the *Indian Act* in 1955 demonstrated the Canadian states' limited efforts to extend the federal franchise to First Nations, as long as they gave up their status as "Indians." So, the awarding of the right to vote to First Nations in federal elections in 1960 without any preconditions was a major milestone in their being able to exercise one of the major privileges of citizenship. The 1969 White Paper, which, amongst other things, proposed a repeal of the *Indian Act* in the supposed goal of making First Nations equal to other citizens, faced such backlash from a highly educated and politically savvy First Nation leadership that the government was forced to concede that First Nations were not citizens just like other Canadians, but "Citizens Plus."[162]

Notes

1. The research for this chapter was conducted while I was the inaugural Avi Arensen Canadian Studies Postdoctoral Fellow in the School of Indigenous and Canadian Studies (SICS) at Carleton University. I am extremely grateful to the International Council for Canadian Studies for their generous financial support through the fellowship and SICS for hosting me.

2. Christina Gabriel, "Citizens and Citizenship," in *Critical Concepts: An Introduction to Politics*, eds. Janine Brodie and Sandra Rein (Toronto: Pearson, 2009), 166.

3. *Ibid.*

4. T. H. Marshall, *Class, Citizenship and Social Development: Essays by T. H. Marshall* (Westport, Connecticut: Greenwood Press, 1964), 84.

5. William Kaplan, "Who Belongs? Changing Concepts of Citizenship and Nationality," in *Belonging: The Meaning and Future of Canadian Citizenship*, ed. William Kaplan (Montreal & Kingston: McGill-Queen's University Press, 1993), 252.

6. Will Kymlicka and Wayne Norman, "Return of the Citizen: A Survey of Recent Work on Citizenship Theory," *Ethics* 104 (1994), 369.

7. Jane Jenson, "Citizenship Claims: Routes to Representation in a Federal System," in *Rethinking Federalism: Citizens, Markets and Governments in a Changing World*, eds. Karen Knop, Sylvia Ostry, Richard Simeon, and Katherine Swinton (Vancouver: UBC Press, 1995), 99.

8. Valerie Knowles, *Forging Our Legacy: Canadian Citizenship and Immigration, 1900–1977* (Ottawa: Citizenship and Immigration Canada, 2000), 88.

9. Gary Caldwell, "Evolution of the Concept of Citizenship (1945–1995): An English Canadian Perspective," in *La Nation Dans Tous Ses Etats: Le Québec en Comparaison*, eds. Yvan Lamonde and Gerard Bouchard (Montreal: Harmattan, 1997), 302.

10. Linda Cardinal and Marie-Joié Brady, "Citizenship and Federalism in Canada: A Difficult Relationship," in *Contemporary Canadian Federalism: Foundations, Traditions, Institutions*, ed. Alain-G. Gagnon (Toronto: University of Toronto Press, 2009), 384.

11. Darlene Johnston, "First Nations and Canadian Citizenship," in *Belonging: The Meaning and Future of Canadian Citizenship*, ed. William Kaplan (Montreal & Kingston: McGill-Queen's University Press, 1993), 349.

12. R. Kenneth Carty and W. Peter Ward, "The Making of a Canadian Political Citizenship," in *National Politics and Community in Canada*, eds. R. Kenneth Carty and W. Peter Ward (Vancouver: UBC Press, 1986), 74.

13. Alan C. Cairns, "Empire, Globalization, and the Fall and Rise of Diversity," in *Citizenship, Diversity, and Pluralism: Canadian and Comparative Perspectives*, eds. Alan C. Cairns, John C. Courtney, Peter Mackinnon, Hans J. Michelmann, and David E. Smith (Montreal & Kingston: McGill-Queen's University Press, 1999), 38.

14. Hamar Foster, "Indian Administration' from the Royal Proclamation of 1763 to Constitutionally Entrenched Aboriginal Rights," in *Indigenous Peoples' Rights in Australia, Canada, & New Zealand*, ed. Paul Havemann (Auckland: Oxford University Press, 1999), 365.

15. Augie Fleras and Jean Leonard Elliott, *The "Nations Within": Aboriginal—State Relations in Canada, the United States, and New Zealand* (Toronto: Oxford University Press, 1992), 221.

16. Joyce Green, "The Impossibility of Citizenship Liberation for Indigenous People," in *Citizenship in Transnational Perspective: Australia, Canada, and New Zealand*, ed. Jatinder Mann (New York: Palgrave Macmillan, 2017), 175–88.

17. For more on the prevalence of Britishness in English-speaking Canada at this time and the French-Canadian reaction to it see Mann, "Anglo-Conformity,'" 253–76. It should be pointed out, though, that English-speaking Canada's Britishness was not a sign of inferiority, rather, English-speaking Canadian Britons saw themselves as superior to those in the "mother-country." It was maintained that the harsh Canadian climate, the realities of colonial life, and a healthier diet had resulted in a fitter and stronger British population in Canada.

18. For more on the *Canadian Citizenship Act of 1947* see Mann, "The Evolution of Commonwealth Citizenship," 293–313.

19. José Igartua, "Ready, Aye, Ready' No More?" in *Rediscovering the British World*, ed. Phil Buckner (Calgary: University of Calgary Press, 2005), 48.

20. Dale C. Thomson, *Louis St. Laurent: Canadian* (New York: St. Martin's Press, 1968), 459.

21. Robert Bothwell, *The Penguin History of Canada* (Toronto: Penguin Canada, 2006), 381–3.

22. Thomson, *Louis St. Laurent*, 459.

23. Canadian Parliamentary Debates, *House of Commons (H of C)*, 1956–57, 27 November 1956, Howard Green cited in Igartua, "Ready, Aye, Ready' No More?" 47.

24. Igartua, "Ready, Aye, Ready' No More?" 61–2.

25. *Ibid.*, 58.

26. Jack L. Granatstein, *Canada 1957–1967: The Years of Uncertainty and Innovation* (Toronto: McClelland and Stewart, 1986), 43.

27. Andrea Benvenuti and Stuart Ward, "Britain, Europe, and the 'Other Quiet Revolution' in Canada," in *Canada and the End of Empire*, ed. Phil Buckner (Vancouver: UBC Press, 2006), 168.

28. This includes R. T. Griffiths and S. Ward, eds., *Courting the Common Market: The First Attempt to Enlarge the European Community* (London: Lothian, 1996); Wolfram Kaiser, *Using Europe, Abusing the Europeans: Britain and European Integration, 1945–1963* (London: Macmillan, 1996); Jacqueline Tratt, *The Macmillan Government and Europe: A Study in the Process of Policy Development* (Basingstoke, Hampshire: Macmillan, 1996).

29. Benvenuti and Ward, "'Britain, Europe, and the 'Other Quiet Revolution' in Canada," 169, 170.

30. *Ibid.*, 171.

31. *Ibid.*, 172, 173.

32. National Archives of the UK, DO 159/52, Fleming, speech at Winnipeg, 19 January 1962, cited in Benvenuti and Ward, "Britain, Europe and the 'Other Quiet Revolution' in Canada," 173.

33. LAC, RG25, vol. 5519, file 12447–40 (pt. 51), record of meeting between Prime Minister Macmillan and Prime Minister Diefenbaker, Ottawa, 20 April 1962, cited in Benvenuti and Ward, "Britain, Europe and the 'Other Quiet Revolution' in Canada," 176–7.

34. Benvenuti and Ward, "Britain, Europe and the 'Other Quiet Revolution' in Canada," 177.

35. Lester Pearson, "Symbols and Realities," in *Mike: The Memoirs of the Right Honourable Lester B. Pearson: Volume 3, 1957–1968*, eds. J. A. Munro and A. I. Inglis (London: Victor Gollancz, 1975), 270.

36. LAC, MG26-N9/Vol. 50—National Unity—1963–1964, Observance of Canada's National Holiday, 28 June 1963.

37. LAC, RG33-80/Acc. 1974–75-039/Box 83/Speeches by PM/1963–1967, Text of the Speech delivered by Lester B. Pearson, Prime Minister of Canada, at the Annual General Meeting of the Canadian French Language Weekly Newspapers' Association, at La Malbaie, on 17 August 1963, 2.

38. *Ibid.*, 3.

39. LAC, RG26/Vol. 76/File 1–5-11/The Foreign Press in Canada/Part 4/1962–1964, Office of the Prime Minister Press Release—Remarks by the Prime Minister Lester B. Pearson at the Third Freedom Festival, O'Keefe Centre, Toronto, Sunday, 10 May 1964, 1.

40. "The Quiet Revolution in Québec," *Citizen* 10, no. 5 (December 1964): 6, 7.

41. *Ibid.*, 10, 11.

42. The first major reference to a "third force" was by Senator Paul Yuzyk, who was of Ukrainian descent, in his maiden speech to the Senate in 1964. He subsequently emerged as one of the strongest proponents of multiculturalism.

43. LAC, MG32-C67/Vol. 91/File 1, Prime Minister Lester Pearson, in the Weekend Magazine, no. 14, 3 April 1965, has seen fit to make the following significant statement to all Canadians.

44. LAC, RG2/Series A-5-a/Vol. 2658—Cabinet Conclusions—Legislation; Canadian Citizenship Act, 22 July 1955, 3.

45. *Ibid.*

46. LAC, RG2/Series A-5-a/Vol. 5775—Cabinet Conclusions—Legislation; possible further amendment to the Canadian Citizenship Act, 25 January 1956, 5.

47. *Ibid.*, 2.

48. *Ibid.*

49. LAC, MG26-M/Vol. 245/Reel M-7900/File 313.3 MI–C, J. R. N., Department of Citizenship and Immigration to the Office of the Prime Minister (including draft Citizenship Day message from Prime Minister), 18 April 1958.

50. LAC, RG2-B-2/Vol. 2741/Cab. Doc. 128–58—Memorandum by E. D. Fulton, Acting Minister of Citizenship and Immigration to the Cabinet—Canadian Citizenship Act. Proposed amendments regarding acquisition and revocation of Canadian citizenship, 10 May 1958, 2.

51. *Ibid.*

52. *Ibid.*

53. *Ibid.*

54. *Ibid.*, 3.

55. *Ibid.*, 4.

56. LAC, RG2/Series A-5-a/Vol. 1898/Cabinet Conclusions—Legislation; amendments to the Canadian Citizenship Act, 27 May 1958, 3.

57. *Ibid.*, 4.

58. LAC, RG26/Vol. 82/File 1–24-27, Part 3, Statement Re: Amendment to the Canadian Citizenship Act, 5 July 1960, 1.

59. *Ibid.*, 2.

60. LAC, MG26-M/Vol. 245/Reel M-7900/File 313.3 MI–C, George F. Davidson, Deputy Minister of Citizenship and Immigration to Claude Gauthier, Secretary to the Prime Minister (including brief Citizenship Day message from Prime Minister for the Toronto Telegram), 15 May 1961, 199767.

61. "Bill to Aid Naturalized Canadians," *The Toronto Star*, 3 July 1961, 10.

62. LAC, MG26-N3/Vol. 210/File 577.2, Michael Lucas, Executive Secretary, Canadian Council of National Groups to Members of the 26th Parliament (including Memorandum on Citizenship Rights, 28 October 1962), June 1963, 8, 9, 10.

63. *Ibid.*, 10.

64. LAC, RG26/Vol. 75/File 1–1-8, Part 3, Memorandum by C. M. Isbister, Deputy Minister to the Minister, 26 February 1964, 2.

65. LAC, MG26-N3/Vol. 210/File 577.2, Hubert Badanai to Rene Tremblay, Minister of Citizenship & Immigration, 26 February 1964, 2.

66. LAC, RG6/Vol. 659/File 1–5-2, Part 1—Acts and Bills—Canadian Citizenship Act—Amendments, Memorandum by John R. Nicholson to Cabinet.

67. LAC, RG6/Vol. 659/File 1–5-2, Part 1—Acts and Bills—Canadian Citizenship Act—Amendments, Notes on proposed amendments to the Canadian Citizenship Act.

68. LAC, RG2/Series A-5-a/Vol. 6264—Cabinet Conclusions—Amendment of the Canadian Citizenship Act, 7 May 1964, 3, 4.

69. LAC, RG2/Series A-5-a/Vol. 6271—Cabinet Conclusions—Proposed amendment to Citizenship Act—Report of security panel, 2 April 1965, 2, 3.

70. LAC, RG6/Vol. 659/File 1–5-2, Part 2, Extract from the *Victoria Daily Times*—"Major Revamp Facing 'Archaic' Act," 26 November 1965.

71. LAC, RG6/Vol. 664/File 3–6-11, Charles A. Lussier, Assistant Deputy Minister (Citizenship) to Donald A. Cameron, 21 July 1965, 2.

72. LAC, RG2/Vol. 660/File 1–16-2, R. E. Williams, Legal Adviser to Registrar of Canadian Citizenship, 4 July 1966.
73. LAC, RG6/Vol. 659/File 1–5-1, J. R. Templeton, Clerk of the Court of Canadian Citizenship to W. P. Simpson, Assessment Commissioner, Ottawa (including Questionnaire), 7 October 1966, 1.
74. LAC, RG6/Vol. 659/File 1–5-1, W. R. Martin, Registrar of Canadian Citizenship to Assistant Under Secretary of State (Citizenship), 27 October 1966.
75. LAC, RG2-B-2/Vol. 6320/Cab. Doc. 700–66, Memorandum by Judy LaMarsh, Secretary of State to the Cabinet—Legislation: Citizenship Act Amendments, 30 November 1966, 1.
76. LAC, RG6/Vol. 664/File 3–6-11, Dr. K. M. Banreti-Fuchs to Jean Marchand, Minister of Manpower and Immigration, 1 December 1966.
77. LAC, RG6/Vol. 664/File 3–6-11, Judy LaMarsh, Citizenship Registration Branch to Dr. K. M. Banreti-Fuchs, 19 December 1966.
78. LAC, RG2-B-2/Vol. 6325/Cab. Doc. 157–67, Memorandum by Judy LaMarsh, Secretary of State to the Cabinet—Canadian Citizenship Act Amendments, 15 March 1967, 1, 3.
79. LAC, RG2/Series A-5-a/Vol. 6323, Amendments to the Canadian Citizenship Act, 16 March 1967, 5.
80. Canadian Parliamentary Debates, H of C, Vol. 1, 1967, 26 May 1967, Mr. Choquette, 642.
81. Canadian Parliamentary Debates, H of C, Vol. 1, 1967, 26 May 1967, Richard Bell, 642.
82. Canadian Parliamentary Debates, H of C, Vol. 1, 1967, 26 May 1967, Robert Stanbury, 647.
83. LAC, RG2/Series A-5-a/Vol. 6436, Citizenship Legislation, 10 January 1974, 11.
84. LAC, RG2-B-2/Vol. 26589/Cab. Doc. 1235–73, Record of Cabinet Decision by R. B. Charron, Supervisor of Cabinet Documents—Citizenship Legislation, 11 January 1974, 2.
85. LAC, RG2/Series A-5-a/Vol. 6436, An Act Respecting Citizenship, 8, 9.
86. Canadian Parliamentary Debates, H of C, vol. IX, 1975, 8 December 1975, Jake Epp, 9802, 9803.
87. Canadian Parliamentary Debates, H of C, vol. IX, 1975, 8 December 1975, Andrew Brevin, 9806.
88. Ibid.
89. Canadian Parliamentary Debates, H of C, vol. IX, 1975, 8 December 1975, Chas L. Caccia, 9807.
90. Canadian Parliamentary Debates, H of C, vol. IX, 1975, 8 December 1975, Bill Jarvis, 9809.
91. Ibid., 9810.
92. Canadian Parliamentary Debates, H of C, vol. IX, 1975, 8 December 1975, D. M. Collenette, 9812.
93. Canadian Parliamentary Debates, H of C, vol. X, 1975–76, 10 December 1975, Walter Baker, 9899.
94. Canadian Parliamentary Debates, H of C, vol. X, 1975–76, 10 December 1975, Len Marchand, 9904.
95. LAC, R11236/Vol. 135/File 148–4-8, A Message from the Secretary of State (including short press release), 23 July 1976.

96. LAC, R11236/Vol. 135/File 148–4-8, J. Hugh Faulkner, The Secretary of State for Canada to Bud Cullen, Minister of National Revenue (including copies of a press release to the ethnic press and women's groups and the bill itself), 6 August 1976, 1.

97. LAC, MG32-B34/Vol. 24/File IA 12A, Part 1, Memorandum by the Director, Indian Affairs Branch for the Deputy Minister, Department of Citizenship and Immigration (including information with respect to views of Indians on the question of voting), 12 April 1950.

98. LAC, MG32-B34/Vol. 24/File IA 12A, Part 1, James Sinclair, MP for Coast-Capilano to Walter E. Harris, Minister of Citizenship and Immigration, 16 May 1950.

99. LAC, MG32-B34/Vol. 24/File IA 12A, Part 1, C. D. Howe, Minister of Trade and Commerce to W. E. Harris, Minister of Citizenship and Immigration, 16 May 1950.

100. LAC, MG32-B34/Vol. 24/File IA 12A, Part 1, W. E. Harris to Prime Minister Louis St. Laurent, 16 May 1950, 1, 2.

101. LAC, RG2/Series A-5-a/Vol. 2645—Cabinet Conclusions, Legislation; Indian Act Revision, 30 May 1950.

102. LAC, MG32-B34/Vol. 24/File IA 12A, Part 1, J. M. Dechene, Member for Athabasca to Walter E. Harris, Minister of Citizenship & Immigration, 31 May 1950, 2.

103. LAC, RG2/Series A-5-a/Vol. 2646—Cabinet Conclusions, Legislation; Indian Act revision; Dominion Elections Act amendment, 6 June 1950, 2, 3.

104. *Ibid.*, 3.

105. Canadian Parliamentary Debates, *H of C*, 19 June 1950, Hon. F. G. Bradley (Secretary of State), 3810.

106. Canadian Parliamentary Debates, *H of C*, 19 June 1950, Hon. Mr. Green, 3811.

107. Canadian Parliamentary Debates, *H of C*, 19 June 1950, Hon. F. G. Bradley (Secretary of State), 3811.

108. Canadian Parliamentary Debates, *H of C*, 19 June 1950, Mr. Gibson, 3811.

109. Canadian Parliamentary Debates, *H of C*, 19 June 1950, Mr. Drew, 3812.

110. Canadian Parliamentary Debates, *H of C*, 19 June 1950, Mr. Ferguson, 3813.

111. Canadian Parliamentary Debates, *H of C*, 19 June 1950, Mr. Applewhaite, 3813.

112. Canadian Parliamentary Debates, *H of C*, 19 June 1950, Mr. Coldwell, 3816.

113. LAC, MG32-B34/Vol. 24/File IA 12A, Part 1, Telegram from Chief William Scow, President, Native Brotherhood of British Columbia to Walter E. Harris, 10 November 1950, 1–2.

114. Walter E. Harris to Chief William Scow, President, Native Brotherhood of British Columbia, 17 November 1950.

115. LAC, RG2/Series A-5-a/Vol. 2653—Cabinet Conclusions, Indian Act; discussions with representatives of Indian bands, 14 October 1953, 15.

116. LAC, MG32-B34/Vol. 24/File IA-12, Part 2, Memorandum by the Legal Advisor, Department of Citizenship and Immigration for the Minister, 26 October 1953, 1.

117. LAC, MG32-B34/Vol. 24/File IA-12, Part 2, A summary of the proceedings of a conference held by Walter Harris, Minister of Citizenship and Immigration, with representative Indians in Ottawa, 26–28 October 1953, 1.

118. LAC, MG32-B34/Vol. 24/File IA 12A, Part 3, James E. Brown, M.P. to J. W. Pickersgill, Minister of Citizenship and Immigration, 22 October 1954, 1.

119. LAC, MG32-B34/Vol. 24/File IA 12A, Part 3, Memorandum by Laval Fortier, Deputy Minister of Citizenship and Immigration for The Minister, 28 October 1954, 2.

120. LAC, MG32-B34/Vol. 24/File IA 12A, Part 3, J. W. Pickersgill to James E. Brown, M.P., Brantford, Ontario, 30 October 1954, 1.

121. LAC, MG26-L/Vol. 382/File 2253—Clippings—Department of Citizenship and Immigration—Hon. J. W. Pickersgill, 1 Jul.–31 Dec. 1954, Extract from the London Free Press —"Federal Minister Opens Indian, Non-Indian School," 20 November 1954.

122. LAC, MG32-B34/Vol. 24/File IA 12A, Part 3, John Laurie, Secretary, Indian Association of Alberta to J. W. Pickersgill, Minister of Citizenship and Immigration, 10 January 1954.

123. LAC, MG32-B34/Vol. 24/File IA 12A, Part 3, J. W. Pickersgill to John Laurie, Secretary, Indian Association of Alberta, 31 January 1955, 1.

124. *Ibid.*, 1–2.

125. LAC, RG2/Series A-5-a/Vol. 2658—Cabinet Conclusions, Legislation; Indian Act amendment, 22 July 1955.

126. LAC, RG2/Series A-5-a/Vol. 2659—Cabinet Conclusions, Franchise for Indians, 30 November 1955, 13.

127. LAC, RG26/Vol. 75/File 1-1-8, Part 1, Indian Conference—Ottawa, December 1955 – Opening Address by J. W. Pickersgill, Superintendent General of Indian Affairs, 2.

128. *Ibid.*

129. LAC, MG32-B1/Vol. 94/File IA-166/File 18, Memorandum by H. M. Jones, Acting Director, Department of Citizenship and Immigration to the Deputy Minister, 20 November 1959, 1–2.

130. LAC, MG32-B1/Vol. 94/File IA-166/File 18, Memorandum by H. M. Jones, Director, Department of Citizenship and Immigration to the Deputy Minister, 25 November 1959, 1.

131. LAC, MG32-B1/Vol. 94/File IA-166/File 18, Ellen L. Fairclough to E. D. Fulton, Minister of Justice, 27 November 1959.

132. LAC, RG2-B-2/Vol. 2745/Cab. Doc. 383–59, Memorandum by Ellen L. Fairclough, Minister for Citizenship and Immigration to the Cabinet Re: Proposed amendment to the Indian Act and Canada Elections Act concerning voting by Indians, 27 November 1959.

133. LAC, RG2/Series A-5-a/Vol. 2745, Legislation—Amendment to the Indian Act and Canada Elections Act concerning voting by Indians, 15 December 1959, 5.

134. This was a major committee set up by the Diefenbaker government to look into relations between First Nations and the Canadian state, with the ultimate goal of revising the Indian Act, which had not been reformed in any significant way since 1950. The awarding of the right to vote on the federal level to First Nations was one of the issues it discussed.

135. LAC, MG32-B1/Vol. 88/File IA-12J, A brief submitted by the Primate of all Canada on behalf of the Anglican Church of Canada to the Joint Committee of the Senate and the House of Commons on Indian Affairs, January 1960, 5.

136. LAC, MG32-B1/Vol. 88/File IA-12J, Brief Prepared by the Aboriginal Native Rights Regional Committee of the Interior Tribes of British Columbia, 20.

137. Generally speaking the Crown concluded treaties with First Nations in parts of Atlantic Canada, Ontario, Québec, Manitoba, Saskatchewan, and Alberta when British settlers first arrived in what became Canada by which the First Nations agreed to surrender large

tracts of their land and live on reservations for compensation of some sort, usually financial. However, there were no treaties with First Nations in British Columbia, the Métis (Indigenous people of mixed First Nation and European descent) and Indigenous peoples in the territories (Inuit). The treaties that did exist between the Crown and the First Nations were often not honoured though, which was a rightful cause of complaint by those First Nations that had signed the treaties in good faith.

138. This was a reference to the continued right of First Nations living on reserves to not pay tax on any income they earned there.

139. LAC, MG32-B1/Vol. 95/File IA-166/File 1, Extract from the *Saskatoon Star-Phoenix*—"Senate Group Approves Federal Vote for Indians," 1 April 1960.

140. LAC, MG32-B1/Vol. 95/File IA-166/File 1, Fred. R. & David Conroy Barristers *et al.*, to Department of Citizenship and Immigration, 2 April 1960.

141. LAC, MG32-B1/Vol. 95/File IA-166/File 1, H. B. M. Best, Private Secretary, Minister to Fred R. & David Conroy Barristers *et al.*, 11 April 1960, 2–3.

142. LAC, MG32-B1/Vol. 95/File IA-166/File 1, Extract from the *Globe and Mail* "The Indian and the Vote," 4 April 1960.

143. LAC, MG32-B1/Vol. 95/File IA-166/File 1, Extract from the *Regina Leader-Post*—"Guarantee Indian's Rights," 14 April 1960.

144. LAC, MG32-B1/Vol. 95/File IA-166/File 1, Letter by Ellen L. Fairclough, Minister of Citizenship and Immigration, 20 May 1960.

145. LAC, MG32-B1/Vol. 95/File IA-166/File 1, Translation of letter from Chief Alphonse T. Picard to Ellen L. Fairclough, Minister of Citizenship and Immigration, 6 June 1960.

146. LAC, MG32-B1/Vol. 95/File IA-166/File 1, Ellen L. Fairclough, Minister, Department of Citizenship and Immigration to Chief Alphonse T. Picard, 20 June 1960.
Ellen L. Fairclough, Minister to Chief Councillor Alex Oakes, 13 June 1960, 2.

147. LAC, MG32-B1/Vol. 95/File 1A-166/File 1, Press Release, 28 June 1960.

148. LAC, RG2/Series A-5-a/Vol. 6338, The Indian Act—Proposed revision, 18 January 1968.

149. *Ibid.*, 3.

150. LAC, RG2/Series A-5-a/Vol. 6338, Indian Act Amendment—Consultation With Indians, 30 April 1968, 14.

151. LAC, RG6/Vol. 662/File 2–12-15, Notes for an Address by the Honourable Robert K. Andras to the National Annual Conference of the Indian-Eskimo Association of Canada, Toronto, 28 September 1968, 3.

152. LAC, RG6/Vol. 662/File 2–12-15, Extract from the *Globe and Mail*—"Cabinet said to be divided over reorganization for Indian affairs," 1 October 1968.

153. LAC, MG26-011/Vol. 22/File 5/635—Speech by Harold Cardinal, 27 October 1968, 9.

154. *Ibid.*, 10, 12.

155. LAC, RG2/Series A-5-a/Vol. 6340, Indian Program, 12 February 1969.

156. LAC, RG2/Series A-5-a/Vol. 6340, Indian policy, 17 June 1969.

157. LAC, RG2-B-2/Vol. 6349/Cab. Doc. 654–69, Memorandum on a "Statement of the Government of Canada on Indian Policy," 1969, 6, 7.

158. LAC, RG2-B-2/Vol. 6354/Cab. Doc. 1007–69, Memorandum by Norbert Prefontaine, Secretary, Cabinet Committee on Social Policy to the Cabinet, 29 October 1969, 1.

159. *Ibid.*, 2.

160. LAC, RG2/Series A-5-a/Vol. 6359, Indians—Presentation to Cabinet, 4 June 1970, 5.

161. This originated from a document with the same name which is more commonly known as the "Red Paper." This was an extremely critical response to the White Paper from Harry Cardinal and the Indian Association of Alberta.

Indian Association of Alberta, *Citizens Plus* ("The Red Paper") (Edmonton: Indian Association of Alberta, 1970).

Cardinal also published a book entitled *The Unjust Society* (Vancouver: Douglas & McIntyre, 1999), which was a play on Prime Minister Pierre Elliott Trudeau's famous catchphrase "The Just Society." Cardinal's widely read book was the first time that many non-Indigenous Canadians learned about the special position of First Nations in the country due to their being the first inhabitants of the country and the treaties they had negotiated with the Crown which ultimately led to the establishment of Canada as a country, and the historical obligations that the state still had towards them.

162. Alan Cairns, *Citizens Plus: Aboriginal Peoples and the Canadian State* (Vancouver: UBC Press, 2001).

· 3 ·

REDEFINING CITIZENSHIP IN AOTEAROA NEW ZEALAND, 1950s–1970s[1]

In the 1950s Aotearoa New Zealand very much identified itself as a British country and an integral part of a wider British World which had the UK at its heart. However, by the 1970s this British World had come to an end, as had Aotearoa New Zealand's self-identification as a British nation. During this period, citizenship in Aotearoa New Zealand was redefined in a significant way from being an ethnic (British)-based one to a more civic-founded one which was more inclusive of other ethnic groups and apparently Māori. This chapter will argue that this redefinition of citizenship took place primarily in the context of this major shift in national identity. After having established the context of the end of the British World in Aotearoa New Zealand (with a focus on the UK's application for entry into the EEC and the British military withdrawal from "East of Suez"), it will explore the popular pressure from mainly Dutch immigrants against distinctions between natural-born and naturalised citizens in 1955, the *British Nationality and New Zealand Citizenship Acts* of 1959 and 1963, and the *Citizenship and Aliens Act* of 1977, to illustrate the ways in which citizenship became more inclusive of other ethnic groups in the country. It will then study the *Māori Affairs Amendment Act* of 1967, the *Race Relations Act* of 1971, the *Māori Affairs Amendment Act* of 1974, and the *Treaty of Waitangi Act* of 1975 to highlight the ways in which citizenship in Aotearoa New Zealand also attempted to incorporate Māori but this proved highly problematic and, at this stage, unresolved.

Theoretical Background

Before exploring these several themes, it will be useful to briefly discuss the theoretical background to citizenship in Aotearoa New Zealand during the 1950s and 1970s—namely the distinction between normative citizenship (legal—citizenship as status) as opposed to substantive citizenship (citizenship as rights and obligations). T. H. Marshall has heavily dominated post-war thinking on citizenship in the western world. He maintained that "Citizenship is a status bestowed on those who are full members of a community....All who possess the status are equal with respect to the rights and duties with which the status is endowed."[2] However, Marshall has not been without his critics, one of the most prominent being Bryan S. Turner.[3] Drawing on Turner's work, Neil Lunt, Paul Spoonley, and Peter Mataira argued that the "Marshallian distinctions of civil, political and social citizenship...are seen as problematic, given the historical treatment of the Chinese community, and the abrogation of the Treaty of Waitangi with respect to European-Maori relationships."[4] Turner commented that Marshall's world has in a very real sense disappeared. From an Aotearoa New Zealand angle, we may debate whether such a world was present; discussions over identity and citizenship that arose in the post-Second-World-War period were directed at achieving a consensus that maintained economic, political, and social advantage.[5] A situation unique to Aotearoa New Zealand, especially in comparison with Australia and Canada, is that there was in reality little difference expressed in obligations and rights between citizens and those who were normally referred to as permanent residents; that is, those with the leave to reside in Aotearoa New Zealand but not citizens, so denizens.[6] This has major ramifications for political and civil aspects of citizenship; whether it undermines the concept of social citizenship is an interesting question—to strengthen the former reduces the latter for permanent residents, but enhancing the rights of many people beyond the exclusivities of formal citizenship might be seen as reducing inequalities. On the Indigenous side, Morgan Godfery argued that for Māori, citizenship is an extremely contested notion and very much related to belonging, and it is only through taking a historical perspective that young Māori can be taught about their position in Aotearoa New Zealand.[7] I agree with this viewpoint, especially the contested notion of citizenship, and the importance of belonging to Māori in terms of their own conception of citizenship, which is very much linked to land. Carwyn Jones and Craig Linkhorn explored the history of citizenship in Aotearoa New Zealand in regard to Māori in depth, from before the Treaty of Waitangi (pre-1840) to the present. One of the key arguments that they made is that Western notions of citizenship have been incompatible with Māori conceptions of citizenship for much of the history of European settlement in Aotearoa New Zealand. It is only in recent decades that there has been a real attempt by Pakeha to try to understand Māori citizenship on its own terms.[8] Again, I wholeheartedly support Jones and Linkhorn's argument. For much of Aotearoa New Zealand's history, Western conceptions of citizenship have been imposed on Māori with varying success. Once the Aotearoa New Zealand state acknowledged that Māori had their own conception of citizenship, which predated the arrival of European settlers and was based very much on their relationship with the land, then progress really started to be made. This is something that this chapter will illustrate, at least the beginning of this process. It was desired that ratification of the Treaty of Waitangi would enable Māori to have equal citizenship rights, as assured under Article Three of the Treaty. The 1966 petition of Rangi Makawe Rangitaura of Waitera and other organisations, for instance, requested ratification of the Treaty, repeal of discriminatory Māori land legislation, review of land claims and other grievances, and closing the paternalistic Department of Māori Affairs.[9] A majority of Māori leaders, especially the so-called "moderates," have been searching for means in which Māori concerns about cultural destruction and land could be dealt with in a structure that defended principles of equal citizenship.[10] One way that Aotearoa New Zealand tried to respond to these expectations was by creating, with the *Treaty of Waitangi Act* of 1975, a fixed commission of inquiry, the Waitangi Tribunal, to look into Māori grievances of Crown Treaty breaches. Petitioners must illustrate that they have been subjected to prejudice through regulations and laws, or by acts, omissions, policies, or practices of the Crown from 1840 in ways that act against the Treaty of Waitangi.[11] Roger Maaka and Augie Fleras put the relationship between citizenship and Indigeneity in a broader perspective: "The politicisation of indigeneity opens up the governing process to contestation....Politicisation confronts white settler dominions with the most quintessential of paradoxes—by forcing them to justify their very right to existence, the legitimacy of their claims to citizenship and their rationale for rule over land and inhabitants."[12] Modern Māori calls for the acknowledgement of their sovereignty appeared in the open on February 6, 1971, at the yearly official commemoration of the signing of the Treaty of Waitangi.[13] Another specific dimension to citizenship and Māori is that alongside the rights awarded by the Treaty of Waitangi, there have been numerous statutes and polices that have given Māori a distinct status as Aotearoa New Zealand citizens. For instance, the statute in 1867 that introduced four Māori seats can be regarded, in modern thinking, as a type of distinct political representation, which guaranteed their participation in the leading decision-making institution in Aotearoa New Zealand.[14] But this was still an instance of Western conceptions of citizenship—representative parliamentary democracy in this case—being imposed on Māori. The bravery and effectiveness of the Māori battalion during the Second World War, particularly in Italy and North Africa, and the ensuing general popular acknowledgement of the Māori war mobilisation, had an immense effect on Māori eligibility for government assistance, broadly, and for welfare benefits, especially. Māori had acted in protection of the state—a core aspect of citizenship—and were now eligible for compensation and the equitable fruits of peace.[15] This underlines the existence of a social citizenship, as opposed to a political or legal citizenship, which illustrates that "citizenship" can be defined in various ways.[16] Joan Metge asserted that "Maoris have the same basic rights as other citizens, but are also distinguished in law for certain purposes....The exact status of these differentiating provisions is a matter of debate."[17] According to Louise Humpage, "Governments in settler societies have conventionally regarded the incorporation of Indigenous peoples into the equal rights of citizenship as an appropriate response to indigenous calls for justice....Indeed, indigenous Maori in New Zealand have been considered fortunate to have had citizenship rights bestowed upon them much earlier than their counterparts in other settler societies."[18] But her central argument is that state nation-building motivations behind citizenship are situated in tension with Indigenous nationalisms which illustrate a different form of nation-building that is not structured by the state.[19] I agree with Humpage here. The Aotearoa New Zealand state had a very much delayed reaction to the fact that a Māori nationalism exists, a sense of being a distinct people, which is separate from its own nation-building efforts. Again, this chapter charts the beginning of this process.

The Context of the End of the British World

Having established this theoretical background, the chapter will now turn to exploring the context of the end of the British World as the major reason for the redefinition of citizenship in Aotearoa New Zealand between the 1950s and 1970s. In the post-Second-World-War period, Aotearoa New Zealand was still very much a British society and an integral part of a wider British World. An excellent and very appropriate example is the *British Nationality and New Zealand Citizenship Act* of 1948. Although this act created the very concept of Aotearoa New Zealand citizenship, it stressed *British Nationality* over *New Zealand Citizenship*. Moreover, the status of British subject was maintained and white immigrants[20] from the British Commonwealth were awarded more generous consideration in terms of naturalisation.[21] The Suez Crisis of 1956 is another example of Aotearoa New Zealand's identification as an integral part of a wider British World. During the episode, the Aotearoa New Zealand government completely backed the UK's policy of overturning President Nasser's decision to nationalise the Suez Canal. Aotearoa New Zealand displayed unconditional support for the UK as it regarded itself as a British country. The UK was still the centre of a wider British World, and thus supporting the UK was still considered as being loyal to the "mother-country."[22]

However, this situation started to change in the 1960s. James Belich asserted with characteristic aplomb that "The process of decolonisation can be dated broadly to the years 1965–88, and more narrowly to 1973–85, when Mother Britain ran off and joined the Franco-German commune known as the European Economic Community."[23] Britain's shift away from the Commonwealth was combined with a move towards Europe. The EEC was in certain ways the protagonist of the British-New Zealand recolonial[24] system. By entering it, Britain would become a part of the Common Agricultural Policy, which considerably subsidised EEC farms. Britain did not join the EEC until 1973, and detailed negotiated temporary arrangements meant the Aotearoa New Zealand economy did not experience the full brunt of this for nearly a decade. Yet the abrupt end of recolonisation was, most certainly, clear well before this. Between 1961, when Britain first announced its plan to become a part of the European Community, and 1988, Aotearoa New Zealand carried out an intensive and lengthy political and diplomatic campaign to maintain the economic foundation of the recolonial system: preferential access for its protein exports. Two recurrent aspects of the Aotearoa New Zealand campaign were blatant appeals to sentiment and sympathy. New Zealander negotiators constantly aimed to elicit European and British sympathy by stressing the country's small size, economic vulnerability, and complete reliance on the British market.[25] Belich emphasised "the depth and reciprocity of the recolonial relationship....Some British politicians even believed that Aotearoa New Zealand could have turned the scale in the 1972 vote on entry, through a direct appeal to the British press, parliament and public."[26]

If Britain's decision to enter the EEC in 1961 was the key benchmark of the decline of Britishness in Aotearoa New Zealand, then its moves to withdraw militarily from "East of Suez" in 1967 only compounded the situation. The British decision took place in the context of a very serious economic situation which meant that it could no longer sustain its military commitments abroad with the financial means it had available. When the new Wilson Labour government came to power in 1964 it received a Treasury report which summarised the economic situation facing Britain—it was even worse than Wilson had imagined. The Labour government undertook a wide-ranging defence review in which there was "agreement that to a far greater extent than in other theatres, Britain's defence spending in the Far East and South-East Asia was out of all proportion to the extent of British economic interests in the area." However, it was not only the military dimensions of the British decision, as Aotearoa New Zealand was under the security umbrella of the Australia-New-Zealand-US mutual-defence treaty and, to a lesser extent, the South East Asian Treaty Organisation.[27] Rather, Britain's military withdrawal from "East of Suez" signalled the end of its global role, which put an end to the idea of a British World with the UK at its centre. However, the emotional ties that remained in Australia (although they can be similarly applied to Aotearoa New Zealand) were on display in a letter from Canberra to London on "The Commonwealth as a British interest" in November 1966:

> Australians are in the vast majority British by origin. They feel and express obvious emotional ties to Britain as "home." With New Zealand, Australia has, for reasons of proximity and common origin, the closest possible relationship; Australians regard the New Zealanders as cousins and share with them a sense of family connection with the mother country.[28]

Kate McMillan explored the decline of the Aotearoa New Zealand-British relationship through the lens of British immigration legislation in the 1960s. According to her, "For New Zealand citizens, these British Immigration Acts emptied any substantive meaning from the term 'British subject'—although the term still appeared in New Zealand passports....Emotional ties to the 'motherland' endured for some, along with a sense of shared Commonwealth identity and a continued allegiance to the Crown, but the major right associated with British subject status—that of entry and abode in the United Kingdom—was gone."[29] The reform of immigration regulations and the reform of citizenship were not immediately linked, but had a relationship, especially in the way that both illustrated a shift in the substance of the connection between Aotearoa New Zealand and the UK.[30] Richard Hill commented on the changed situation in Aotearoa New Zealand in the 1970s, "By the 1970s, the old 'politics of stability and consensus' in New Zealand was rapidly being superseded by a 'politics of volatility and increasing political polarization'....While this reflected an international western phenomenon, it was given an antipodean edge by a growing propensity among Pakeha[31] citizens to see themselves as New Zealanders rather than 'British.'"[32]

The unravelling of British race patriotism in the 1970s led to a supposed void in the national identity of Aotearoa New Zealand—the "new nationalism" was offered as a potential alternative to replace it. The first Aotearoa New Zealand-born Governor-General, Sir Arthur Porritt, proudly declared in 1970 that "the events of the last year or two have given New Zealand a new sense of national entity."[33] Within three years, New Zealanders would have a political leader able to take advantage of the rhetoric and language of the "new nationalism" in Labour's Norman Kirk. When political commentators spoke about the "new nationalism," they referred to a process of redefining settler-colonial communities for a post-imperial period. It was a nationalism divorced from its British foundations—a more assertive effort for a more longlasting concept of the people, instead of the "old" nationalism with its connections in wider groupings of Britishness.[34] In Aotearoa New Zealand, there are echoes of Canadian historian Douglas Cole in Belich's two-volume history, especially in his interpretative opposition to the nationalist generation of historians headed by Keith Sinclair. Belich's idea of "recolonisation" is almost precisely identical to Australian historian Neville Meaney's "nationalist era," and mirrors Cole in arguing that during this time, "collective [New Zealand] identity was intense, but not nationalist."[35]

Stuart Ward put the whole concept of the "new nationalism" in a broader British World context: "The experience of 'new nationalism' in the 1960s and early 1970s is particularly instructive here, because it underlines the necessary adjustments that had to be made when Britishness could no longer serve as a key determinant of belonging to the settler-colonial state....As Britishness was slowly consumed by the receding break up of empire, it was widely assumed that

Canada, Australia, and New Zealand were somehow incomplete as national entities —that they were in urgent need of a national-cultural makeover."[36] The 1960s in Aotearoa New Zealand brought growing calls for a complete re-structuring of the nation's key traditions and symbols. Sinclair admitted in a 1963 lecture that "for us to want to be British is a poor adjective, like wanting to be an understudy or a caretaker—or an undertaker."[37] The demand for new national symbols was based on the belief that Aotearoa New Zealand was not "truly" a nation. W. B. Sutch regularly emphasised this theme throughout the 1960s in talks, publications, and essays such as *Colony or Nation?* (1965) and *Take Over New Zealand* (1972).[38] According to Ward, "Like [Australian Prime Minister] Gorton a few years earlier, Kirk pointed to the direct causal relation-ship between the fraying ties to Britain, and the urgency of putting the na-tional house in order….It was the unavoidable fact that New Zealanders could no longer ground their ethnic selves within an imagined community of British peoples that brought the fundamental flimsiness of their nationhood sharply into focus."[39] This was the major context in which nationality and citizenship legislation was amended during the 1950s and 1970s.

Popular Pressure From Mainly Dutch Immigrants Against Distinctions Between Natural-Born and Naturalised Citizens in 1955

In 1955 there was popular pressure from mainly Dutch immigrants in New Zealand against distinctions between natural-born and naturalised citizens. This was illustrated in a translated article in *De N. Z. Hollander* in August 1955:

> In some respects a distinction is made between a naturalized New Zealander and a natural born New Zealander….A…difference between a "British born" and a "nat-uralized" New Zealander is that the latter always needs a re-entry permit in order to return to New Zealand, which is not necessary for the former. That a naturalized New Zealander may lose his New Zealand citizenship by leaving this country and staying abroad during more than six years….In this connection it is perhaps advisable to point out that by naturalization and acquiring the status of a New Zealander you will lose your Netherlands nationality and that according to Dutch law you will then be an alien without any further rights.[40]

So, Dutch immigrants in Aotearoa New Zealand were being warned against applying for Aotearoa New Zealand citizenship, as they could lose it under circumstances not applicable to natural-born Aotearoa New Zealanders, and if this occurred, then they could find themselves stateless, as neither citizenship allowed their citizens to be dual citizens.

The Aotearoa New Zealand government responded to this popular pressure in a Press Statement:

> "There has recently been comment in the Press about discrimination in our nationality legislation between natural born and naturalized citizens", said the Minister of Internal Affairs, Mr. S. W. Smith, today. In particular, the statement had been made that New Zealand citizenship acquired by naturalization "can be cancelled by a stroke of the pen"....."Few countries in the world impose so little restrictions on aliens as New Zealand," said Mr. Smith. "Apart from the facts that they could not vote in general elections or hold a New Zealand passport and were subject to police registration, they were virtually unrestricted"...."This state of affairs, very different from that obtaining in many other countries, means there is little pressure on a foreign resident to become a citizen."[41]

However, it did concede that:

> "It was true," the Minister went on "that naturalized persons could be deprived of New Zealand citizenship in circumstances now applicable to the natural born citizen"...."With minor variations, our legislation is similar in this respect to that of other Commonwealth countries. There are very few if any bodies of nationality legislation in the world which do not contain deprivation provisions."[42]

So, the New Zealand government was emphasising here that its deprivation provisions were in line with its sister Commonwealth states of Australia and Canada, which is not surprising, as their nationality and citizenship legislation had the same origins after the Second World War, as outlined above.

The story was picked up in the English-speaking press later that year, in an article in *The Evening Post*: "As more and more Dutchmen in New Zealand become eligible for naturalisation more and more of them are deciding not to change their old nationality." It added that "Their argument is that there is little sense in exchanging a perfectly valid passport for what has become known among immigrants as a '50 per cent passport.'"[43] This was of course a reference to the fact that Dutch people were reluctant to give up their Dutch citizenship for Aotearoa New Zealand citizenship, when they could lose the latter under circumstances that did not apply to natural-born citizens.

The pressure continued to be applied, as demonstrated through a petition presented to the Minister for Women and Children in April 1956:

> We, the undersigned, respectfully wish to bring to your attention the discrimination made between *born* New Zealanders and *naturalised* New Zealanders, as laid down in

the Naturalisation Act of 1948....We women, mothers of future New Zealanders, are very much aware of the responsibility which rests on our shoulders. Are we entitled to change our nationality, knowing that by doing so we will put our children in a position of disadvantage for the rest of their lives? It is for this reason, that we beg you most respectfully to do your utmost to rectify the status of a naturalised New Zealander, so that in future he or she not only has the same *duties* but also the same *rights* as a New Zealand born citizen.[44]

The apparent success of this continued pressure was commented on by *The Evening Star* a few months later: "The Government is understood to be taking another look at the legislation covering the naturalisation of alien immigrants....This move is reported to be the result of protests, particularly from Dutch new settlers, that the existing provisions do not give them the opportunity to become 100 per cent New Zealanders."[45] The Secretary for Internal Affairs outlined official government thinking on the issue in a Memorandum for the Minister of Internal Affairs, Sidney Walter Smith, on 29 June 1956:

The basic differences between the status of a naturalized citizen and of a natural born citizen are two. Firstly under the Immigration Restriction Amendment Act 1920, any person not of British birth and parentage requires permission to enter New Zealand and a naturalized citizen is defined in the Act specifically as not being of British birth and parentage....The second difference is that naturalized people are liable to lose their citizenship in certain conditions that do not apply to natural born people. The main grounds for deprivation are: (a) Disloyalty or disaffection towards Her Majesty. (b) Unlawful trading with an enemy during war. (c) Being sentenced within 5 years after naturalization in any country to imprisonment for a term of not less than 12 months. (d) If naturalization or registration has been gained by means of fraud, misrepresentation etc. (e) If the person has been ordinarily resident in foreign countries for a continuous period of 6 years.[46]

The Secretary for Internal Affairs added that "once a person is naturalized he should be on exactly the same footing as a natural born citizen, particularly in view of the very careful enquiries that are made before naturalization is granted." But they did not feel that there was any "special urgency about this particular question, but I think it should be carefully examined in conjunction with other aspects of the naturalization law which the Department now has under consideration.... At the appropriate time a submission will be made to Government covering all these matters."[47]

The President of the Canterbury Council for Civil Liberties wrote to Smith, to add his voice to calls for the government to take action to remove distinctions between naturalised and natural-born Aotearoa New Zealand citizens. The President centred his argument on three main points. Firstly, he criticised the deprivation of citizenship of a naturalised citizen if they were away for more than six years in a non-Commonwealth country. Secondly, he pointed out that the UN Study on Statelessness in 1949 had suggested that nationality should not be removed from someone who might have decided to live in a foreign country, however long they were away, unless they had taken up a new nationality. And thirdly, he drew attention to the fact that the current law allowed naturalised citizens to be deprived of citizenship for disaffection with, or disloyalty to, the Queen. In light of the possibility of these clauses being broadened so as to include lawful political activity, the association believed that this clause could discourage naturalised citizens from expressing ideas that were considered "extreme" by officials or the community.[48]

However, Dutch immigrants were also lobbying their MPs to put pressure on government, as illustrated by a letter from J. G. Barnes, MP, to Attorney General Jack Marshall in September 1956:

> Please find attached a copy of a statement I have received from a Dutch immigrant, who has applied for naturalisation. He claims that many more Dutch people would apply but for the Act of 1948, wherein it is possible for a person applying for naturalisation to have it cancelled for certain offences. It is considered that such action would make those who had received naturalisation stateless if their New Zealand naturalisation were cancelled. It is fully appreciated that wrongdoers should be punished, but it is felt that when a New Zealander commits an offence and serves his penalty, he is then completely free to rejoin society. It is considered by Dutch people, who have consulted me, that they are placed at a distinct disadvantage and many are afraid to apply for naturalisation.[49]

But the government was not to be moved into taking action at that time. Nevertheless, the growing public pressure certainly contributed to changes in Aotearoa New Zealand citizenship legislation a few years later.

The *British Nationality and New Zealand Citizenship Act* of 1959

The *British Nationality and New Zealand Citizenship Act* was very rarely amended since its inception in 1948. The two major points of reforms were in 1959 and 1977. The latter is rightly given the most attention due to the significant changes it introduced. However, the former also involved some important reforms, and in many ways paved the way for the 1977 legislation. Therefore, I will focus on this first. In the late 1950s there was continued criticism from naturalised Aotearoa New Zealand citizens, particularly the Dutch, about the different ways in which they were treated compared to their natural-born counterparts. A prominent example was naturalised Aotearoa New Zealand citizens not being permitted to enlist in the Aotearoa New Zealand Navy.[50] This feeling of grievance even reached National Prime Minister Keith J. Holyoake, who asked the Minister of Internal Affairs, Sidney Walter Smith, to produce a "report on the statement that 'New Zealand citizenship may be withdrawn by a simple decision of the Minister of Internal Affairs'" in September 1957.[51] Smith duly complied a month later and pointed out that the deprivation provisions of the *British Nationality and New Zealand Citizenship Act* of 1948 were "almost identical with those of the United Kingdom, being if anything less severe....They are certainly less severe than similar provisions in Canadian and Australian law."[52] He drove his point home with the argument that no naturalised Aotearoa New Zealander should fear losing their citizenship so long as they acted within the law and maintained their affirmation of loyalty to the Queen.[53] However, in response to the Aotearoa New Zealand Police Force changing its policy of admitting naturalised New Zealanders into its ranks in late 1957, Secretary for Internal Affairs, A. G. Harper, wrote to the Controller General of Police and argued that "When applicants are told baldly that they are not acceptable for a position because they are naturalized, it gives strength to the feeling that has gained some currency and publicity recently, that the status of a naturalized person is below that of a natural born one, in other words, it is second-class citizenship."[54]

In early 1958 the Department of Internal Affairs finally decided to act on the alleged discrimination between natural-born and naturalised New Zealanders. The Australian government's moves in this direction certainly seem to have been a motivating factor, and the Aotearoa New Zealand government was very keen to discover what changes its Australian counterpart intended to make in this area, particularly in terms of the deprivation of citizenship provisions.[55] The Australian government replied that they intended to remove all deprivation of citizenship provisions that only applied to naturalised citizens, from the nationality and citizenship legislation, with the exception of those provisions relating to obtaining citizenship through fraud or if the minister believed that their continuing to be an Australian citizen was not in the public interest.[56]

The Secretary for Internal Affairs wrote a memorandum to the Labour Minister of Internal Affairs, Bill Anderton, in July 1958, in which he drew attention to the problems with the existing nationality and citizenship legislation in Aotearoa New Zealand in regard to the deprivation provisions between natural-born and naturalised citizens. The two major criticisms were that the current four main ways in which a citizen could be stripped of their citizenship only applied to naturalised citizens, and if any of these took place, they could become potentially stateless.[57] But it was not until early the following year that the Secretary for Internal Affairs circulated memoranda on proposed changes to the *British Nationality and New Zealand Citizenship Act*. Secretary of External Affairs, A. D. McIntosh, responded in June 1959. He expressed concern over two features of the suggested amendments: "The general tendency to weaken the significance of the status of British Subject or Commonwealth Citizen" and "The proposal that existing rights possessed by New Zealand Citizens (including New Zealand born Citizens) should be taken away."[58] However, McIntosh's most significant remarks related to the changes in the deprivation provisions in relation to naturalised citizens:

> While I feel that the existing provisions are not unreasonable (apart from the provisions dealing with absence from New Zealand all the other grounds require some element of disloyalty) I appreciate your desire to remove any apparent discrimination between naturalized and natural-born citizens and see no objection to the repeal of the provisions concerned.[59]

An explanatory note on the *British Nationality and New Zealand Citizenship Amendment Bill* a few months later emphasised that two of the most important changes were that the legislation allowed for the minister to possibly demand citizens of other Commonwealth countries, Irish citizens, and British protected persons to take the oath of allegiance before they were awarded Aotearoa New Zealand citizenship. And it also limited the range of situations in which naturalised citizens could be deprived of their Aotearoa New Zealand citizenship.[60] Cabinet approved the text of the *British Nationality and New Zealand Citizenship Amendment Bill* at a meeting on 18 August 1959.[61]

Newspaper coverage of the introduction of the bill on 27 August 1959 was generally very positive. *The Dominion* commented that "Naturalised and natural-born citizens of New Zealand are placed on the same footing, with regard to the grounds on which they may be deprived of New Zealand citizenship, by the British Nationality and New Zealand Citizenship Amendment Bill." It added that the "The Minister of Internal Affairs, Mr. Anderton, told the House that the Act was being amended for the first time since it came into force on January 1, 1949."[62] The *Evening Post* expressed similar sentiments in its editorial: "In the deprivation of New Zealand citizenship naturalised and natural-born citizens will have equal rights under a British

Nationality and New Zealand Citizenship Amendment Bill."[63] It did though point out that one exception remained: obtaining citizenship through fraud or misrepresentation. The *New Zealand Herald* also highlighted the other significant change in the legislation: "The bill also confers on the Minister a discretion in connection with granting New Zealand citizenship to citizens of other Commonwealth countries and Irish citizens."[64] So, the previous automatic situation in this regard was going to be changed. The *Gisborne Herald* argued that the effect of all these changes was that "A greater number of alien migrants are likely to become fully-fledged New Zealanders as a result of the British Nationality and New Zealand Citizenship Amendment Bill now before Parliament."[65] It also pointed out that the new citizenship legislation brought Aotearoa New Zealand into line with Australia and Canada and met the international standard for aliens determined by the UN.[66]

In his second reading speech on the bill, Anderton emphasised that the most significant feature of the bill was clause 8, which related to the deprivation of citizenship of naturalised citizens:

> The position in short is that at present a naturalised New Zealand citizen may be deprived of his citizenship on grounds that do not apply to the natural born....The clause largely follows similar amending legislation in Australia and Canada. It gives me great pleasure to introduce this Bill because it deals with matters which have caused concern to many of our immigrants who will now be on exactly the same basis as natural-born citizens....Not only the Dutch people, but a number of Dutch people have raised the point that by accepting citizenship under the present Act they become second-rate citizens of this country while losing their own nationality, and I can understand their position.[67]

However, the National member for Hobson, and former Minister of Internal Affairs, Sidney W. Smith, despite supporting the amendments, could not "help but feel that the grievances of any alien desiring naturalisation to which the Minister referred was purely imaginary."[68] The Labour member for Napier, Jim Edwards, also commented on clause 6 of the bill, which required those prospective citizens from Commonwealth countries which did not acknowledge the sovereignty of the Throne, i.e., republics, to take an oath of allegiance. He highlighted the importance of this in terms of "we should ask citizens of such Commonwealth countries to take the same oath of allegiance as aliens because that puts them on an equal basis as full New Zealand citizens."[69] The National Party MP for Manawatu, Blair Tennant, emphasised that "in this Bill we are discussing one of the country's most valued possessions, our British and New Zealand citizenship....As citizens that is the greatest possession we can have."[70] He added that he was saddened that the Minister mentioned the term "second class citizenship." This was something that Dutch migrants had used in their protests about the previous citizenship legislation several years ago.[71]

The *British Nationality and New Zealand Citizenship Act* of 1963

Despite the changes adopted in the 1959 Act there were still distinctions remaining between naturalised and natural-born Aotearoa New Zealand citizens, especially when it came to deprivation of citizenship. The situation as it existed, particularly in relation to dual citizenship, was discussed in a memorandum issued in September 1962, which firstly pointed out that it was incorrect to state (as numerous pronouncements in the departmental files had previously come very near to stating) that dual nationality was, in the thinking of Aotearoa New Zealand nationality law, an unwelcome thing. If the legislation desired to do so, it would be relatively simple to prevent the creation of dual nationality by confining the usage of both the jus soli and the jus sanguinis principles to those individuals who held no other citizenship at birth. The memorandum then went on to discuss UK nationality legislation, which was the basis for Aotearoa New Zealand legislation: "The United Kingdom seems to have concluded in 1948 that dual nationality from its point of view was more often desirable in effect than undesirable, in spite of its 19th century experience; or at least to have concluded that no effect was sufficiently undesirable to warrant the power of obviating it." But there was no logical inconsistency in arguing that, while dual nationality overall might be harmless from the national perspective, there could be situations where it became undesirable. This was the perspective of Aotearoa New Zealand and numerous other Commonwealth nations; and these nations had offered various solutions.[72]

In contrast to UK law, Australian law was absolutely intolerant of dual nationality (or citizenship) obtained by an adult by voluntary action while the individual concerned was outside Australia. Loss was automatic and took place after the adoption of another Commonwealth citizenship, just like the adoption of a foreign nationality. The memorandum added that "While intolerant of dual nationality acquired by voluntary election, the Australian legislation has taken no power...to deal with voluntary exercise of the rights attaching to a second nationality acquired otherwise than by voluntary action, e.g. by birth, descent or marriage." Australia allowed for automatic loss of citizenship in another specific situation. Section 19 of the Act stated: "An Australian citizen who, under the law of a country other than Australia, is a national or citizen of that country and serves in the armed forces of a country at war with Australia shall, upon commencing so to serve, cease to be an Australian citizen." Section 23(1) of the Australian Act included a further aspect not seen in the Aotearoa New Zealand legislation: "Where an Australian citizen, being the responsible parent of a child who is also an Australian citizen, automatically loses his Australian citizenship if he is, or thereupon becomes, a national or citizen of another country."[73]

The memorandum asserted that the Canadian deprivation law was essentially the same as Australia's. But it had specific points of difference that were notable:

> The main provision (section 15 of the Canadian Citizenship Act 1946) is almost identical with the Australian....It reads "15(1) A Canadian citizen who, when outside of Canada and not under a disability, by any voluntary and formal act other than marriage acquires the nationality of citizenship of a country other than Canada, thereupon ceases to be a Canadian citizen."[74]

Furthermore, the memorandum elaborated upon further relevant sections of the Canadian citizenship legislation:

> Section 17 of the Canadian Act contains a provision similar to that of section 19 of the Australian Act...but more restricted in effect: "17(1) A Canadian citizen, who, under the law of another country, is a national or citizen of such country and who serves in the armed forces of such country when it is at war with Canada, thereupon ceases to be a Canadian citizen. (2) This section does not apply to a Canadian citizen who, under the laws of another country, became a national or citizen of such country when it was at war with Canada."[75]

Having surveyed the situation in other major Commonwealth countries, the memorandum argued that:

> In considering the desirability of any changes in section 22 of the New Zealand Act, one must admit that one would be led in the direction of change by considerations more of academic than of urgent practical character. The total number of persons deprived of New Zealand citizenship under the 1948 Act is extremely small, and of that number the great majority has been of persons naturalized in New Zealand and deprived under the provisions of section 23 of the Act as it stood before the 1959 Amendment.[76]

In mid-1963 Secretary to the Cabinet, A. R. Perry, wrote to the National Minister of Internal Affairs, Leon Götz, reminding him that "At the meeting on 4 June Cabinet *agreed* that a Press Statement should be made explaining the position in relation to the status and rights of naturalised citizens." He added that "it was the understanding that the Minister of Finance would consider whether the provision in the Reserve Bank Act, restricting the appointment of naturalized persons to the Board of the Bank, could be amended if there was another reason to amend the Act this year."[77] This latter point was subsequently discussed that same month by C. Barker, Secretary to the Treasury to Harry Lake, the National Minister of Finance. Barker argued that the Governor of the Reserve Bank was agreeable to the legislation being changed to remove this last source of statutory discrimination. Specifically, this would involve replacing the last part of the current wording of Section 32 of the act—"No person shall be appointed or continue to hold office as a member of the Board, whether as Governor, Deputy Governor, or otherwise who (a) *Is not a British subject by birth*"[emphasis added by author]—with simply "Is not a British subject."[78]

Changing the title of the *British Nationality and New Zealand Citizenship Act* was also under consideration:

> Our review of terms used in our citizenship law takes into account the fact that the word "British" has over recent years been used by authorities in the United Kingdom to refer to the United Kingdom itself. For example, their representation in New Zealand, formerly called the United Kingdom High Commission, is now called the British High Commission. In order on the one hand to respect this seeming preference of the United Kingdom and on the other to avoid confusion between New Zealand and the United Kingdom citizens the New Zealand Government decided not to enface its passports with the words "British passport." At a later stage it changed the national description of its passport holders from "British subject and New Zealand citizen" to "New Zealand citizen."[79]

However, the Aotearoa New Zealand government was quick to refute any suggestion that it had downgraded Commonwealth citizenship: "Commonwealth citizenship has *not* been down-graded in New Zealand and we would resist this suggestion....Our 1948 Act shows predominant emphasis on common status, born out also by passport references to 'British subject and New Zealand citizen.'"[80]

This was reiterated in a memorandum on "Nationality and Citizenship":

> Section 3 of the 1948 Act as amended in 1959 carries out this decision by providing that New Zealand citizens shall have the status of British subjects and that the

citizens of other Commonwealth countries shall be recognised in New Zealand as possessing that same status....Under present legislation the status of British subject, or loosely British nationality, can be acquired only through possession of citizenship of one or other of the Commonwealth countries.[81]

It went on to argue that:

It is Government policy nevertheless, to place the emphasis on the Commonwealth-wide status of British Nationality rather than on the regional status of citizenship in public statements....In matters of internal administration however, it makes for clearness and conciseness if a person's specific citizenship only is stated without the redundant reference to British nationality....A person possessing the citizenship of two Commonwealth countries is a dual citizen, As his two regional citizenships are only sub-classes of the one British nationality, he is not a dual national.[82]

The above illustrates that a British-centred identity was still very much prevalent in Aotearoa New Zealand at this time.

The *Citizenship and Aliens Act* of 1977

The next major reform of nationality and citizenship legislation took place fourteen years later in 1977, with the *Citizenship and Aliens Act*. One of the most important features of the bill outlined in April of that year was the elimination of the distinction between British subjects and aliens in terms of applying for citizenship: "the present twin procedures of obtaining citizenship by registration (British subjects) and by naturalisation (aliens) are discontinued....The Bill provides for the grant of New Zealand citizenship to any person who satisfies the prescribed requirements, irrespective of whether he is a British subject or an alien."[83] But in a submission on the bill, the academics C. W. Gardiner and H. J. Gardiner from the University of Waikato criticised the deprivation of citizenship, a penalty which still existed in the bill, as "archaic, and surely unnecessary." They argued that "The actions referred to are some kind of low grade treason, which are better dealt with in The Crime Act, and punished by some procedure other than this deprivation procedure." But they were especially concerned over "the lack of clear definition of acting against the interests of New Zealand....Could this mean criticizing the Government? Or working for a British Butter Marketing Firm which sells non Zealand butter?"[84] That same month, the Secretary of Foreign Affairs wrote to the Secretary for Internal Affairs and suggested that a copy of the bill might be sent to the British government before its introduction. The main motivation for this was that "it would be very much in keeping with the traditionally intimate relationship which we have shared with Britain in citizenship and nationality matters."[85] This illustrates that the unravelling of Britishness in Aotearoa New Zealand was a gradual process, and remnants of it could still be seen as late as the 1970s. And this did not just apply in one direction, as when the Aotearoa New Zealand prime minister visited London, he received from Prime Minister James Callaghan an advance copy of a "Green Paper" on potential changes to the British Nationality legislation.[86]

So, at a meeting of the Cabinet on 7 June 1977 it was agreed that in relation to the legislation on citizenship:

> Three years' residence in New Zealand be the standard requirement for both alien and British applicants for citizenship but that the present provisions for reduction to one year's residence at Ministerial discretion for British subjects and Irish citizens... copies of the draft Citizens and Aliens Bill be made available on a confidential basis to the Governments of the Cook Islands, Niue,[87] and the United Kingdom and that the comments of the Cook Islands and Niue Governments be invited as a matter of urgency.[88]

In his second reading speech on the bill that same month, National Minister of Internal Affairs David Highet underlined the reforms the proposed legislation intended in relation to British subjects and aliens:

> Hitherto, British subjects have been required to have resided in New Zealand for 3 years—and this has been reducible to a minimum of 1 year in special circumstances, at the Minister's discretion—before being eligible to apply for citizenship, whereas aliens have been required to have lived here for a minimum of 5 years. It is proposed henceforth there will be a common period of 3 years minimum residence....There was another distinction, too, between British subject applicants and aliens which it is proposed to do away with. The legislation has referred to the registration of British subjects as New Zealand citizens and to the naturalisation of aliens.[89]

The Labour member for Henderson, Dr. Martyn Finlay, commented on the ministerial discretionary provisions of the bill: "The retention of ministerial discretion, at least for those of British descent, is desirable, but I would like to see ministerial discretion extended to the whole lot, right across the board." But he also believed that "there should be some avenue of appeal against the exercise of this discretion, which could be capricious and oppressive."[90] This suggestion was supported by the Labour member for Grey Lynn, Eddie Isbey, who asked if there was allowance in the Bill for an individual who was declined Aotearoa New Zealand citizenship to appeal to a body and receive a justification for the refusal.[91] This echoed sentiments expressed by Gardiner and

Gardiner in their submission on the bill. Several parliamentarians expressed the view that the government should either look at entering into reciprocal arrangements with other countries or pursue the idea of the universality of nationality and citizenship laws at the Commonwealth or the UN.[92] The Labour member for New Lynn, Jonathan Hunt, also added that he was "in favour of the use of the term 'Commonwealth citizenship,'" but he was surprised that "the second schedule talks about 'British subjects'; I would have liked to see the words 'Commonwealth citizens' used."[93] This is an excellent illustration of the end of the British World in Aotearoa New Zealand, as previously, strong sentiments would have been expressed to the contrary. The Labour member for Porirua, Dr Gerard Wall, also asserted that "The definition of what is contrary to New Zealand's interests is a problem."[94] Highet replied that he thought Hunt's point was a good one and that it should be raised with the Statutes Revision Committee. However, he was not willing to budge on the question of the appeal authority: "The Minister's decision is final."[95]

In their submission to the Statutes Revision Committee on the bill, the National Council of Women of New Zealand pursued the issue of an appeal body to ministerial discretion: "We consider that if a person has a right to apply to the Supreme Court for a declaration that there are insufficient grounds for deprivation of citizenship, there should also be equivalent recourse to the Court if an application for citizenship is refused."[96] Unsurprisingly, in its submission to the committee, the Salvation Army focused its attention on the provisions regarding limiting Aotearoa New Zealand citizenship by descent: "We are…seriously concerned over the proposed restrictions on the acquisition of New Zealand Citizenship by descent, particularly since these restrictions will affect Christian families with a missionary tradition.…It is difficult to see the justification for restricting the rights of our Citizens in this way?"[97]

Nevertheless, when the bill returned to Parliament from the committee, the Opposition pressed the issue of appeal rights:

> I draw the attention of the House to the fact that rights held by citizens are normally protected by our courts or some special tribunal, and that Parliament has recognised that a politician, even though he may be acting in good faith, should not have absolute discretion over the rights and liberties of the citizens of New Zealand.…Appeal rights for citizens have been established in other countries, and have worked very well. I believe there is an overwhelming case for the setting up of appeal rights so that a person who is turned down when he applies for citizenship can receive a fair hearing before a court or special tribunal, and get a decision on properly laid down and properly known criteria.[98]

But Highet remained unmoved on the issue[99]; when the second reading of the bill was passed in November 1977, Highet again emphasised that "The Bill will implement the Government's manifesto promise to place citizenship on an equal footing for all prospective New Zealanders and to reduce the residential requirement for non-British subjects from 5 years to 3 years,"[100] and the *Citizens and Aliens Act* of 1977 subsequently came into force. The significance of this was reiterated by Richard Bedford, who maintained that "The *Citizenship Act* put an end to the distinction between British subjects (including New Zealand citizens) and 'aliens' that had been retained in New Zealand's foundation *Citizenship Act* of 1948."[101] This was supported by Megan Hutching, who argued that the "Citizenship Act 1977…repealed both the British Nationality and New Zealand Citizenship Act 1948 and much of the Aliens Act 1948, which had requested aliens resident in New Zealand to register with the Police and notify changes of name, address and occupation….The same criteria now applied to all applicants for New Zealand citizenship."[102] So, I have shown above how the end of the British World led to a redefinition of citizenship in Aotearoa New Zealand between the 1950s and 1970s in relation to other ethnic groups. As the chapter outlined in the introduction, it focuses on the redefinition of citizenship between the 1950s and 1970s in terms of both ethnicity and Indigeneity. Whereas the above has substantiated attempts for greater inclusion of other ethnic groups, the situation with the Māori was very different. What the following four sections of the chapter will show is that incorporating Māori was, and still is, hugely contested, as it continues to reflect inherent power and asset imbalances.

The *Māori Affairs Amendment Act* of 1967

Due to a shift away from an ethnic-centred national identity to a "new nationalism," Pakeha New Zealanders were now more willing to apparently incorporate Māori in ideas of citizenship. However, the *Māori Affairs Amendment Act* of 1967 was an extremely controversial piece of legislation. One of the major reasons why it was so contentious is that many Māori argued that it flew in the face of the Treaty of Waitangi, which they believed had enshrined their distinct citizenship rights, particularly in relation to land ownership. On introducing the bill in May 1967, National Minister of Māori Affairs, Ralph Hanan, emphasised that "This Bill proposes very important and fundamental changes in laws relating to Maoris and Maori land….To a considerable extent the Bill follows the recommendations of the committee set up in 1964 to inquire into a number of questions dealing with Maori land titles and the use of Maori land." This was a reference to the Pritchard Committee. Hanan did not go into detail about the provisions of the bill as there were 147 clauses— unusually long for a bill at the time. But its main motivation was to deal with the problem, as he saw it, of Māori land being owned in common by a number of owners in various, and quite often very small, plots.[103] The bill had the supposedly lofty aim of placing Māori and Pakeha on an equal basis in terms of land ownership. The Labour leader of the Opposition, Norman Kirk, pointed out, however, that not all recommendations of the Pritchard Report, which the minister had admitted the current bill before the house was based on, were universally approved.[104] The Labour member for Northern Māori, Matiu Rata, also piped up and jumped on the comment by Hanan that the bill was extremely complicated: "If the Bill is so complicated for members of this House, how much more difficult would it be for the Maoris to understand the effects of what is proposed."[105] Hanan responded by trying to undermine Kirk's point that the Pritchard Report had not been universally acclaimed by stating that the Aotearoa New Zealand Māori Council and a university group in Auckland opposed nearly all its recommendations, but the mass of "ordinary" Māori had supported them.[106]

Newspaper coverage of the bill was predominantly positive. The *New Zealand Herald* remarked that:

> The boldest bid yet to check multiplying problems of Maori land ownership— succession, fragmented titles and uneconomic interests—is now before Parliament....A massive Maori Affairs Amendment Bill of eight parts and 147 sections...if passed will make some 1.4 million acres—or more than a third of the 3.9 million acres of Maori holdings which remain—virtually the same in law as ordinary land.[107]

The Dominion put the proposed changes in the status of Māori land even more bluntly: "More than one-third of present Maori land holdings will be 'Europeanised' if a Bill presented to Parliament yesterday is passed." It added that the bill was "based largely on the 1965 Pritchard-Waetford report on Maori land law."[108]

One of the major features of the bill, and certainly one of the most controversial, was the "giving of the status of European land to blocks of Maori land owned by not more than four persons." This was essentially the privatisation of collective Māori land, which would then allow it to be sold to Pakeha. Other aspects of the bill related to "Promotion of better use and administration of

Maori land," "Amendments to Maori Affairs Act 1953 relating to partition and planning," "Incorporations," "Wills and succession," and "Provisions relating to alienation."[109] Various submissions were made regarding the bill to the Parliamentary Māori Affairs Select Committee. In September 1967 the Tuwharetoa Māori Trust Board commented that: "It has...been suggested in some quarters that the existing law treats the Maori as a child or, in some ways, as a second class citizen." Though the Trust Board's main issue with the bill was "the element of compulsion which marks so many of its provisions.... We would like to see a little less 'must' and a little more 'may.'" However, the most astonishing parts of the bill to them were those that tended to increase discrimination, those that caused them the most concern.[110] The Aotearoa New Zealand Māori Council also sent a submission to the Māori Affairs Committee. It began by drawing attention to the fact that it represented Māori across the country, adding greater authority and gravitas to its subsequent comments. However, its main points were that the "strong tie between the [Maori] people and their land still persists." It added that "it would wish to see land currently owned by Maoris retained in their possession." Though its most stinging criticism was that "the land should be fully utilised for the benefit of the owners and of the national economy, but the rights of the owners should be paramount and should not be outweighed by any economic argument."[111]

Younger Māori also made submissions to the Parliamentary Committee on Māori Affairs on the bill. This included the Association of Māori University Graduates in late 1967. One of the central arguments made by the association was the centrality of the Treaty of Waitangi to Māori and the belief that the present bill was the latest in a long line of legislation which acted directly against it:

> Many of the laws of this country affecting Maori land have been designed to increase their effective use and occupation, but not necessarily for the direct benefit of the Maoris and the arbitrary implementation of such laws has caused the Maori people to consider them as successive erosions of the rights guaranteed them under the Treaty of Waitangi, whereas it is probable that the same ends could have been achieved by negotiation on the partnership principle.[112]

They also particularly criticised the loss under the bill of the Māori land courts, which had upheld the principle of the inviolability of Māori lands. They actually suggested that "All Maori land that is not under active development should be regarded as the same as crown Land, and should be free from rating imposts....This would then have the effect of preserving Maori land until the Maori people of another generation have gained the financial and technological resources to proceed with the development."[113] The association acknowledged that the Māori view of Turangawaewae was slowly shifting; however, the point had not yet been reached when the Māori connection to their ancestral rights to their land should be ignored, and overridden without their permission. The association also lamented the failure of the bill to provide a modern definition of a Māori, which had been recommended by the controversial Hunn Report of 1960, which had called for the integration of Māori into Pakeha society.[114]

When the bill was returned to Parliament later that month there was heated debate in the chamber. Rata took the Opposition lead and quickly moved a counter-amendment to the government's calling for the bill to proceed as amended, insisting that the bill be returned to the Parliamentary Māori Affairs Select Committee. His main argument for this was that the bill went far beyond what was recommended in the Pritchard Report and "flies in the face of informed Maori and other opinion, and representations made to the committee were not only critical but suggested constructive alternatives."[115] But Hanan was having none of it, maintaining that the "Bill provides for the most far-reaching and progressive reform of the Maori land laws this century." He attempted to counter Rata's point about heavy Māori opposition to the bill by stating that "Almost every progressive move over the years to further the real progress of the Maori people has been opposed by Maori members of Parliament….I instance the right of the Maori to sit on juries; even this was opposed when it was first brought into the House."[116] This exchange set the tone for the subsequent debates surrounding the progress of the bill in the house over the next few weeks. Newspapers followed its passage closely, commenting on the united action of the four Māori MPs in the house (Rata, Iriaka Ratana [Western Māori], Paraone Reweti [Eastern Māori], and Whetu Tirikatene-Sullivan [Southern Māori]) in taking the lead to block the passage of the bill, supported by their Labour colleagues. There were 28 divisions in total on the bill. The government won the last division by 36 votes to 29. So, the bill was an extremely divisive measure—votes coming down along partisan lines. Despite the opposition's heroic efforts, the *Māori Affairs Amendment Bill* received its third reading on 22 November 1967.[117] It can be argued that acts of Aotearoa New Zealand nationalism were aimed at "finishing" the settler project in the name of progress. So, the attempted "Europeanisation" of remaining Māori land was, in actual fact, an attempt to impose Western conceptions of citizenship on Māori and highlighted the very contested nature of citizenship in Aoteareo New Zealand, particularly between Māori and Pakeha.

The *Race Relations Act* of 1971

The existence of racial discrimination in Aotearoa New Zealand was high-lighted by National Minister of Māori Affairs, Ralph Hanan, in the *Dominion Herald* in July 1968: "The Minister of Māori Affairs, Mr. Hanan, gave a sharp warning last night about racial discrimination...[he] said that if discrimination against the Maori arose in New Zealand it must be promptly handled, with all the censure and public disapproval that people could muster, and if need be, with all the power of the law."[118] However, the limitations of the latter were emphasised a few months later:

> Legislation to prevent racial discrimination in the letting and selling of properties would be almost impossible to enforce and hence ineffective to put an end to the evil, the Minister of Justice (Mr. Marshall) told Parliament yesterday. Mr. Marshall made the comment in replying to a question by the Opposition Member for Northern Maori (Mr. M. Rata), seeking an amendment to the Property Law Act outlawing discrimination on similar lines to a provision in the Sale of Liquor Act.[119]

However, the government's attitude seems to have changed, as in early 1971 *The New Zealand Herald* reported that "Racial discrimination in all its forms may soon become an offence punishable by law, if the Government goes ahead with its intention to ratify the International Convention on the Elimination of All Forms of Racial Discrimination." It added that "The Cabinet has decided that the highest priority should be given to preparing draft legislation to be introduced into Parliament this year, as part of New Zealand's contribution to the International Year for Action to Combat Racism and Discrimination."[120] The newspaper elaborated on the proposals the following day:

> While its precise content is not yet clear and, indeed, has apparently still to be set-tled, the proposed Race Relations Bill will deserve thorough and objective scrutiny by Parliament and the community. The measure will appear following an upsurge of interest in the Treaty of Waitangi and in its legal implications. Those implications are sufficiently obscure to have encouraged a separate official study. The intention of the bill, however, is to ratify not the Treaty of Waitangi but a United Nations convention on the elimination of racial discrimination.[121]

So, it was quick to emphasise that the motivation for the Race Relations Bill was not in fact the ratification of the Treaty of Waitangi but, rather, ful-filling New Zealand's international obligations. The move did, though, have the support of the opposition: "It was a Bill that would be welcome by every thinking person in the country, said the Leader of the Opposition (Mr. Kirk) in speaking to the Race Relations Bill....It would be welcomed for the declarations and its attempts to establish good race relations, or remove the cause of bad race relations."[122]

The proposed Race Relations legislation also had broader popular support. The National Council of Churches Commission on Church and Society submitted their views in August 1971:

> At the outset we plan to commend the Government very sincerely for recognising the need to enact this Act to affirm and promote racial equality in New Zealand and to implement the International Convention on the Elimination of all Forms of Racial Discrimination. This country has been spared from the racial disharmony prevalent in many parts of the world and it is our firm belief that the enactment of this Act will assist to continue the harmonious race relations that prevail in this society.[123]

The Citizen's Association for Racial Equality also expressed their support for the *Race Relations Bill* in a submission:

> The Citizen's Association for Racial Equality welcomes the introduction of the Race Relations Bill. If enacted in an effective form this measure could do a great deal to remove most manifestations of racial discrimination in this country, to prevent any more extensive pattern of discrimination developing in the future and to promote racial equality and racial harmony generally....This Bill if enacted would, in our view, result in substantial progress toward these objectives but these gains would be considerably greater if many of its provisions were extended, strengthened or modified along the lines we shall suggest. In its provisions the Bill shows that many lessons have been learnt by those drafting it from experience in Britain and the United States of the operation of their race relations and many provisions appear among the most progressive in the world.[124]

The submission of the Aotearoa New Zealand Māori Graduates Association in October 1971, although also generally positive, included some suggestions to improve the legislation:

> The Maori Graduates Association's examination of the Race Relations Bill took place on the assumption that the Bill would be passed into legislation. Therefore the Association's immediate concern was to examine the Bill clause by clause, in order to determine its strengths and weaknesses in the light of its prior purpose— i.e. the promotion of racial equality in New Zealand—and having regard to its effects upon the Maori people....In the Association's view, one of the most significant factors to emerge was the possibility that the creation, existence and maintenance of Maori institutions and organisations would be seen to be incompatible with a Race Relations Act as such....In presenting these submissions, the Maori Graduates make known their recognition of the need for some form of legal sanction against racial discrimination. It assumes that the introduction of this Bill also

reflects Government's recognition of the need to protect ethnic minority groups against discrimination.[125]

The submission went on to argue that the "preceding submissions have been made on the premise that like other social legislation the effectiveness of this Bill will depend not only on the acceptability of the standards it enacts but also on the strength of its procedures for enforcement." The submission added that "The nub of the problem of enforcing laws against discrimination is to make a choice between criminal prosecution, civil remedies and administrative implementation...[it] affirm[ed] the concept of conciliation as the first forum of reference so long as a just and speedy remedy is available to an individual victim where conciliation has failed."[126] The Māori Graduates Association ended their submission with broader points about the position of Māori in Aotearoa New Zealand Society and their relationship to Pakeha:

> The Maori Graduates Association states strong support for the creation (as the need arises), existence and maintenance of Maori institutions and organizations. Further, the Association firmly believes the maintenance of Maori institutions and organizations to be justified by the purpose they serve in bridging the continuing social, economic and cultural gap between Maori and European New Zealanders....That there is a growing number of Europeans who regard Maori institutions and organisations as "racist" or "instruments of separation," is becoming increasingly more obvious to members of this Association. To people who hold this view, integration means New Zealand should have one political system, one set of laws, one education system, one language and one culture "after-all, we are all New Zealanders."[127]

The Manifesto of the Aotearoa New Zealand Māori Council on the Race Relations Bill, prepared by Dr. Ranginui Walker, University of Auckland, continued this approach, but also connected it to the Treaty of Waitangi:

> The New Zealand Maori Council submits on behalf of the Maori people of New Zealand, that the Race Relations Bill presents an opportunity to recapture the ideals embodied in the Treaty of Waitangi, and set the course for the future of our nation. Although New Zealand takes pride in its reputation for racial harmony, there is a feeling of unease in the land that somehow we have lost out way. The time has come for a reappraisal of our situation before we pass as law, a Race Relations Bill designed to give us the right to accede to the International Convention, rather than to chart the destiny of our people. Our ancestors who were present at the signing of the Treaty of Waitangi were fully aware of its implications. The first chief who objected to the Treaty demanded equality as a precondition for his signing.[128]

In their actual submission on the *Race Relations Bill*, the Aotearoa New Zealand Māori Council continued with this theme of linking it with the Treaty of Waitangi:

> The New Zealand Maori Council has prepared proposals which aim at making all New Zealanders aware of the place this legislation should have in our country; it is our considered view that the Race Relations Act be at least a charter of human relations at least as inspiring the first Race Relations Bill, the Treaty of Waitangi. The Maori people still seek legal recognition of that Treaty, and a comparison of its intentions with those of the Bill under review would show that the parallels are in fact close.[129]

The *Māori Affairs Amendment Act* of 1974

Once the Labour Party returned to power in 1972 it found itself in a position to reverse the controversial reforms of the *Māori Affairs Amendment Act* of 1967 and fulfil other election pledges in the field of Māori affairs with its own act. Labour Minister of Māori Affairs, Matiu Rata, outlined the background to the *Māori Affairs Amendment Bill* to his cabinet colleagues in a memorandum in late 1973:

> The forthcoming proposals are based primarily on the stated policy of Government on Maori Affairs in our Election Manifesto with respect to land wherein we started, "with the strong ties between people and their land, Labour recognises the rights of kin-groups to remain proprietors of their land and firmly believes in the retention of Maori land in Maori ownership and management in every practicable instance," thus the changes proposed are generally to give effect to the Government's policy and the long standing grievance of the Maori people in this field. As already indicated, the proposed Bill will enable wide and extensive discussions, which not only affects the Maori people but will have effect on the community in general and deals principally with those expressions over a long period of time.[130]

The Cabinet agreed to the preliminary drafting of the bill on a departmental level on 24 October 1973.[131] However, due to shortage of time in the current parliamentary session and a heavy workload by the parliamentary draftsmen, the drafting of the bill could not be completed in time to be introduced that session.[132] So, the following month Rata suggested that a white paper on the bill instead be forwarded to the Parliamentary Māori Affairs Select Committee, which would contain a copy of the preliminary draft of the bill during the parliamentary recess for study.[133] The Cabinet agreed to these proposals on 20 November 1973.[134]

The *Māori Affairs Amendment Bill* was finally introduced into Parliament on 5 July 1974. In his introductory speech on the bill, Rata outlined that one of its most important features was "to restore the principle of hereditary ownership of land and to recognise the right of the Māori people to succeed to and perpetuate ownership in common in accordance with Māori customs."[135] The National Opposition did not waste any time in expressing their dissatisfaction with the bill—with the National member for Manuwatu, Allan McCready, taking point: "We have had only a short time to study the Bill, but judging from a quick glance at it, it appears to put the clock back many years."[136] This was a reference to the situation that existed before the previous National Government's own *Māori Affairs Amendment Act* of 1967. The Labour member for Eastern Māori, Paraone Reweti, responded immediately to McCready's comment that the proposed legislation was taking New Zealanders back a number of years: "I assure the member that it takes us back to 1967 when the National Government introduced the 1967 amendment Act, and the representatives of the Maori people indicated in their submissions at that time that the Bill was designed to enforce measures on the Maori people."[137] McCready's National Party colleague, David Highet, the member for Remuera (and former Minister of Internal Affairs), commented that "Some of my constituents who are interested in the Maori people are deeply concerned about the ramifications of this Bill....I believe that we are now one people in this country and the sooner those of European or Maori origin recognise that fact the better."[138] Labour Prime Minister Norman Kirk also weighed in, remarking that "This Maori Affairs Amendment Bill represents a consensus of the opinion of the Maori people....The Minister of Maori Affairs and his colleagues, the members for the Maori electorates, visited practically every marae in New Zealand." He contrasted this situation with the bill's predecessor: "The complaints poured in through the House when the 1967 Bill was being debated in this Parliament....The Maoris said, 'When will we have a voice in legislation affecting us?'"[139] Rata responded to the remarks made to his introductory speech, eluding to the broader thrust of the government's initiatives in Māori affairs: "The Bill establishes, probably for the first time, that the Labour Government is committed to a policy of promoting equality in New Zealand, but that equality must be reached on the Maori people's terms....They are fully entitled to have their say in setting the terms, and as long as this Government is in power it will ensure that they do."[140] He also attempted to counter the "emotional humbug," as he referred to it, expressed by the two Opposition members over the new, more inclusive definition of Māori in clause 2 of the bill. He quite

rightly pointed out that the definition followed the example of earlier legislation actually enacted by previous National governments, for example, the
Māori Education Foundation Act of 1961, which defined a Māori as "a person
belonging to the aboriginal race of New Zealand; and includes any descend-
ent of a Maori."[141] Newspapers commented on the significance of the changes
proposed by the government. According to the *New Zealand Herald*:

> Legislation covering a wide range of subjects relating to Maori social and economic
> affairs was introduced to Parliament yesterday by the Minister of Maori Affairs, Mr.
> Rata....The Maori Affairs Amendment Bill brings into effect many of the proposals
> published last year in the Government's White Paper on Maori and related matters.[142]

The Dominion referred to the important changes in the definition of a Māori
included in the bill: "For most purposes, a Maori in future will be a person
with any Maori blood according to the Maori Affairs Amendment Bill introduced in Parliament yesterday afternoon....The bill...amends the previous definition which said that a Maori was someone of half or more Maori
blood."[143] The bill was then forwarded to the Parliamentary Māori Affairs Select Committee where it received submissions from a wide range of groups.
This included P. H. E. Bloomer, a solicitor from Hastings in July 1974 who
countered the anticipated objections of some individuals as to why Māori
people should have special land laws by arguing that they were needed due
to historical land ownership reasons. However, his most poignant remarks
were that "The argument that unused Maori Land should be made productive
is, I submit, fallacious....Until there is a universal policy to ensure all people
and institutions use their land efficiently is there any moral or even public
justification to single out Maori Land?"[144] The Aotearoa New Zealand Māori
Council also presented a submission the following month. The Council was,
perhaps unsurprisingly, extremely supportive of the bill:

> The Council wishes it to be known that it welcomes the philosophy enunciated in
> Part II wherein one of the objects of the Department of Maori Affairs is stated to be:
> "The retention of Maori land in the hands of its owners, and its use or administration
> by them for their benefit." This has been a principle which the Council has steadfast-
> ly held....Indeed the spirit which animates the Bill is one with which the Council
> finds itself completely in harmony.[145]

The tone of the majority of the submissions was in stark contrast to those on
the *Māori Affairs Amendment Act* of 1967, although not all the views expressed
were positive. P. J. H. Southern, a Customs Officer in Auckland, heavily criticised the changes in the definition of Māori in the bill in his submission

that same month. He argued that "The proposed redefinition would enable a large number of people who are not primarily Maoris by family background, or educational influence, or traditional association with Maoritanga to secure the benefits and advantages which the Maori Affairs Amendment Bill, 1974 has been designed to provide."[146] But the government countered such sentiments when expressed in Parliament by maintaining that the new definition of Māori in the bill reflected the current situation.

The *Māori Affairs Amendment Bill* was returned to Parliament in October 1974. The National Opposition continued to criticise it, insisting that it should be circulated to a wider group of people. The Labour Māori MPs, in particular, pointed out that the bill had initially been introduced as a White Paper and had received widespread circulation, not to mention the numerous submissions to the Parliamentary Māori Affairs Select Committee, of which the vast majority were extremely supportive of the bill. Thus, the *Māori Affairs Amendment Act* of 1974 was passed soon after.[147] Its departure from its extremely unpopular predecessor could not have been more extreme. However, though the *Māori Affairs Amendment Act* was a significant improvement on its controversial predecessor and attempted to engage with Māoridom on its own terms, in regard to citizenship, it was the beginning of the process. It would be later, in the 1980s, with the settling of land claims, that the Aotearoa New Zealand state really accepted that Māori actually had a very distinctive conception of citizenship, which was based on their relationship with the land, and this actually predated the arrival of the first European settlers in Aoteareo New Zealand. It is not a coincidence that it was at this very time that the British World finally ended in Aotearoa New Zealand.

The *Treaty of Waitangi Act* of 1975

The *Treaty of Waitangi Act* of 1975 finally saw the legislative enshrinement of the treaty and led to the establishment of the *Treaty of Waitangi Tribunal*, which had the power to adjudicate on cases brought before it of supposed breaches of the treaty. Discussion about it began in early 1971, as illustrated by P. J. Brooks, Secretary of the Cabinet to Dan Riddiford, National Minister of Justice: "You agreed in Cabinet today to arrange for a paper to be submitted on the reasons why successive Governments had not given the Treaty of Waitangi the force of law....No doubt you will recommend to Cabinet whether any action should not be taken on this matter."[148] A few months later a joint memorandum by Riddiford and his National colleague, Minister of Māori Affairs, Duncan Macintyre, was presented to cabinet on the issue:

> Formal ratification of the Treaty now by the Government would…at most be a superfluous action for if the Waitangi Treaty is a treaty of international law the Government is clearly bound by it despite the fact that it was not ratified….Apart from this the following objections may be made to expressing the Treaty in statutory form: (a) It would lower the force and dignity of the Treaty of Waitangi if it became just another statute or a schedule to a statute. (b) At present it is possible in any situation to appeal to the Treaty, which has a moral force that Governments will be less and less able to put aside.[149]

In light of the above, it is not surprising that they recommended to the Cabinet that it should "decline to take any steps to ratify the Treaty of Waitangi or to incorporate it in legislation."[150] However, the Labour Party conference at the time contrarily supported "incorporating the Treaty of Waitangi into statute law," although this was criticised by *The Dominion* as "an appeasing gesture to a vocal political Maori group."[151]

It was therefore not until early 1974 that the issue was raised again, this time in a Labour Party government. The Report of the Government Caucus Committee of Māori Affairs on the Treaty of Waitangi outlined why it was so important to take action on the issue:

> Accepting that the social, economic and cultural wellbeing of all New Zealand citizens is the responsibility of Government and Parliament to foster, encourage and promote, the Treaty has provided a basis and an enduring link within the New Zealand people. The Government considers that it is equally important to have the Treaty of Waitangi seen in its proper perspective and that both its symbol and spirit may be given practical application.[152]

And their key recommendation was that: "legislation providing for the recognition of the Treaty of Waitangi be introduced and further that a Tribunal to be known as the Treaty of Waitangi Tribunal be established for the purpose of maintaining, upholding, advising and hearing any matters related to the Treaty to which existing laws offer no redress."[153] The Labour government, unlike its National predecessor, wholeheartedly supported the thrust of the report and its major recommendation.[154]

In late 1974 the *New Zealand Herald* announced that "A bill to give formal and statutory recognition to the terms of the Treaty of Waitangi was introduced into Parliament yesterday by the Minister of Maori Affairs, Mr. Rata." It went on to outline that the bill "would establish a three-man tribunal with powers to investigate and make recommendations on complaints by Maoris against activities by the Crown which the complainants consider prejudicial." The tribunal would also act as a watchdog on legislation to determine whether it adhered to the ideals of the Treaty. Furthermore, "The new tribunal to be known as the Waitangi Tribunal, would comprise the Chief Judge of the Maori Land Court as chairman, plus two others to be appointed by the Governor-General on the recommendations of the Ministers of Justice and of Maori Affairs." The article ended with a comment that "Mr. Rata, in introducing the bill said it would give physical sustenance to the long-held view that the spirit of the Treaty more than warranted continued support."[155]

The second reading of the bill did not take place until September 1975, and the parliamentary debate surrounding it proved to be extremely lively. Rata moved that the bill be read a second time. In moving the second reading of the bill he was "conscious of the importance the treaty has played and the influence it has had for the Maori people."[156] But his more substantive comments were that:

> Members will recall that the Bill was introduced on 8 November last year and referred to the Maori Affairs Committee, which heard numerous submissions from Maori organisations as well as the legal fraternity and private individuals...Perhaps the most important feature of the Bill, and one which the Maori Affairs Committee heard strong views on was the need to provide for retrospective jurisdiction on outstanding grievances of the past. After considerable thought the Government has taken the view that there are overwhelming difficulties at this stage.[157]

Rata ended with "the Maori Affairs Committee has made amendments to the representation on the tribunal by ensuring the appointment of one person being a Maori....The Law Society has also expressed the view that the right of counsel to appear before the tribunal should be clarified."[158]

However, the National opposition did not waste any time in expressing their concerns with the bill. After voicing his displeasure at the second reading of the bill being initiated at such a late hour (11.30 p.m.), National MP for Egmont, Venn Young, made some more substantive remarks. These were initially positive: "The Treaty of Waitangi was a unique agreement for those colonial years in which it was signed....It was not a peace treaty with a vanquished race, but more an unusual bond between two civilisations." And he added that "It is true that the treaty has been regarded by many New Zealanders as a solemn pact....It is also true that many have seen subsequent events, particularly those surrounding the land wars of the 1860s as an abrogation of the treaty."[159] But then things took a decisively negative turn:

To many persons recent statements by the Minister of Maori Affairs have resulted in an unnecessary divisiveness within our society, and before I am convinced that unity in citizenship is a prime object of the Bill I will need to have more evidence than has so far been put before me. Too often under this Government have we seen legislation, such as the Electoral Amendment Act, that divides rather than unites....So far as the Waitangi Tribunal has a responsibility to protect the rights of all citizens of New Zealand, it could become an integral part of a wider human rights commission. I suggest that the Waitangi Tribunal could be integrated with a human rights commission that has authority to review the whole field of civil rights, supervising and co-ordinating the work of different tribunals that specialise in their respective fields.[160]

But one of Rata's colleagues, Whetu Tirikatene-Sullivan, who was the Minister of Tourism and the Labour member for Southern Māori, came to his defence. She emphasised that several submissions to the Māori Affairs Committee "commended the Minister for introducing this measure."[161] She went on to outline some of the most prominent submissions:

First of all there was one from the Te Reo Maori Society of Victoria University, which on the whole considered the Bill to be a satisfactory one....The New Zealand Maori Council also congratulated the Minister of Maori Affairs on what it described as the bold and imaginative set of proposals embodied in this Bill....The New Zealand Maori Graduates Association warmly approves the motives of the Government in introducing the Treaty of Waitangi Bill, and believes that, in the circumstances, legislative support for the principles of the treaty is an acceptable alternative to proper ratification of the Treaty of Waitangi.[162]

However, she also supported Rata in his position that the Treaty of Waitangi Tribunal should not investigate any possible retroactive breaches of the Treaty of Waitangi, for the time being at least: "I go along with the Minister... that, while the responsibility for dealing with past grievances is one for Parliament and Governments, provisions for retroactive consideration of these grievances may well be made in the future...At the present moment it would be unrealistic to incorporate such provisions in this Bill."[163] Both Rata and Tirikatene-Sullivan were most likely conscious of the need to avoid the creation of a popular panic about largescale transfers of land back to Māori, which a retrospective remit on land claims could possibly have entailed, as the vast majority of Māori lands were confiscated in the second half of the nineteenth and first half of the twentieth century.

In conclusion, this chapter has shown how the end of the British World led to a redefinition of citizenship in Aotearoa New Zealand between the 1950s and 1970s. The UK's first application for entry into the EEC in 1961, and the announcement of its military withdrawal from "East of Suez" in 1967, were particular highlights which signalled the end of the British self-identification of Aotearoa New Zealand. Through focusing on the popular pressure from mainly Dutch immigrants against distinctions between natural-born and naturalised citizens in 1955, the *British Nationality and New Zealand Citizenship Acts* of 1959 and 1963, and the *Citizenship and Aliens Act* of 1977, the chapter has demonstrated the way in which naturalised British subjects were put on a much more equal basis to their natural-born counterparts in being able to attain Aotearoa New Zealand citizenship and exercise the benefits of Aotearoa New Zealand citizenship. It has also illustrated how the *Māori Affairs Amendment Act* of 1967 was supposedly aimed at placing Māori on an equal basis with Pakeha in terms of the selling of their land. But as one group had the money to buy (Pakeha) and the other did not (Māori), this was nothing less than the commodification of Indigenous collective land and territorial identity. Nevertheless, there was considerable opposition to this from Māori, and the subsequent *Māori Affairs Amendment Act* of 1974 actually reversed the main features of its predecessor, and was widely advocated as treating Māoridom on its own terms, although it was the beginning of the process, and it was not until the 1980s that major shifts took place. This illustrates the continued, hugely contested nature of citizenship in Aotearoa New Zealand when it comes to Māori and the Aotearoa New Zealand state. The *Race Relations Act* of 1971 attempted to counter the imbalance between Māori and Pakeha in terms of social citizenship. And the *Treaty of Waitangi Act* of 1975 was aimed at providing a forum, through the Treaty of Waitangi Tribunal, for Māori to attempt to secure redress for breaches against the treaty.

Notes

1. The research for this chapter was conducted while I was a Resident Scholar in the Stout Research Centre for New Zealand Studies at the Victoria University of Wellington. I am grateful to the Stout Research Centre for all its support, both material and intellectual.
2. Marshall, *Class, Citizenship and Social Development*, 84.
3. Bryan S. Turner, "Contemporary Problems in the Theory of Citizenship," in *Citizenship and Social Theory*, ed. Bryan S. Turner (London: Sage, 1993), 1–18.
4. Neil Lunt, Paul Spoonley, and Peter Mataira, "Past and Present: Reflections on Citizenship Within New Zealand," *Social Policy & Administration* 36, no. 4 (August 2002), 346.
5. *Ibid.*, 359.

Mike O'Brien and Chris Wilkes, *The Tragedy of the Market: A Social Experiment in New Zealand* (Palmerston North: The Dunmore Press, 1993) and John E. Martin, *Honouring the Contract* (Wellington: Victoria University Press, 2010) present different angles on these questions.

6. Malcolm McKinnon, *Immigrants and Citizens: New Zealanders and Asian Immigration in Historical Context* (Wellington: Institute of Policy Studies, Victoria University of Wellington, 1996), 44.

7. Morgan Godfery, "Whose Citizenship Anyway?" *Set: Research Information for Teachers* 3 (2009), 4.

8. Carwyn Jones and Craig Linkhorn, "'All the Rights and Privileges of British Subjects': Māori and Citizenship in Aoteareo New Zealand" in Jatinder Mann (ed.), *Citizenship in Transnational Perspective: Australia, Canada, and New Zealand*, Politics of Citizenship and Immigration Series (New York: Palgrave Macmillan, 2017) 139.

9. Richard S. Hill, *Maori and the State: Crown-Maori Relations in New Zealand/Aotearoa, 1950–2000* (Wellington: Victoria University Press, 2009), 154.

10. Richard Mulgan, "Multiculturalism: A New Zealand Perspective," in Chandran Kukathas (ed.), *Multicultural Citizens: The Philosophy and Politics of Identity* (The Centre for Independent Studies Limited, 1993), 85.

11. Roger Maaka, "Maori and the State: Diversity Models and Debates in New Zealand," in *Belonging? Diversity, Recognition and Shared Citizenship in Canada*, eds. Keith Banting, Thomas J. Courchene, and F. Leslie Seidle (Montreal: The Institute for Research on Public Policy (2007), 289–90.

12. Roger Maaka and Augie Fleras, "Engaging with Indigeneity: Tino Rangatiratanga in Aotearoa," in *Political Theory and the Rights of Indigenous Peoples*, eds. Duncan Ivison, Paul Patton, and Will Sanders (Cambridge: Cambridge University Press, 2000), 95.

13. *Ibid.*, 103.

14. Augie Fleras and Paul Spoonley, *Recalling Aotearoa: Indigenous Politics and Ethnic Relations in New Zealand* (Auckland: Oxford University Press, 1999), 62.

15. Bronwyn Labrum, "Developing 'the Essentials of Good Citizenship and Responsibilities' in Maori Women: Family Life, Social Change, and the State in New Zealand, 1944–70," *Journal of Family History* 29, no. 4 (October 2004), 447–8.

16. Mamari Stephens' recent work is an excellent example of this. "'A Useful and Self-respecting Citizenship': Maori as Citizens in the Quest for Welfare in the Modern New Zealand State," in *Citizenship in Transnational Perspective: Australia, Canada, and New Zealand*, ed. Jatinder Mann (New York: Palgrave Macmillan, 2017), 189–208.

17. Joan Metge, *Rautahi: The Maori of New Zealand* (London: Routledge, 2004), 289.

18. Louise Humpage, "Revision Required: Reconciling New Zealand Citizenship With Maori Nationalisms," *National Identities* 10, no. 3 (September 2008), 247.

19. *Ibid.*

20. The White New Zealand Policy which had been established in the early twentieth century and was primarily aimed at preventing Asian immigration to New Zealand was very much alive and well at this time.

21. For more on the wider changes in Commonwealth citizenship that this legislation was a part of see Mann, "The Evolution of Commonwealth Citizenship," 293–313.

22. Rolf Pfeiffer, "New Zealand and the Suez Crisis of 1956," *The Journal of Imperial and Commonwealth History* 21, no. 1 (1993), 126–52.

23. Belich, *Paradise Reforged*, 425.
    However, Belich has had his critics: J. G. A. Pocock, *The Discovery of Islands: Essays in British History* (Cambridge: Cambridge University Press, 2005), 181–98, although largely sympathetic, did critique Belich.
    Jim McAloon, "Unsettling Recolonization: Labourism, Keynesianism and Australasia from the 1890s to the 1950s," *Thesis Eleven* 92 (February 2008): 50–68, and *Judgements of all Kinds: Economic Policy-Making in New Zealand, 1945–1984* (Wellington: Victoria University Press, 2013), 13–31, provides a stronger counter argument for suggesting the New Zealand/British economic relationship was already changing earlier than Belich said.

24. This was the relationship between New Zealand and the UK that emerged in the late nineteenth century, whereby, because it regarded itself as a British nation, the former viewed itself economically as a supplier of primary products to the "mother-country," and the latter as the main buyer of New Zealand produce.

25. *Ibid.*, 431, 432–3, 433, 434.

26. *Ibid.*, 434.

27. S. R. Ashton and Wm Roger Louis, eds. *East of Suez and the Commonwealth 1964–1971: Part I East of Suez*, British Documents on the End of Empire series edited by S. R. Ashton (Norwich: The Stationary Office, 2004), xxxiii, xxxvi, xl.

28. S. R. Ashton and Wm Roger Louis, eds. *East of Suez and the Commonwealth 1964–1971: Part II Europe, Rhodesia, Commonwealth*, British Documents on the End of Empire series edited by S. R. Ashton (Norwich: The Stationary Office, 2004), 348.

29. Kate McMillan, "Developing Citizens: Subjects, Aliens and Citizens in New Zealand since 1840," in *Tangata Tangata: The Changing Ethnic Contours of New Zealand*, eds. Paul Spoonley, Cluny Macpherson, and David Pearson (Southbank, Victoria: Thomson, 2004), 279.

30. McKinnon, *Immigrants and Citizens*, 43.

31. These were New Zealanders of European descent.

32. Hill, *Maori and the State*, 149.

33. *Evening Post* (Wellington), 2 January 1969, cited in Ward, "The 'New Nationalism' in Australia, Canada and New Zealand," 232.

34. Ward, 232.

35. *Ibid.*, 234.

36. *Ibid.*, 235–6.

37. Keith Sinclair, "The Historian as Prophet," cited in Ward, 241.

38. Ward, 241.

39. *Ibid.*, 242.

40. ANZ R19964588, Translation of Article in the Dutch Language from "N. Z. Hollander," 1 October 1955.

41. ANZ R19964588, Press Statement, 1

42. *Ibid.*, 2.

43. ANZ R19964588, "Many Immigrants Prefer Own Nationality—Barbs in Process of Naturalisation," *Evening Post*, 12 November 1955.

44. ANZ R19964588, Petition to the Minister for Women and Children, 17 April 1956.

45. ANZ R19964588, "Citizenship of New Settlers," *The Evening Star*, Monday 25 June 1956.
46. ANZ R19964588, Memorandum by the Secretary for Internal Affairs for the Minister of Internal Affairs, 29 June 1956, 1, 2.
47. *Ibid.*, 3.
48. ANZ R19964588, President, Canterbury Council for Civil Liberties to the Hon. S. W. Smith, Minister of Internal Affairs (including copy of a statement by Council to Christchurch Press), 28 August 1956.
49. ANZ R19964588, J. G. Barnes, MP to the Hon. J. R. Marshall, Attorney General (including copy of a statement from a Dutch immigrant), 4 September 1956.
50. ANZ R19964589, T. L. Macdonald, Office of the Minister of External Affairs to S. W. Smith, Minister of Internal Affairs, 10 May 1957.
51. ANZ R19964589, K. J. Holyoake, Prime Minister to S. W. Smith, Minister of Internal Affairs, 23 September 1957.
52. This is but one of numerous examples where the Aotearoa New Zealand government compared its nationality and citizenship legislation with its Australian and Canadian counterparts especially. This is not surprising, however, as all three countries' nationality and citizenship legislation was drawn from the same starting point after the Second World War. For more on this see Mann, "The Evolution of Commonwealth Citizenship."
53. ANZ R19964589, Memorandum by S. W. Smith, Minister of Internal Affairs to the Prime Minister, 3 October 1957, 1.
54. ANZ R19964589, A. G. Harper, Secretary for Internal Affairs to The Controller General of Police, 27 September 1957.
55. ANZ R20761248, R. W. Sharp, Secretary of External Affairs to the First Secretary, Office of the High Commissioner for New Zealand, 11 February 1958; R. W. Sharp to the First Secretary, Office of the High Commissioner for New Zealand, 15 April 1958; R. W. Sharp to P. Cotton, Office of the High Commissioner for New Zealand, Canberra, 30 July 1958.
56. ANZ R20761248, T. H. E. Heyes, Commonwealth of Australia Department of Immigration to P. Cotton, Office of the High Commissioner for New Zealand, Canberra.
57. ANZ R20969491, Secretary for Internal Affairs to The Minister of Internal Affairs, 23 July 1958, 5.
58. ANZ R20969491, A. D. McIntosh, Secretary of External Affairs to The Secretary for Internal Affairs, 30 June 1959, 1.
59. *Ibid.*, 2.
60. ANZ R20969491, British Nationality and New Zealand Citizenship Amendment Bill — Explanatory Note, 10 August 1959, ii.
61. ANZ R20969491, A. R. Perry, Secretary of the Cabinet to Prime Minister, 18 August 1959.
62. "Bill on Nationality and N.Z. Citizenship," *The Dominion*, 28 August 1959, 8.
63. "Citizenship Bill Amendments—Equal Treatment for Two Classes," *Evening Post*, 28 August 1959.
64. "Grounds for Loss of N.Z. Citizenship," *New Zealand Herald*, 29 August 1959.
65. "Aid Towards Acquiring Citizenship," *Gisborne Herald*, 15 September 1959.
66. *Ibid.*

67. Aotearoa New Zealand Parliamentary Debates, *House of Representatives (H of R)*, Vol. 320, 9 September 1959, William Anderton (Minister of Internal Affairs), 1738–9.

68. Aotearoa New Zealand Parliamentary Debates, *H of R*, Vol. 320, 9 September 1959, Sidney Smith, 1740.

69. Aotearoa New Zealand Parliamentary Debates, *H of R*, Vol. 320, 9 September 1959, Jim Edwards, 1743.

70. Aotearoa New Zealand Parliamentary Debates, *H of R*, Vol. 320, 9 September 1959, Mr. Tennant, 1744.

71. *Ibid.*

72. ANZ R12323366, Memorandum on British Nationality and New Zealand Citizenship Bill 1963—Deprivation of New Zealand Citizenship, 19 September 1962, 19.

73. *Ibid.*, 20, 21, 22.

74. *Ibid.*

75. *Ibid.*, 23.

76. *Ibid.*, 25.

77. ANZ R10764767, A. R. Perry, Secretary to the Cabinet to the Minister of Internal Affairs, 5 June 1963.

78. ANZ R10764767, C. Barker, Secretary to the Treasury to the Minister of Finance, 7 June 1963.

79. ANZ R22013510, Letter by J. F. Cavanagh for Secretary for Internal Affairs.

80. ANZ R22013510, Department of External Affairs to New Zealand High Commission, London, 22 June 1965, 1.

81. ANZ R10764764, Memorandum on "Nationality and Citizenship," 2–3

82. *Ibid.*, 3.

83. ANZ R20761257, *Citizens and Aliens Bill*, 1 April 1977, i.

84. ANZ R20761257, Submission on the *Citizens and Aliens Bill* by C. W. Gardiner and H. J. Gardiner, 2.

85. ANZ R20761257, Secretary of Foreign Affairs to The Secretary for Internal Affairs, 27 April 1977, 3.

86. ANZ R20761257, Secretary of Foreign Affairs to The Minister of Foreign Affairs, 27 April 1977, 1.

87. The Cook Islands and Nieu were dependencies of Aotearoa New Zealand and nationality and citizenship legislation on the mainland was applicable to them, although their respective parliaments had the opportunity to approve any amendments.

88. ANZ R20761257, Secretary of Foreign Affairs to Minister of Internal Affairs, 8 June 1977.

89. Aotearoa New Zealand Parliamentary Debates, *H of R*, Vol. 410, 10 June 1977, David Highet (Minister of Internal Affairs), 554.

90. Aotearoa New Zealand Parliamentary Debates, *H of R*, Vol. 410, 10 June 1977, Dr. Martyn Finlay, 554.

91. Aotearoa New Zealand Parliamentary Debates, *H of R*, Vol. 410, 10 June 1977, Mr. Isbey, 555.

92. Aotearoa New Zealand Parliamentary Debates, *H of R*, Vol. 410, 10 June 1977, Dr. Gerard Wall and Jonathan Hunt, 555.

93. Aotearoa New Zealand Parliamentary Debates, H of R, Vol. 410, 10 June 1977, Jonathan Hunt, 555.

94. Aotearoa New Zealand Parliamentary Debates, H of R, Vol. 410, 10 June 1977, Dr. Gerard Wall, 555.

95. Aotearoa New Zealand Parliamentary Debates, H of R, Vol. 410, 10 June 1977, David Highet (Minister of Internal Affairs), 557.

96. ANZ R20761257, Submission to the Statutes Revision Committee on the Citizens and Aliens Bill by the National Council of Women of New Zealand, 4 July 1977, 2.

97. ANZ R20761257, Submission by the Salvation Army in the matter of the Citizens and Aliens Bill and in the matter of the Statutes Revision Committee, July 1977, 1.

98. Aotearoa New Zealand Parliamentary Debates, H of R, Vol. 412, 22 July 1977, Richard Prebble, 1583–4.

99. Aotearoa New Zealand Parliamentary Debates, H of R, Vol. 412, 22 July 1977, David Highet (Minister of Internal Affairs), 1748.

100. Aotearoa New Zealand Parliamentary Debates, H of R, Vol. 415, 9 November 1977, David Highet (Minister of Internal Affairs), 4379.

101. Richard Bedford, "Citizenship in New Zealand: Tougher Criteria for a New Century," Canadian Diversity 6, issue 4 (Fall 2008): 95.

102. Megan Hutching, New Zealanders by Choice (Wellington: Identity Services, 1998), 84. However, national origin as a basis for immigration was not formally abolished until 1986, so British people were actually still advantaged until then, and, of course, the strong English-language provisions still advantage them.

103. Aotearoa New Zealand Parliamentary Debates, H of R, Vol. 350, 3 May 1967, Ralph Hanan (Minister of Maori Affairs), 46. This was something that went all the way back to the Treaty of Waitangi as a device for obtaining access to Maori land. For connections of this to citizenship see David Pearson, "The 'Majority Factor': Shaping Chinese and Māori Minorities" in Manying Ip (ed.), The Dragon and The Taniwha (Auckland: Auckland University Press, 2009) 32–55.

104. Aotearoa New Zealand Parliamentary Debates, H of R, Vol. 350, 3 May 1967, Norman Kirk, 47.

105. Aotearoa New Zealand Parliamentary Debates, H of R, Vol. 350, 3 May 1967, Matiu Rata, 48. This again has strong echoes of the Treaty of Waitangi.

106. Aotearoa New Zealand Parliamentary Debates, H of R, Vol. 350, 3 May 1967, Ralph Hanan, Minister of Maori Affairs, 49–50.

107. "New bill alters definition of term 'Maori,'" The Dominion, 6 July 1974, 10.

108. "Maoris may have to part with land," The Dominion, 4 May 1967, 6.

109. ANZ R20827493, Maori Affairs Amendment Bill—Explanatory Note, pp. i–vi.

110. ANZ R19524601, Submission to Parliamentary Maori Affairs Committee on 20 September 1967 by The Tuwharetoa Maori Trust Board, 1.

111. ANZ R19524601, Submission in respect of Maori Affairs Amendment Bill 1967 by The New Zealand Maori Council, 1–2.

112. ANZ R19524601, Submission in respect of The Maori Affairs Amendment Bill, 1967 by the Association of Maori University Graduates, 11 October 1967, 1.

113. ANZ R19524601, Submission in respect of The Maori Affairs Amendment Bill, 1967 by the Association of Maori University Graduates, 11 October 1967, p. 2.

114. *Ibid.*, 2, 5.

115. Aotearoa New Zealand Parliamentary Debates, H *of R*, Vol. 353, 26 October 1967, Matiu Rata, 3656.

116. Aotearoa New Zealand Parliamentary Debates, H *of R*, Vol. 353, 26 October 1967, Ralph Hanan, Minister of Maori Affairs, 3657.

117. "Move to delay Maori land Bill resisted," *The Dominion*, 27 October 1967, 5.
"Important Changes made to Maori Affairs Bill," *New Zealand Herald*, 28 October 1967, 3.
"Controversial Bill 'Talked Out,'" *New Zealand Herald*, 28 October 1967, 3.
"Govt's close win on Maori Affairs Bill," *The Dominion*, 28 October 1967, 6.
"Maori Bill Is Worst Affray since Culloden," *Evening Post*, 8 November 1967.
"Unhappy With Bill Says Sir Turi," *New Zealand Herald*, 8 November 1967.
"Maori affairs amendment," *The Dominion*, 15 November 1967, 2.
"Controversy in Parliament—Maori Affairs Bill Meets with Dogged Resistance," *New Zealand Herald*, 16 November 1967, 3.
"Opposition attacks Maori land law amendments," *The Dominion*, 16 November 1967, 6.
"Divisions on Bill total 27," *The Dominion*, 17 November 1967, 6.
"Land Bill now law," *The Dominion*, 22 November 1967, 3.
"Last-ditch stand against land Bill," *The Dominion*, 22 November 1967.

118. ANZ R22473534, "Mr. Hanan warns on racialism," *Dominion Herald*, 23 July 1968.

119. ANZ R22473534, "Hard to police laws against racial basis in housing," *Evening Post*, 18 September 1969.

120. ANZ R21581910, "Top Priority For Bill On Racial Legislation," *The New Zealand Herald*, 3 March 1971, 12.

121. "Race Relations by Law," *New Zealand Herald*, 4 March 1971.

122. ANZ R21581910, "Opposition Feels Bill Will Be Welcomed By All," *The Evening Post*, 9 July 1971.

123. ANZ R21581910, Submission on the Race Relations Bill by The National Council of Churches Commission on Church and Society, 19 August 1971, 4.

124. ANZ R21581910, Submission on the Race Relations Bill by the Citizen's Association for Racial Equality, 1.

125. ANZ R21581910, Submission of the New Zealand Maori Graduates Association on the Race Relations Bill, October 1971, PART I, 1.

126. *Ibid.*, 8.

127. ANZ R21581910, Submission of the New Zealand Maori Graduates Association on the Race Relations Bill, October 1971, PART II, 1.

128. ANZ R21581910, Manifesto of the New Zealand Maori Council on the Race Relations Bill, 1971, prepared by Dr. Ranginui Walker, University of Auckland, 3.

129. ANZ R21581910, Race Relations Bill, 1971—The Submissions of the New Zealand Maori Council Presented to the Parliamentary Statutes Revision Committee, 1.

130. ANZ R20825943, Memorandum by Matiu Rata, Minister of Maori Affairs for Cabinet, 18 October 1973 (including Maori Affairs Amendment Bill 1973 and other appendices), 1.

131. ANZ R20825943, Secretary of the Cabinet to the Minister of Maori Affairs, 24 October 1973.

132. ANZ R20825943, "Proposed Maori Affairs Amendment Bill 1973."

133. ANZ R20825943, Memorandum by Matiu Rata, Minister of Maori Affairs for Cabinet, 16 November 1973, 1–2.

134. ANZ R20825943, Secretary of the Cabinet to the Minister of Maori Affairs, 20 November 1973.

135. Aotearoa New Zealand Parliamentary Debates, *H of R*, Vol. 391, 5 July 1974, Matiu Rata, Minister of Maori Affairs, 2688.

136. Aotearoa New Zealand Parliamentary Debates, *H of R*, Vol. 391, 5 July 1974, Mr. Reweti, 2689.

137. Aotearoa New Zealand Parliamentary Debates, *H of R*, Vol. 391, 5 July 1974, Allan McCready, 2689.

138. Aotearoa New Zealand Parliamentary Debates, *H of R*, Vol. 391, 5 July 1974, David Highet, 2690.

139. Aotearoa New Zealand Parliamentary Debates, *H of R*, Vol. 391, 5 July 1974, Norman Kirk (Prime Minister), 2691.

140. Aotearoa New Zealand Parliamentary Debates, *H of R*, Vol. 391, 5 July 1974, Matiu Rata, Minister of Maori Affairs, 2994.

141. *Ibid.*

142. "Major Changes to Maori Affairs Act," *New Zealand Herald*, 6 July 1974.

143. "New bill alters definition of term 'Maori,'" *The Dominion*, 6 July 1974, 10.

144. ANZ R4533837, Maori Affairs Amendment Bill 1974—Submissions of P. H. E. Bloomer, Solicitor, Hastings, 26 July 1974, 1.

145. ANZ R22155366, Submissions in respect of the Maori Affairs Amendment Bill 1974—New Zealand Maori Council, Wednesday 14 August 1974, 1.

146. ANZ R4533837, Submissions on Maori Affairs Amendment Bill, 1974 by P. J. H. Southern, 6 August 1974, 1.

147. Aotearoa New Zealand Parliamentary Debates, *H of R*, Vol. 394, 2 October 1974, 4775–86, Vol. 395, 16 October 1974, 5096–111.

148. ANZ R20827493, P. J. Brooks, Secretary of the Cabinet to the Minister of Justice, 1 March 1971.

149. ANZ R20827493, Memorandum by D. J. Riddiford, Minister of Justice and D. Macintyre, Minister of Maori Affairs to Cabinet (including appendices), 24 May 1971, 2, 3.

150. ANZ R20827493, Note to Cabinet, 27 May 1971.

151. NLNZ 88–070-17/01, "Waitangi: Treaty or act?" *The Dominion*, Saturday 29 May 1971.

152. ANZ R20825944, Report of the Government Caucus Committee of Maori Affairs on the Treaty of Waitangi, 2.

153. *Ibid.*, 22.

154. ANZ R20825944, Memorandum by Matiu Rata, Minister of Maori Affairs for Cabinet, 7 March 1974, 2.

155. "Tribunal Guardian of Treaty," *New Zealand Herald*, 9 November 1974, 5.

156. Aotearoa New Zealand Parliamentary Debates, *H of C*, Vol. 401, 10 September 1975, M. Rata, 4343.

157. *Ibid.*
158. *Ibid.*
159. Aotearoa New Zealand Parliamentary Debates, H *of* R, Vol. 401, 10 September 1975, V. S. Young, 4343, 4344.
160. *Ibid.*, 4345, 4346.
161. Aotearoa New Zealand Parliamentary Debates, H *of* R, Vol. 401, 16 September 1975, Mrs. T. W. M. Tirikatene-Sullivan, 4495.
162. *Ibid.*, 4495, 4496.
163. *Ibid.*, 4496.

· 4 ·

COMPARISONS

Between the 1950s and 1970s, Britishness declined as the foundation of national identity in Australia, English-speaking Canada, and Aotearoa New Zealand. This was primarily due to several external shocks for the three countries: the Suez Crisis of 1956 was the starting point of the process in Canada. The UK's application for entry into the EEC was a common turning point for all three countries. The UK's withdrawal from East of Suez in 1967 was the end point of the process in Australia and Aotearoa New Zealand. The decline of the British connection led to a shift from an ethnic-centred (British) citizenship to a more civic-based one that was more inclusive of other ethnic groups and apparently Indigenous peoples in Australia, Canada, and Aotearoa New Zealand. The highlights in Australia were the *British Nationality and Australian Citizenship Act* of 1967, the *Australian Citizenship Act* of 1973, the awarding of the right to vote to Aborigines in 1960, and the 1967 referendum, which gave the Commonwealth power to legislate for Aborigines. In Canada, the key points were the *Canadian Citizenship Acts* of 1967 and 1977, the awarding of the right to vote for First Nations on the federal level, and the White Paper of 1969. The highlights in Aotearoa New Zealand were the *British Nationality and New Zealand Citizenship Act* of 1959, the *Citizenship and Aliens Act* of 1977, and the *Maori Affairs Amendment Acts* of 1967 and 1974.

This chapter will draw comparisons between the Australian, Canadian, and Aotearoa New Zealand experiences and offer some explanations for any similarities and differences.

The theoretical background to the redefinition of citizenship in all three countries is similar—the distinction between normative (citizenship as status) as opposed to substantive (citizenship as rights and responsibilities) citizenship. T. H. Marshall's theory of citizenship rights has profoundly impacted upon ideas of post-war citizenship. He argued that citizenship is a designation awarded to those who are complete members of a group. All who have this designation are supposedly the same in terms of the rights and responsibilities with which the designation is given.[1] However, this was not the case in post-war Australia, Canada, and Aotearoa New Zealand. Natural-born British subjects in all three countries actually had preferential status in comparison with their "alien" or naturalised counterparts, not only in terms of the naturalisation process itself (in the case of Australia and Canada) but also the rights to apply for public service jobs, stand for election, and so on.[2] Though unique to Aotearoa New Zealand, especially when compared with Australia, there was very little difference between the rights and obligations of citizens and permanent residents.[3] Things were even more complicated on the Indigenous side, as in theory, Indigenous groups in both Australia and Canada were considered citizens, and by extension, British subjects, but they did not actually have the rights associated with this, i.e., the right to vote and stand for election.[4] The situation in Aotearoa New Zealand was quite different, however, with Māori having both the franchise and the right to stand for elected office.[5] Therefore, Māori had many of the rights associated with citizenship, unlike their Indigenous counterparts in other former British settler societies. There were still differences though, in terms of social citizenship. So, citizenship in the three countries at the beginning of the 1950s was extremely restrictive in terms of other ethnic and Indigenous groups. However, by the end of the 1970s, this situation had changed drastically. Natural-born British migrants were put on the same level as their alien counterparts in Australia, Canada, and Aotearoa New Zealand.[6] And in fact, "British subject" status was finally removed from citizenship acts in all three countries. Australian, Canadian, and Aotearoa New Zealand citizens were solely that now. Furthermore, Indigenous peoples in Australia and Canada were also finally given the rights associated with their longstanding status as citizens. This included the awarding of the federal franchise and being allowed to stand for election.[7]

In terms of the context of the end of the British World in the three countries—developments followed a broadly similar trajectory in both Australia and Aotearoa New Zealand, although Britishness lingered perhaps longer in the latter in comparison with the former. I believe that this was a reflection of the greater hold the identity had in Aotearoa New Zealand in comparison with Australia, although it also had a firm grip on the latter's self-identification. A very appropriate example of the strength of British race patriotism in both countries is their first citizenship legislation introduced in 1948. Although both the *British Nationality and Australian Citizenship Act* and the *British Nationality and New Zealand Citizenship Act* introduced local citizenships in Australia and Aotearoa New Zealand for the very first time, *British* nationality was prioritized over *Australian* or *New Zealand* citizenship. And in any case, both countries very grudgingly introduced the legislation, and only did so because Canada's unilateral action in defining its own citizens jeopardised the entire common code system, which enshrined the status of British subjects across the British Empire.[8]

This was due to the problems Britishness faced in a bicultural society such as Canada, with its competing European founding group—the French-Canadians, in contrast to Australia and Aotearoa New Zealand, which had no comparable experience. The Suez Crisis of 1956 marked the beginning of the unraveling of Britishness in Canada. The Liberal government at the time opposed the Anglo-French action in Egypt against Nasser and argued instead for UN intervention. Once this took place it then actually took a leading role in the UN Emergency Force that was established. Jose Igartua argued that the Suez Crisis was a litmus test of Canada's automatic loyalty to the British Empire, and it showed to some Canadians that the British connection was not what it once was.[9] However, the Progressive Conservative opposition adopted a contrary view to the government and maintained that Canada should support the British in their action against Nasser's abrogation of an international contract, and that Canada's vocal opposition instead represented a disgraceful point in the country's history. In Australia, in contrast with the Canadian government, the Liberal-Country Coalition government backed the position of their conservative brethren and supported the British action in Suez. In Aotearoa New Zealand the National government was of a similar mindset and supported the British action in Suez. The Labour opposition also backed Britain. But it should be pointed out that the Australians and New Zealanders were duped, as were the British people, over the secret Anglo-French collusion with Israel to invade Egypt, thereby allowing the two European powers to in- turn intervene in the country on the pretext of separating the warring parties.[10] However, "Australian" support for the British should be qualified, as the Labor opposition there (contrary to Aotearoa New Zealand) held a similar position to the Liberal government in Canada. Although I would argue that the strength of British race patriotism still in Australia at this time implies that this opposition was against *British policy* in Egypt, not against *Britishness*, per se.

But by the time of Britain's first application for entry into the EEC, Australia's and Aotearoa New Zealand's Britannic self-identity was also challenged for the first time, and English-speaking Canada's threatened even more. This was a major psychological shock to the Australians, Canadians, and New Zealanders, as the British government had made repeated assurances to the effect that it was not considering full membership of the community. However, by the early 1960s, these promises were shown to be hollow, as the Australian, Canadian, and Aotearoa New Zealand governments got the distinct impression that the British government had indeed determined to join the EEC. This was confirmed by the British decision to send out the Secretary for Commonwealth relations: Duncan Sandys, to the far reaches of the Commonwealth to gauge opinion on the British decision. The Australian, Canadian, and Aotearoa New Zealand governments made it very clear that they considered it a detrimental blow to the integrity and future of the Commonwealth. If Britain were to join the EEC, how would it then consider Australia, Canada, and Aotearoa New Zealand? The British decision acted directly against the interests of the British World.[11] Aotearoa New Zealand felt particularly vulnerable, as it was so dependent on the British market, primarily in terms of its protein exports, although the impact of the British decision on Australia was far from negligible. However, the latter had already started diversifying its trade interests away from Britain before the 1960s. A prominent example was the trade treaty signed in the 1950s between Australia and its former wartime enemy, Japan.[12]

Therefore, it is very interesting that Australia and Aotearoa New Zealand adopted different strategies to limit the impact on their economies. Australia attempted to be part of the British negotiations but was rebuffed. They did, though, still try their best to encourage the British government to secure concessions for their exports. But these efforts proved to be largely unsuccessful as there was not much sympathy amongst the EEC members for Australia's "plight" as it was a reasonably sized economy which was developing trade relations in its own region. In contrast, Aotearoa New Zealand was much more successful in securing concessions for its protein exports well into the 1980s, as it played on the sympathy of both Britain and the EEC that it was a very small economy completely dependent on Britain for its exports.

In Canada there was also strong opposition to the British decision despite the economic impact being less than on Australia or Aotearoa New Zealand, as Canada's economic links with the US had far outgrown those with the UK long ago. But it was for this very reason that the Canadian government was even more vocal than its Australian or Aotearoa New Zealand counterparts in expressing its opposition. Canada did not want to become even more dependent on the US, which would ensue if the UK joined the EEC and diverted its economic interests to the European mainland. Of greater concern in Canada, though, was the growing military and political dominance of the US in the country. Thus, the Canadian government, personified by Prime Minister John Diefenbaker (who was an open Anglophile), strongly asserted that British membership of the EEC would only lead to Canada becoming even more linked to the US, to the detriment of the British World.[13] But whereas Britain's application to join the EEC in 1961 was the beginning of the process of the unravelling of the British World in Australia and Aotearoa New Zealand (its end point being signalled by Britain's announcement of its withdrawal militarily from "East of Suez" in 1967), it was the nail in the coffin in Canada. As argued above, this was due to the bicultural nature of Canada, in particular the presence of the French-Canadians in that country. Things came to a head in the 1960s as Britain's turning away from the British World occurred at the exact same time as the Quiet Revolution in Québec, which involved the complete modernization of Québec society (culturally, economically, politically, and socially), the driving force of which was a strident Québec nationalism. So, Québécois were defining themselves as a distinct people at the very same time as English-speaking Canadians were struggling with their self-identity due to external shocks. Therefore, I argue that this shift in national identity was the context in which citizenship legislation and policy was redefined in Australia, Canada, and Aotearoa New Zealand. It is to this transformation that I will now turn.

On the ethnic groups side, Australia actually took the lead in breaking down the distinctions between natural-born British subjects and aliens in citizenship legislation in 1973—Canada did not do this until 1976, and Aotearoa New Zealand not until 1977. This is quite unusual, as from my previous research, which compared the rise of multiculturalism in Canada and Australia between the 1890s and 1970s,[14] Canada consistently took the lead over Australia when it came to immigration policy and migrant policy. This is particularly notable, as Canada had experienced mass non-British migration much earlier than Australia and Aotearoa New Zealand—in the late nineteenth century, compared with the second half of the twentieth century in Australia and Aotearoa New Zealand. However, Canadian, Australian, and Aotearoa New Zealand legislation removed the preferential status of natural-born British subjects and placed all citizens on an equal basis. I would argue, though, that one of the reasons why Australia took the lead in this compared with Canada is because the provinces in the latter have more powers than their Australian counterparts. So, governments in the English-speaking provinces in Canada took some time to remove the special privileges they had for British subjects in their jurisdictions. This was, of course, not an issue in Québec, especially after the Quiet Revolution in the early 1960s. Contrarily, the Australian federal government was much more able to introduce national legislation which changed the situation.

Furthermore, Australia reformed its citizenship legislation more frequently than Aotearoa New Zealand. This is perhaps an indication of the different political cultures in the two countries, in that there was a belief in Australia that national issues could be addressed through positive legislative action, whereas in Aotearoa New Zealand the feeling was more that governments should trudge along unless something really had to be changed, coming up with stop-gap measures in the meantime. Also, Aotearoa New Zealand kept a close eye on what Australia did in terms of amending its citizenship and nationality legislation, as its own legislation was broadly similar. Moreover, both countries introduced legislation breaking down the final distinctions between natural-born British subjects and aliens around the same time; this is interesting, as Australia had received mass non-British migration somewhat earlier than Aotearoa New Zealand—the 1940s and 1950s in the former as opposed to the 1950s and 1960s in the latter. Nevertheless, both Australian and Aotearoa New Zealand legislation removed the preferential status of natural-born British subjects and placed all citizens on an equal basis. I would argue, though, that one of the reasons why this occurred around the same time is the different political systems in the two countries: federal as opposed to unitary. So, state governments in Australia took some time to remove the special privileges they had for British subjects in their jurisdictions. In contrast, in Aotearoa New Zealand, once the decision was made, the central government there could simply introduce legislation in the national parliament to put it into effect.

Before all of these major pieces of legislation in the 1970s in Australia, Canada, and Aotearoa New Zealand, however, the latter introduced important legislation in 1959, and the former two in 1967, which went some way towards removing some of the glaring disadvantages experienced by naturalised citizens in contrast with natural-born British subjects. This was primarily in terms of the revocation of citizenship. Previously, in all three countries, aliens could lose their Australian, Canadian, or Aotearoa New Zealand citizenship under revocation provisions which did not apply to natural-born British subjects. A prominent example of this was time spent away from their adopted countries. However, under the new legislation, these distinctions in regard to revocation were removed in all three countries—the only one remaining referring to obtaining citizenship through fraud. However, natural-born British subjects still retained preferential terms in regard to naturalisation compared with their alien counterparts. Nevertheless, the 1959 legislation in Aotearoa New Zealand and the 1967 legislation in both Australia and Canada show that the redefinition of citizenship in terms of other ethnic groups was a gradual process—it did not take place overnight in one sweeping piece of legislation. The fact that Aotearoa New Zealand took the lead in this respect, though, should be emphasised, especially since Britishness had a greater hold in that country. I believe that the explanation is mainly related to the point made earlier about the different political cultures between it and Australia, in terms of how they regarded legislative action in a positive way or not in terms of dealing with national issues.

Moving on to Indigenous groups in Australia, Canada, and Aotearoa New Zealand, there were differences between the former two in terms of their federal systems. In Australia, initially only the States had the power to legislate for Aborigines. Hence, a national plebiscite was required to confer this power to the Commonwealth government as well. In contrast, in Canada, the federal government was primarily responsible for the Indigenous people in its territory, and could therefore simply introduce legislation itself. The famous 1967 referendum in Australia asked the Australian people whether the Commonwealth government should be given the right to legislate for Aborigines as well as asking Australians whether Aborigines should be counted in the census. There was a resounding "Yes" on both questions. It was through this mechanism that the Commonwealth government was able to assume legislative powers for Aborigines, which there had been much clamour for over several decades. Contrarily, in Canada, the federal government already had legislative powers for Indigenous peoples.

Thus, it was able to award all of them the federal franchise through a simple act of parliament in 1960, although the Commonwealth government could extend the federal franchise to Aborigines in the same year as the constitution allowed this. The Trudeau Liberal government's introduction of the infamous White Paper of 1969 (which recommended dismantling the *Indian Act* which governed relations between the federal government and a large number of First Nations, as well as generally trying to make Indigenous peoples the "same" as all other citizens), however, illustrates the opposition that the federal government faced from Indigenous groups when it attempted to utilise its powers without due consultation.

The Māori in Aotearoa New Zealand were much more active themselves at an earlier stage, compared with both Australia and Canada, in lobbying the government to improve their situation, and the government had to negotiate with them in implementing policies. This was not the case in Australia due to the different political relationships between the settler colonial state and its Indigenous peoples, i.e., the lack of any treaties with Aborigines and the legal doctrine of "Terra Nullius" [land belonging to no one], which operated in Australia as late as 1992. The situation was also different in Canada, as the state there had only negotiated treaties with First Nations, not Inuit or Métis, and even then, only with certain First Nations. In Aotearoa New Zealand, due to their political representation in Parliament and the existence of the Māori Council, Māori opinion on policies that affected them could not be dismissed. The Māori Affairs Select Committee was an important vessel in which to express this opinion. The 1967 *Maori Affairs Act* is an excellent example of the impact of Māori opinion on policy. This was an extremely controversial piece of legislation, the primary aim of which was to "Europeanise" large tracts of Māori land. However, there was such a huge backlash to it from Māori parliamentarians and various organisations across the country that the act was repealed and replaced by another *Maori Affairs Act* in 1974. This is a major point of difference between Aotearoa New Zealand and Australia especially. In contrast, in Australia, the awarding of the federal franchise and the holding of the referendum in 1967 were acts of the Commonwealth government, which were certainly encouraged by Aboriginal rights organisations. But the key difference was that non-Aboriginal Australians very often, if not always, headed these organisations. It was only really in the 1970s and 1980s that the leadership changed to actual Aborigines themselves. As mentioned above, this was primarily due to the different political relationships between the settler colonial state and the Indigenous people within its territory.

Indigenous groups in Canada were much more active at an earlier stage, though, in comparison with Australia, in lobbying the government to improve their situation, and the federal government had to negotiate with them in implementing policies. This is a major point of difference between the two countries. As early as 1960, First Nations were often extremely vocal in their opposition to the federal government's moves to extend the federal franchise to them (as they were concerned about losing their status as "Indians" under the *Indian Act*). The federal government was forced to take notice and went to some pains to reassure First Nations that they would not lose any rights through their extension of the franchise. The strong Indigenous opposition to the White Paper of 1969 actually led to the federal government essentially abandoning its plans and acknowledging that Indigenous peoples were not like all other Canadian citizens and were indeed actually "Citizens Plus" (due to their treaties with the Crown which predated the existence of the state of Canada and the fact that they were actually the First Nations to inhabit the territory which later became known as Canada). As mentioned above, in Canada, there were treaties signed with many, but not all, Indigenous groups—the Inuit and Métis being prominent examples—but even amongst First Nations, bands and tribes in British Columbia had no treaties. Although, of course, it is openly acknowledged that the federal government often did not act in good faith when it came to the treaties that had been concluded with Indigenous groups and the Crown. You also had the overarching *Indian Act*, which managed relations between the federal government and First Nations. But in Australia there were firstly no treaties and no overarching act governing the relations between the Commonwealth and the Aborigines. This was sadly due to the ignorance British settlers had of Aboriginal culture—which was so alien to western hierarchical structures that they took the mistaken view that Aborigines had a primitive, nomadic culture with no social structure, and therefore treaties could not be concluded with them. The irony, of course, being that the Aborigines had one of the longest continuous cultures in the world. Linked to this, as stated above, Australia was declared "Terra Nullius" [land belonging to no one], which meant there was no need to conclude treaties with anyone in any case.

As stated above there are differences between Australia, Canada, and Aotearoa New Zealand in terms of their political systems: the former two possessing federal systems, as opposed to unitary in the latter. The federal and state governments in Australia and federal and provincial governments in Canada were both responsible for elements of Indigenous citizenship policy in their respective countries, whereas in Aotearoa New Zealand it was only the central government in Wellington which had power in these areas. However, the most fundamental point of difference between Australia, Canada, and Aotearoa New Zealand in terms of Indigenous peoples is the different historical and political experiences of the three countries. Māori in Aotearoa New Zealand had political representation (although not proportionate to their numbers in the population) through the four original Māori seats from 1868, and the extension of the franchise to Māori men and women followed the same broad trajectory as Pakeha. In direct contrast, Aboriginal groups in Australia and Canada did not have these until much later. In fact, Aborigines and First Nations did not gain the right to vote in federal elections until 1960. Part of the explanation for this difference is the fact that Māori have consistently formed a much larger proportion of the population compared with their Indigenous counterparts in Australia and Canada: approximately 15 % today compared with 2 or 3 % in Australia, or 3 or 4 % in Canada. The second reason, I believe, is the existence of the Treaty of Waitangi in Aotearoa New Zealand, and the lack of an equivalent in Australia or even Canada. Of course the terms of the treaty, and even its spirit, have not always been honoured, or acted on in good faith by Pakeha, but the fact that it exists has certainly had an impact, especially as a means with which Māori have been able to argue, especially in recent decades, that previous legislation had abrogated the terms of the treaty and their rights as equal citizens in Aotearoa New Zealand. This relates to another point about the difference between the Indigenous populations of the two countries. Although there are various tribes, the Māori are ethnically one people. In contrast, in Australia and Canada, you have numerous Aboriginal groups with their own languages, not to mention the Torres Strait Islanders who are ethnically a different people from Aborigines in Australia, and the three different Indigenous groups in Canada: First Nations, Inuit, and Métis. Thus, it was possible for British settlers to conclude the Treaty of Waitangi with the majority (but certainly not all) of Māori Chiefs in the nineteenth century. But in Australia, there were no treaties between the Commonwealth and the Aborigines for the reasons outlined above. And in Canada, there were treaties with some First Nations, but not with Inuit or Métis. Another explanation, in my opinion, relates to the geography of the three countries: although Aotearoa New Zealand is not insignificant in terms of land mass (being approximately the size of the UK), it is considerably smaller than Australia and Canada. Hence, Māori were not as isolated as their Indigenous counterparts in Australia and Canada; consequently, there was no comprehensive reservation system in Aotearoa New Zealand akin to that found in Australia and Canada. The great Māori migration to urban areas in the 1950s only brought Pakeha and Māori in even closer interaction.

Having said all of the above, it is even more fascinating, then, that both Canada and Aotearoa New Zealand saw the introduction of extremely unpopular and controversial legislation which was supposedly aimed at making their Aboriginal populations more equal citizens: the White Paper of 1969 and the *Maori Affairs Amendment Act* of 1967. The former had the supposedly lofty aim of making Indigenous peoples the "same" as other Canadian citizens, through the repealing of the *Indian Act*, and the provinces taking over the responsibility for Indigenous peoples along with other citizens. The latter "Europeanised" over a third of the remaining Māori land in Aotearoa New Zealand, specifically, land that was owned by not more than four owners. But although there was Indigenous opposition in both countries, it was more effective in Canada in derailing the plans. First Nation opposition to the White Paper or the "Red Paper," as it was referred to by many of them, actually led to the Trudeau Liberal government changing track and instead advocating the concept that First Nations were "Citizens plus," due to the treaties that existed between many of them and the Crown and the fact that they were the first people to inhabit what later became known as Canada. In contrast, although there was also considerable Māori opposition to the *Maori Affairs Amendment Act*, the National government at the time still decided to go ahead with its plans. However, the subsequent Kirk Labour government reversed many of the controversial features of the legislation in their own *Maori Affairs Amendment Act* of 1974. Part of the explanation for this could again be the different political systems between the two countries. In Canada, with the federal government keen to offload many of its responsibilities towards First Nations under the *Indian Act* to the provinces under the White Paper, the latter insisted that they would not commit to this unless First Nations were also present on the negotiating table and agreed to it as well. When it became clear that this would not be the case, the federal government backtracked. Contrarily, the lack of a federal system in Aotearoa New Zealand meant that the National government could introduce its controversial legislation in 1967 despite such opposition, and similarly, its Labour successor could reverse this when it came to power.

In conclusion, this chapter has compared the end of the British World and the redefinition of citizenship in Australia, Canada, and Aotearoa New Zealand, between the 1950s and 1970s. Through firstly establishing a common theoretical background—in that unlike T. H. Marshall's famous linkage of the rights and responsibilities of citizenship, Australia, Canada, and Aotearoa New Zealand in the 1950s actually had several distinctions in this respect between natural-born British subjects and naturalised citizens, and non-Indigenous and Indigenous citizens. In terms of the context of the unravelling of Britishness in the three countries, the process began earlier in Canada compared with Australia and Aotearoa New Zealand, although the trajectory was similar. The difference in terms of timing relates to the bicultural nature of Canada compared with a predominantly monocultural Australia and Aotearoa New Zealand. However, by the 1970s, all three countries had largely resigned themselves to the end of the British World. It was in this context that citizenship legislation and policy was redefined in Australia, Canada, and Aotearoa New Zealand. On the ethnic groups side, the trajectory was broadly similar. Australia took the lead in removing the last remnants of the preferential treatment of natural-born British subjects compared with aliens, although interestingly, both Australia and Aotearoa New Zealand removed the last remnants of the preferential treatment of British subjects compared with naturalised citizens around the same time, this despite Australia having experienced mass non-British migration earlier than Aotearoa New Zealand. There were more differences on the Indigenous side, however. In 1967 the Commonwealth government had to hold a referendum in order to be given the power to legislate for Aborigines. In contrast, in Canada, the federal government already had this power. And Indigenous groups in Canada were much more active themselves in pushing for change from the government compared with Australian Aborigines, due to the different political relations between the settler colonial state and its original Indigenous inhabitants in the two countries. On the surface, the Māori had already had for a long time many of the rights associated with citizenship: the franchise and the ability to stand for parliament. This did not take place in Australia and Canada until much later.

Notes

1. Marshall, *Class, Citizenship, and Social Development*, 84.
2. Hudson and Kane, "Rethinking Australian Citizenship," 2. Gabriel, "Citizens and Citizenship," 166.
3. McKinnon, *Immigrants and Citizens*, 44.
4. Johnston, "First Nations and Canadian Citizenship," 349.

Dodds, "Citizenship, Justice and Indigenous Group-Specific Rights-Citizenship and Indigenous Australia," 106.

5. Humpage, "Revision Required," 247.
6. Jordens, *Alien to Citizen: Settling Migrants in Australia, 1945–75,* 189.
   Knowles, *Forging our Legacy: Canadian Citizenship and Immigration, 1900–1977,* 88.
   Mulgan, "Multiculturalism: A New Zealand Perspective," 85.
7. Chesterman and Galligan, "Indigenous Rights and Australian Citizenship," 67.
   Cardinal and Brady, "Citizenship and Federalism in Canada: A Difficult Relationship," 384.
8. Mann, "The Evolution of Commonwealth Citizenship," 293–313.
9. Igartua, "'Ready, Aye, Ready' No More?"
10. Hudson, *Blind Loyalty.*
    Pfeiffer, "New Zealand and the Suez Crisis of 1956," 126–52.
11. Ward, *Australia and the British Embrace.*
12. *Ibid.*
    Belich, *Paradise Reforged.*
13. Benvenuti and Ward, "Britain, Europe, and the 'Other Quiet Revolution' in Canada."
14. Mann, *The Search for a New National Identity: The Rise of Multiculturalism in Canada and Australia, 1890s–1970s.*

CONCLUSION

This book has explored the way in which citizenship was redefined between the 1950s and 1970s in Australia, Canada, and Aotearoa New Zealand, in terms of ethnicity and Indigeneity. The overall context in which this all took place was the end of the British World in the three countries.

Chapter 1 showed how the end of the British World and its replacement with a "new nationalism" led to a redefinition of citizenship in Australia between the 1950s and 1970s. The UK's first application for entry into the EEC in 1961 and the announcement of its military withdrawal from "East of Suez" in 1967 were particular highlights, which signaled the end of the British self-identification of Australia. Through focusing on the *Nationality and Citizenship Acts* of 1955 and 1960, the *Citizenship Act* of 1969, and the *Australian Citizenship Act* of 1973, the chapter demonstrated the way in which non-British migrants were gradually put on a much more equal basis to their British counterparts in terms of being able to attain Australian citizenship and exercise the benefits of Australian citizenship, such as employment in the public services. It also illustrated how Aboriginal policy during the 1950s, the awarding of the right to vote for Aborigines in 1961, the 1967 Referendum, and the International Convention on the Elimination of All Forms of Racial Discrimination during the 1960s and 1970s, collectively led to the removal of the constitutional discriminations against Aborigines and actually allowed them to exercise the rights of Australian citizenship which they had theoretically held since 1948.

Chapter 2 illustrated how the end of the British World led to a redefinition of citizenship in Canada between the 1950s and 1970s. The key highlights of the unravelling of Britishness in Canada were the Suez Crisis of 1956 and the UK's decision to apply for membership of the EEC in 1961. This resulted in a shift away from a British-centred citizenship to one that was more inclusive of other ethnic groups and apparently Indigenous peoples. The *Canadian Citizenship Acts* of 1957, 1962, 1967, and 1977 demonstrated the gradual shift in terms of greater inclusivity towards ethnic groups, as, especially with the final Act, the last distinctions between British subjects and other migrants were removed from Canadian citizenship legislation. And on the Indigenous side, the amendment of the *Elections Act* in 1950 and the *Indian Act* in 1955 demonstrated the Canadian states' limited efforts to extend the federal franchise to First Nations, so as long they gave up their status as "Indians." So, the awarding of the right to vote for First Nations in federal elections in 1960 without any preconditions was a major milestone in their being able to exercise one of the major privileges of citizenship. The 1969 White Paper, which, amongst other things, proposed a repeal of the *Indian Act*, with the aim of making First Nations equal to other citizens, faced such a backlash from a highly educated and politically savvy First Nation leadership that the government was forced to concede that First Nations were not citizens just like other Canadians, but "Citizens Plus."[1]

Chapter 3 showed how the end of the British World led to a redefinition of citizenship in Aotearoa New Zealand between the 1950s and 1970s. The UK's first application for entry into the EEC in 1961, and the announcement of its military withdrawal from "East of Suez" in 1967, were particular highlights which signalled the end of the British self-identification of Aotearoa New Zealand. Through focusing on the popular pressure from mainly Dutch immigrants against distinctions between natural-born and naturalised citizens in 1955, the *British Nationality and New Zealand Citizenship Acts* of 1959 and 1963, and the *Citizenship and Aliens Act* of 1977, the chapter demonstrated how naturalised British subjects were put on a much more equal basis to their natural-born counterparts in being able to attain Aotearoa New Zealand citizenship and exercise the benefits of Aotearoa New Zealand citizenship. It also illustrated the way in which the *Māori Affairs Amendment Act* of 1967 was supposedly aimed at placing Māori on an equal basis with Pakeha in terms of the selling of their land. But as one group had the money to buy (Pakeha) and the other did not (Māori), this was nothing less than the commodification of Indigenous collective land and territorial identity. Nevertheless, there was considerable opposition to this from Māori, and the subsequent *Māori Affairs Amendment Act* of 1974 actually reversed the main features of its predecessor and was widely advocated as treating Māoridom on its own terms. It was only the beginning of the process, however, and it was not until the 1980s that major shifts took place. This illustrates the continued hugely contested nature of citizenship in Aoteareo New Zealand when it comes to Māori and the Aoteareo New Zealand state. The *Race Relations Act* of 1971 attempted to counter the imbalance between Māori and Pakeha in terms of social citizenship. And the *Treaty of Waitangi Act* of 1975 was aimed at providing a forum, through the Treaty of Waitangi Tribunal, for Māori to attempt to secure redress for breaches against the treaty.

Chapter 4 compared the end of the British World and the redefinition of citizenship in Australia, Canada, and Aotearoa New Zealand between the 1950s and 1970s. Through firstly establishing a common theoretical background—in that unlike T. H. Marshall's famous linkage of the rights and responsibilities of citizenship, Australia, Canada, and Aotearoa New Zealand in the 1950s actually had several distinctions in this respect between natural-born British subjects and naturalised citizens, and non-Indigenous and Indigenous citizens. In terms of the context of the unravelling of Britishness in the three countries, the process began earlier in Canada when compared with Australia and Aotearoa New Zealand, although the trajectory was similar. The difference in terms of timing relates to the bicultural nature of Canada compared with a predominantly monocultural Australia and Aotearoa New Zealand. However, by the 1970s, all three countries had largely resigned themselves to the end of the British World. It was in this context that citizenship legislation and policy was redefined in Australia, Canada, and Aotearoa New Zealand. On the ethnic groups side, the trajectory was broadly similar. Australia took the lead in removing the last remnants of the preferential treatment of natural-born British subjects compared with aliens. Although interestingly, both Australia and Aotearoa New Zealand removed the last remnants of the preferential treatment of British subjects compared with naturalised citizens around the same time, this despite Australia having experienced mass non-British migration earlier than Aotearoa New Zealand. On the Indigenous side, however, there were more differences. The Commonwealth government had to hold a referendum in 1967 in order to be given the power to legislate for Aborigines. In contrast, in Canada, the federal government already had this power. And Indigenous groups in Canada were much more active themselves in pushing for change from the government compared with Aborigines in Australia, due to the different political relations between the settler colonial state and its original Indigenous inhabitants in the two countries. On the surface, the Māori had already had for a long time many of the rights associated with citizenship, including the franchise and the ability to stand for parliament. This was not the case in Australia and Canada until much later.

Bringing the development of citizenship policy in the three countries up to the present, on the ethnicity side in Australia, in the 1970s the Commonwealth removed racism from its policies, using a new series of discourses on human distinction: ethnicity and a transformed nationalism in which race still remained below the surface. Regardless of the shift, allegiance continued to be a significant measure by which citizens were differentiated with strangers.[2] This illustrates that when it came to citizenship, the last remnants of Britishness were not abandoned until as late as the end of the 1980s. Kim Rubenstein has shown that there has recently been much vulnerability for dual citizens. This has led to Australian citizens reverting back to their "subject"-like status in principle, if not in name.[3] The larger difference between British subjects and aliens, which conceptualised Australian citizenship in the first 48 years of the country's existence, has been maintained to the present day with the existing difference between citizen and non-citizen.[4]

On the Indigeneity side, from the late 1970s, "self-determination" increasingly became the rhetoric for reform, utilised to explain the limitations of assimilation. As an administrative concept, self-determination was closely linked to decentralisation—an effort to shift further from dominant paternalistic central control. Up to now, conversations between Indigenous people and governments about what type of government organisation could be the best for giving service and access to Aboriginal groups have been ad hoc and few and far between. Beginning in the 1970s, after the 1967 referendum, the federal government tried to have a conversation with Indigenous people when the National Aboriginal Consultative Conference and National Aboriginal Conference were established and then disestablished.[5]

Jeremy Beckett argued that "The reconstituting of the Aboriginal community coincided with the demand for Land Rights, which had become the focal issue for the Tent Embassy....The demand could be made in several modes: minimally as a plea for Aboriginal people to enjoy the same security of occupancy as other Australians—a serious issue in view of Queensland's relocation of the Mapoon mission a few years before; in terms of economic justice, as partial or token restitution for the original act of expropriation; in religious terms, as a recognition of the Aborigines' spiritual relationship to the land, manifest in the performance of ceremonies by the 'traditionally orientated' in northern and central Australia, but also said to persist in the psychic makeup of Aboriginal people everywhere."[6]

In Canada, reflecting on the legacy of the 1977 *Canadian Citizenship Act*, on the ethnicity side, it certainly played a part in the formation of new calls for inclusion and the acknowledgement of identities and social rights, as illustrated by the *Multiculturalism Act* in 1988. Indeed, the introduction of the Canadian Charter of Rights and Freedoms in 1982 was the consequence of this drive towards a more inclusive citizenship.[7] Yasmeen Abu-Laban has demonstrated that policy reforms in the past decade have included numerous changes introduced by Prime Minister Stephen Harper's Conservative government (in power from 2006 to 2015), which combined to make Canadian citizenship harder to obtain (and easier to lose), and intensified the surveillance of borders and belonging in ways that are racialised and gendered.[8] Audrey Macklin has also illustrated that the Conservatives systematically resiled from the citizenship policies that typify a settler society. Citizenship law furnished an ideal platform for staging the rebranding of Canada as Warrior Nation, a pet Conservative project. The role played by one particular citizenship policy during the Fall 2015 federal election (the ban on face covering while swearing the citizenship oath) reveals a lingering, and perhaps chronic, ambiguity regarding Canadian citizenship in an era where forces of globalisation and nationalist retrenchment impose competing pressures on state citizenship regimes.[9]

In Aotearoa New Zealand, growing Māori calls for acknowledgement of rangatiratanga combined with notable challenges to the establishment from numerous sections, with the "founding myths" of New Zealand (including those of paradisal race relations), in particular, facing criticism across the board. It was a lively social and intellectual time for numerous (especially young) people, including Māori youth living in urban areas with access to educational opportunities not available to their ancestors. The Māori movement to "reconcile Aotearoa with New Zealand" took place together, impacted and influenced postcolonial nationalist debate and "nation building" terminology and discourse. Large numbers of non-Māori were starting to regard themselves as "Pakeha" instead of "European" or "British."[10] Michael King also made reference to the view of Aotearoa New Zealand as having paradisal race relations, "For Pakeha, the matching myth was that New Zealand had the best race relations in the world, a verdict Pakeha politicians trumpeted at every possible opportunity."[11]

Also in the 1970s, a journey of introspection started in government departments: encompassing the Department of Māori Affairs, The "Tu Tangata" policy (translated literally as "people standing tall") was introduced by Kara Puketapu, who was appointed as the Secretary for Māori Affairs in 1977.[12] Alan Ward and Janine Hayward argued, though, that "While some sectors of the Māori community appeared to support the principle of Tu Tangata as an expression of Māori autonomy, others remained sceptical about the department's intentions and were suspicious that Māori would not be adequately resourced in their new role."[13]

The Māori land march movement began as a hui organised at Mangere Marae in early 1975 by the prominent Māori leader, Whina Cooper. The main drive of the movement was increasing anger towards the continued control and alienation of the remaining 1.2 million hectares of Māori land by Pakeha laws.[14] M. H. Durie maintained that "In the same year that Whina Cooper led the historic land march from Te Hapua to Parliament, the Treaty of Waitangi Act 1975 became law under the sponsorship of the Minister of Māori Affairs, Matiu Rata....While its significance as a vehicle for reform was to pass unnoticed until the Motunui case in 1983, the Act was a further signal that Māori leadership would not be bound by the agendas of previous governments or the conservative wishes of mainstream New Zealand."[15]

Nevertheless, motivated by an all-encompassing drive for social cohesion in a nation where Indigenous Māori form a major proportion of the populace (currently 15 %), Aotearoa New Zealand administrations have had to provide a symbolic acknowledgement of Māori nationhood. This illustrates how, in reality, the activities of administrations heading liberal-democratic status customarily have to go beyond the boundaries of liberal theory to respond to the challenge of national and cultural diversity.[16]

Paul Spoonley maintained that by the 1970s, the country had begun to debate nationality and citizenship in ways that differed (in part) from other modern liberal (including settler) societies. It has two key elements: a pre-eminent focus on a biculturalism which recognises the Indigeneity of the original settlers, Māori; and the shift in in the ethnic diversity that resulted from changes to immigration policy in the 1980s so that a significantly enhanced diversity has altered debates about identity, nationality, and citizenship.[17] Carwyn Jones and Craig Linkhorn considered the nature of Māori citizenship today in the era of Treaty of Waitangi settlements, exploring how citizenship in this period of transitional justice is informed by political, social, and justice dimensions of conceptions of Māori citizenship over time.[18] Mamari Stephens highlighted that an examination of welfare law and development in New Zealand can reveal both Māori persistence in having Māori notions of citizenship fully heard, and the sheer difficulty in having such notions broadly recognised.[19]

Notes

1. Cairns, *Citizens Plus*.
2. Dutton, *One of Us? A Century of Australian Citizenship*, 157.
3. Kim Rubenstein, "The Vulnerability of Dual Citizenship: From Supranational Subject to Citizen to Subject?" in *Citizenship in Transnational Perspective: Australia, Canada, and New Zealand*, ed. Jatinder Mann, Politics of Citizenship and Immigration Series (New York: Palgrave Macmillan, 2017), 245–62.
4. Rubenstein, *Australian Citizenship Law in Context*, 10.
5. Fletcher, "Living Together but not Neighbours," 342, 343.
6. Jeremy Beckett, "Aboriginality, Citizenship and Nation State," *Social Analysis*, no. 24 (December 1988): 13.
7. Cardinal and Brady, "Citizenship and Federalism in Canada," 384.
8. Yasmeen Abu-Laban, "Building a New Citizenship Regime? Immigration and Multiculturalism in Canada," in *Citizenship in Transnational Perspective: Australia, Canada, and New Zealand*, ed. Jatinder Mann (New York: Palgrave Macmillan, 2017), 263–84.
9. Audrey Macklin, "From Settler Society to Warrior Nation and Back Again," in *Citizenship in Transnational Perspective: Australia, Canada, and New Zealand*, ed. Jatinder Mann (New York: Palgrave Macmillan, 2017), 285–314.
10. Hill, *Maori and the State*, 149, 151.
11. King, *The Penguin History of New Zealand*, 471.
12. Alan Ward and Janine Hayward, "Tino Rangatiratanga: Maori in the Political and Administrative System," in *Indigenous Peoples' Rights in Australia, Canada & New Zealand*, ed. Paul Havemann (Auckland: Oxford University Press, 1999), 394.
13. *Ibid.*
14. Ranginui Walker, *Ka Whawhai Tonu Matou—Struggle Without End* (Auckland: Penguin Books, 1990), 212.
15. Mason H. Durie, *Te Mana Te Kāwanatanga—The Politics of Māori Self-Determination* (South Melbourne, Victoria: Oxford University Press, 1998), 175.
16. Humpage, "Revision Required," 247.
17. Paul Spoonley, "Renegotiating Citizenship: Indigeneity and Superdiversity in Contemporary Aotearoa/New Zealand," in *Citizenship in Transnational Perspective: Australia, Canada, and New Zealand*, ed. Jatinder Mann (New York: Palgrave Macmillan, 2017), 209–24.
18. Jones and Linkhorn, "'All the Rights and Privileges of British Subjects,'" 139–58.
19. Mamari Stephens, "'A Useful and Self-Respecting Citizenship'—Maori as Citizens in the Quest for Welfare in the Modern New Zealand State," in *Citizenship in Transnational Perspective: Australia, Canada, and New Zealand*, ed. Jatinder Mann, Politics of Citizenship and Immigration Series (New York: Palgrave Macmillan, 2017), 189–208.

BIBLIOGRAPHY

Primary Sources

Archives New Zealand

R4533837: Maori Affairs Amendment Bill, 1974.

R10764764: Naturalisation—British Nationality and New Zealand Citizenship, 1961–1966.

R10764767: Naturalisation—British Nationality and New Zealand Citizenship, 1962–1963.

R12323366: Naturalisation—British Nationality and New Zealand Citizenship Act 1948—Proposed revision and consolidation—British Nationality and New Zealand Citizenship Bill 1963, 1962–1963.

R19524601: Committee of Inquiry—Proposed Amendments to Maori Affairs Bill, 1967.

R19964588: British Nationality and New Zealand Citizenship Act 1948—Legislation—Policy etc.

R19964589: British Nationality and New Zealand Citizenship Act 1948—Legislation—Policy etc.

R20761248: Commonwealth Affairs: Legislation and Constitutional Affairs—Nationality—Australian Citizenship [01/45–01/72], 1945–1972.

R20761257: Commonwealth Affairs: Legislation and Constitutional Affairs—Nationality—NZ Citizenship: General [09/76–08/77], 1976–1977.

R20825943: Maori Affairs—General, 1972–1974.

R20825944: Maori Affairs—General, 1974–1975.

R20827493: Maori Affairs—General, 1965–1972.

R20969491: British Nationality and New Zealand Citizens Amendment Bill 1959, 1959.

R21581910: Race Relations.

R22013510: Naturalisation—British Nationality and New Zealand Citizenship Act 1948—"Commonwealth Citizen," 1965.

R22155366: Miscellaneous—Legislation—Maori Affairs Amendment Bill '74—Submission to Maori Affairs Committee, 1974–1975.

R22473534: New Zealand Affairs: Maori Affairs—General—Discrimination Against the Maoris, 1965–1971.

Library and Archives Canada

MG26-L/Vol. 382/File 2253: Clippings. General Series, 1935–1957.

MG26-N9/Vol. 50: National Unity, 1963–1965.

MG26-M/Vol. 245/Reel M-7900/File 313.3 MI–C.

MG26-M/Vol. 245/Reel M-7900/File 313.3 MI–C, J.R.N.

MG26-N3/Vol. 210/File 577.2: Immigration and Citizenship—Citizenship—Act, June 1963-November 1965.

MG26-O11/Vol. 22/File 5/635: Prime Minister's Office Secret Documents, 1968–1984.

MG32-B1/Vol. 88/File IA-12J: Policy and Case Files—Joint Committee on Indian Affairs—Correspondence, 1959–1960.

MG32-B1/Vol. 94/File IA-166/File 18: Policy and Case Files—Indians' Right to Vote, 1957–1959.

MG32-B1/Vol. 95/File IA-166/File 1: Policy and Case Files—Indians' Right to Vote, 1960.

MG32-B34/Vol. 24/File IA 12A, Part 1: Citizenship and Immigration. Indian Affairs Branch—Indian Act Sub-Series, 1936–1957.

MG32-B34/Vol. 24/File IA 12A, Part 2: Citizenship and Immigration. Indian Affairs Branch—Indian Act Sub-Series, 1936–1957.

MG32-B34/Vol. 24/File IA 12A, Part 3: Citizenship and Immigration. Indian Affairs Branch—Indian Act Sub-Series, 1936–1957.

MG32-C67/Vol. 91/File 1: Files Received in 1986 From Senate, 1946–1986.

R11236/Vol. 135/File 148-4-8: Secretary of State—Citizenship, 1976–1979.

RG2/Series A-5-a/Vol. 1898: Cabinet Conclusions, 1944–1979.

RG2/Series A-5-a/Vol. 2645: Cabinet Conclusions, 1944–1979.

RG2/Series A-5-a/Vol. 2646: Cabinet Conclusions, 1944–1979.

RG2/Series A-5-a/Vol. 2653: Cabinet Conclusions, 1944–1979.

RG2/Series A-5-a/Vol. 2658: Cabinet Conclusions, 1944–1979.

RG2/Series A-5-a/Vol. 2659: Cabinet Conclusions, 1944–1979.

RG2/Series A-5-a/Vol. 2745: Cabinet Conclusions, 1944–1979.

RG2/Series A-5-a/Vol. 5775: Cabinet Conclusions, 1944–1979.

RG2/Series A-5-a/Vol. 6264: Cabinet Conclusions, 1944–1979.

RG2/Series A-5-a/Vol. 6271: Cabinet Conclusions, 1944–1979.

RG2/Series A-5-a/Vol. 6323: Cabinet Conclusions, 1944–1979.

RG2/Series A-5-a/Vol. 6338: Cabinet Conclusions, 1944–1979.

RG2/Series A-5-a/Vol. 6340: Cabinet Conclusions, 1944–1979.

RG2/Series A-5-a/Vol. 6359: Cabinet Conclusions, 1944–1979.

RG2/Series A-5-a/Vol. 6436: Cabinet Conclusions, 1944–1979.

RG2-B-2/Vol. 2741/Cab. Doc. 128–58: Cabinet Documents 101–150, 1958.

RG2-B-2/Vol. 2743/Cab. Doc. 383–59: Cabinet Documents 351–400, 1959.

RG2-B-2/Vol. 6320/Cab. Doc. 700–66: Cabinet Documents 651–769, 1966.

RG2-B-2/Vol. 6325/Cab. Doc. 157–67: Cabinet Documents 151–275, 1967.

RG2-B-2/Vol. 6349/Cab. Doc. 654–69: Cabinet Documents 616–691, 1969.

RG2-B-2/Vol. 6354/Cab. Doc. 1007–69: 967–1039, 1969.

RG2-B-2/Vol. 26589/Cab. Doc. 1235–73: 1226–1311, 1973.

RG6/Vol. 659/File 1–5-1: Acts and Bills—General 66–67, 1966–1967.

RG6/Vol. 659/File 1–5-2, Part 1: Acts and Bills—Canadian Citizenship Act—Amendments, 1965–1969.

RG6/Vol. 659/File 1–5-2, Part 2: Acts and Bills—Canadian Citizenship Act—Amendments, 1965–1969.

RG6/Vol. 660/File 1–16-2: Legal—Oath of Allegiance—General, 1965–1966.

RG6/Vol. 662/File 2–12-15: Indian Organizations (Canadian)—General, 1965–1968.

RG6/Vol. 664/File 3–6-11: Citizenship Cases—Loss and Resumption of Canadian Citizenship—Policy and Instructions 65–69—1965–1969.

RG25/Vol. 5519/File 12447–40 (pt. 51): European Common Market (EEC), 1962/03/09–1962/04/30.

RG26/Vol. 75/File 1–1-8, Part 1: Minister of Citizenship and Immigration—General File [Report on symposium at McMaster University in April 1949 entitled "Population Growth and Immigration into Canada"; statistics and memoranda relating to immigration and the labour force; copies of speeches delivered by the Minister of Immigration; assorted material relating to Indian Affairs; translations of articles/editorials from foreign language periodicals published in Canada; temporary docket entitled "Trip of the Minister to Immigration Offices overseas and proposed visit in British Columbia; copy of booklet" Caritas-Canada"; other material, 1954–1957.

RG26/Vol. 75/File 1–1-8, Part 3: Minister of Citizenship and Immigration—General File [Report on symposium at McMaster University in April 1949 entitled "Population Growth and Immigration into Canada"; statistics and memoranda relating to immigration and the labour force; copies of speeches delivered by the Minister of Immigration; assorted material relating to Indian Affairs; translations of articles/editorials from foreign- language periodicals published in Canada; temporary docket entitled "Trip of the Minister to Immigration Offices overseas and proposed visit in British Columbia; copy of booklet" Caritas-Canada"; other material, 1954–1957.

RG26/Vol. 76/File 1–5-11: The Foreign Press in Canada—Part 4, 1961–1962.

RG26/Vol. 82/File 1–24-27, Part 3: Human Rights—Draft Convention on Prevention of Discrimination and Protection of Minorities [United Nations releases; reports of General Assembly re: draft covenants; government statements re: draft covenants and suggested amendments; correspondence, etc. relating to the Commission on the Status of Women; other material], 1954–1957.

RG33-80/Acc. 1974-75-039/Box 83: Speeches by PM, 1963–1967.

National Archives of Australia

A432 1960/1196: Nationality and Citizenship Bill, 1960.

A432 1960/3289 PART 2: Aboriginal natives—voting at Federal elections, 1960–1965.

A432 1961/3191: Census returns—Nationality, 1954–1961.

A432 1967/3321 PART 1: Aborigines—Commonwealth powers with regard to Constitution—correspondence in relation to provisions of Constitution—general file, 1958–1967.

A432 1968/3377: Revision of Nationality and Citizenship Act, 1968.

A406 E1967/30: 1967 Referendum—Constitution alteration—Main file, 1967–1968.

A446 1957/66699: Suggested amendments to Nationality and Citizenship Acts, 1950–1978.

A446 1965/45441: Nationality and Citizenship Act 1955, 1954–1978.

A446 1965/45472: Amendments to the Nationality and Citizenship Act 1960, 1959–1966.

A446 1965/46671: Canadian Citizenship Act—part 2, 1958–1967.

A446 1967/72349: Nationality and Citizenship Act 1967—Review of, 1966–1968.

A446 1969/70341: Citizenship Act 1969, 1969–1970.

A446 1978/75530: Nationality and Citizenship Act 1967—review of, 1968–1994.

A446 1978/75531: Citizenship Act 1969—part 2, 1970–1973.

A446 1978/75532: Citizenship Act 1969—part 3, 1973.

A463 1957/2783: Citizenship rights under naturalisation—General—1954–1961, 25 Mar 1954–14 Sep 1961.

A463 1957/3309: Australian Citizenship Convention—1958—General, 19 Sep 1957–10 Jan 1958.

A463 1966/793: Voting rights for Aborigines, 22 Nov 1960–22 Mar 1962.

A1838 555/10/9 PART 2: Publicity—Racial discrimination, 1961–1973.

A1838 557/1 PART 2: Publicity on Australian Aborigines, 1956–1967.

A1838 557/2 PART 3: Publicity abroad relating to Australian Aborigines, 1961–1962.

A1838 557/2 PART 4: Publicity abroad relating to Australian Aborigines, 1962–1965.

A1838 557/5 PART 1: Aborigines—Inter-Departmental Committee on Racial Discrimination, 1960–1964.

A1838 929/5/6 PART 1: United Nations—Human Rights—Discrimination and minorities—Convention on racial discrimination, 1964–1965.

A1838 929/5/6 PART 5: United Nations—Human Rights—Discrimination and minorities—International Convention on racial discrimination, 1965–1966.

A1838 929/5/6 PART 7: United Nations—Human Rights—Discrimination and minorities—International Convention on racial discrimination, 1968–1969.

A4940 C3496: Voting rights for Aborigines, policy, 1961–1962.

A5827 VOLUME 31: Cabinet submissions 991–1020 vol. 31, 1963–1966.

A5840 79: Cabinet Minute—Constitutional Amendment—Aborigines—SUBMISSIONS 46 and 64, 1967.

A5840 507: Cabinet Minute—Aborigines—SUBMISSION 432, 1967.

National Library of Australia

MS 2683/Series 10/Box 27/Folder 3: Papers of Jessie Street, circa 1914–1968.
MS 2683/Series 10/Box 27/Folder 4: Papers of Jessie Street, circa 1914–1968.
MS 2683/Series 10/Box 27/Folder 7: Papers of Jessie Street, circa 1914–1968.
MS 2683/Series 10/Box 27/File 9: Papers of Jessie Street, circa 1914–1968.
MS 2683/Series 10/Box 28/Folder 16: Papers of Jessie Street, circa 1914–1968.
MS 2683/Series 10/Box 28/Folder 23: Papers of Jessie Street, circa 1914–1968.
MS 4965/Series 1/Folder 5275: Papers of Brian Fitzpatrick, 1921–1965.
MS 5274/Series III/Box 32/Folder 2: Papers of Sir Paul Hasluck, 1925–1989.
MS 5274/Series III/Box 33/Folder 10: Papers of Sir Paul Hasluck, 1925–1989.
MS 6690/Series 12/Box 40/File 22: Papers of Jerzy Zubrzycki, 1919–2006.
MS 7798/Series 3/Box 40: Papers of Al Grassby, 1965–1984.
MS 8256/Series II/Sub-Series II/Box 175: Papers of Gordon Bryant, 1917–1991.

National Library of New Zealand

NLNZ 88–070-17/01: David Watt Balantye Papers.

Parliamentary Debates

Debates, *House of Commons*, vol. I, 1950.
Debates, *House of Commons*, vol. I, 1967.
Debates, *House of Commons*, vol. IX, 1975.
Debates, *House of Commons*, vol. X, 1975–76.
Debates, *Representatives* (Australian), vol. 4, 1954.
Debates, *Representatives* (Australian), vol. 5, 1954.
Debates, *Representatives* (Australian), vol. 6, 1954–55.
Debates, *Representatives* (Australian), vol. 54, 1967.
Debates, *Representatives* (Australian), vol. 63, 1969.
Debates, *Representatives* (Australian), vol. 83, 1973.
Debates, *Representatives* (New Zealand), vol. 320, 1959.
Debates, *Representatives* (New Zealand), vol. 350, 1967.
Debates, *Representatives* (New Zealand), vol. 353, 1967.
Debates, *Representatives* (New Zealand), vol. 391, 1974
Debates, *Representatives* (New Zealand), vol. 401, 1975.
Debates, *Representatives* (New Zealand), vol. 410, 1977.
Debates, *Representatives* (New Zealand), vol. 412, 1977.
Debates, *Representatives* (New Zealand), vol. 415, 1977.

Newspapers

Age, 17 May 1967; 26 May 1967.

The Canberra Times, 25 May 1967.

The Courier-Mail, 20 January 1954; 14 June 1954.

The Dominion, 28 August 1959; 4 May 1967; 27 October 1967; 15 November 1967; 16 November 1967; 17 November 1967; 22 November 1967; 6 July 1974.

Evening Post, 28 August 1959; 8 November 1967.

Gisborne Herald, 15 September 1959.

New Zealand Herald, 29 August 1959; 28 October 1967; 8 November 1967; 16 November 1967; 4 March 1971; 6 July 1974; 9 November 1974.

Sydney Morning Herald, 17 November 1965; 28 February 1967; 13 May 1967; 16 May 1967; 17 May 1967; 22 May 1967; 24 May 1967; 26 May 1967; 29 May 1967.

The Toronto Star, 3 July 1961.

The West Australian, 2 February 1950; 16 June 1950; 28 December 1954.

Others

Citizen, vol. 10, no. 5, December 1964.

Secondary Sources

25 Years On: Marking the Anniversary of the Aboriginal Referendum of 27 May 1967. Canberra: Aboriginal and Torres Strait Islander Commission, 1992.

Abu-Laban, Yasmeen. "Building a New Citizenship Regime? Immigration and Multiculturalism in Canada." In *Citizenship in Transnational Perspective: Australia, Canada, and New Zealand*, edited by Jatinder Mann, 263–84, Politics of Citizenship and Immigration Series. New York: Palgrave Macmillan, 2017.

Adamoski, Robert, Dorothy E. Chunn, and Robert Menzies, eds. *Contesting Canadian Citizenship: Historical Readings*. Peterborough, Ontario: Broadview Press, 2002.

Armitage, Andrew. *Comparing the Policy of Aboriginal Assimilation: Australia, Canada, and New Zealand*. Vancouver: UBC Press, 1995.

Ashton, S. R., and Wm Roger Louis, eds. *East of Suez and the Commonwealth 1964–1971: Part I East of Suez*. British Documents on the End of Empire series edited by S. R. Ashton. Norwich: The Stationary Office, 2004.

Ashton, S. R., and Wm Roger Louis, eds. *East of Suez and the Commonwealth 1964–1971: Part II Europe, Rhodesia, Commonwealth*. British Documents on the End of Empire series edited by S. R. Ashton. Norwich: The Stationary Office, 2004.

Attwood, Bain, and Andrew Markus. *The 1967 Referendum, or When Aborigines Didn't Get the Vote*. In collaboration with Dale Edwards and Kath Schilling. Canberra: Australian Institute of Aboriginal and Torres Strait Islander Studies, 1997.

Attwood, Bain, and Andrew Markus. "Representation Matters: The 1967 Referendum and Citizenship." In *Citizenship and Indigenous Australians: Changing Conceptions and Possibilities*, edited by Nicolas Peterson and Will Sanders, 118–40. Cambridge: Cambridge University Press, 1998.

Bandler, Faith. *Turning the Tide: A Personal History of the Federal Council for the Advancement of Aborigines and Torres Strait Islanders.* Canberra: Aboriginal Studies Press, 1989.

Banting, Keith, Thomas J. Courchene, and F. Leslie Seidle, eds. *Belonging? Diversity, Recognition and Shared Citizenship in Canada.* Montreal: The Institute for Research on Public Policy (IRPP), 2007.

Beaumont, Joan. "Australian Citizenship and the Two World Wars." *Australian Journal of Politics and History* 53, no. 2 (2007): 171–82.

Beckett, Jeremy. "Aboriginality, Citizenship and Nation State." *Social Analysis* 24 (December 1988): 3–18.

Bedford, Richard. "Citizenship in New Zealand: Tougher Criteria for a New Century." *Canadian Diversity* 6, no. 4 (Fall 2008): 95–8.

Belich, James. *Paradise Reforged: History of the New Zealanders from the 1880s to the Year 2000.* Auckland: Penguin Books, 2002.

Bennett, Scott. "The 1967 Referendum." *Australian Aboriginal Studies*, no. 2 (1985): 26–31.

Bennett, Scott. *Aborigines and Political Power.* Sydney: Allen & Unwin, 1989.

Benvenuti, Andrea, and Stuart Ward. "Britain, Europe, and the 'Other Quiet Revolution' in Canada." In *Canada and the End of Empire*, edited by Phil Buckner. Vancouver: UBC Press, 2006.

Blake, Raymond B. "A New Canadian Dynamism? From Multiculturalism and Diversity to History and Core Values." *British Journal of Canadian Studies* 26, no. 1 (May 2013): 79–103.

Bohaker, Heidi, and Franca Iacovetta. "Making Aboriginal People 'Immigrants Too': A Comparison of Citizenship Programs for Newcomers and Indigenous Peoples in Postwar Canada, 1940s–1960s." *Canadian Historical Review* 90, no. 3 (September 2009): 427–62.

Boyer, Pierre, Linda Cardinal, and David Headon, eds. *From Subjects to Citizens: A Hundred Years of Citizenship in Australia and Canada.* Ottawa: University of Ottawa Press, 2004.

Bridge, Carl, and Kent Fedorowich, eds. *The British World: Diaspora, Culture and Identity.* Abingdon, Oxford: Routledge, 2003.

Brodie, Janine. "Three Stories of Canadian Citizenship." In *Contesting Canadian Citizenship: Historical Readings*, edited by Robert Adamoski, Dorothy E. Chunn, and Robert Menzies, 43–66. Peterborough, Ontario: Broadview Press, 2002.

Brodie, Janine, and Sandra Rein, eds. *Critical Concepts: An Introduction to Politics.* Toronto: Pearson, 2009.

Broome, Richard. *Aboriginal Australians: Black Responses to White Dominance 1788–2001.* Crows Nest, NSW: Allen & Unwin, 2001.

Buckner, Phil, ed. *Canada and the End of Empire.* Vancouver: UBC Press, 2005.

Bulmer, Martin, and Anthony M. Rees, eds. *Citizenship Today: The Contemporary Relevance of T. H. Marshall.* London, England: UCL Press, 1996.

Byrnes, Giselle, ed. *The New Oxford History of New Zealand.* South Melbourne, Victoria: Oxford University Press, 2009.

Cairns, Alan C. "Empire, Globalization, and the Fall and Rise of Diversity." In *Citizenship, Diversity, and Pluralism: Canadian and Comparative Perspectives*, edited by Alan C. Cairns,

John C. Courtney, Peter MacKinnon, Hans J. Michelmann, and David E. Smith, 23–57. Montreal & Kingston: McGill-Queen's University Press, 1999.

Cairns, Alan. *Citizens Plus: Aboriginal Peoples and the Canadian State*. Vancouver: UBC Press, 2001.

Cairns, Alan C., John C. Courtney, Peter MacKinnon, Hans J. Michelmann, and David E. Smith, eds. *Citizenship, Diversity, and Pluralism: Canadian and Comparative Perspectives*. Montreal & Kingston: McGill-Queen's University Press, 1999.

Caldwell, Gary. "Evolution of the Concept of Citizenship (1945–1995): An English Canadian Perspective." In *La Nation Dans Tous Ses États: Le Québec en Comparaison*, edited by Yvan Lamonde and Gérard Bouchard, 297–310. Montreal: Harmattan, 1997.

Cardinal, Linda, and Marie-Joié Brady. "Citizenship and Federalism in Canada: A Difficult Relationship." In *Contemporary Canadian Federalism: Foundations, Traditions, Institutions*, edited by Alain-G. Gagnon, 381–404. Toronto: University of Toronto Press, 2009.

Carty, R. Kenneth, and W. Peter Ward, eds. *National Politics and Community in Canada*. Vancouver: UBC Press, 1986.

Carty, R. Kenneth, and W. Peter Ward. "The Making of a Canadian Political Citizenship." In *National Politics and Community in Canada*, edited by R. Kenneth Carty and W. Peter Ward, 65–79. Vancouver: UBC Press, 1986.

Chesterman, John, and Brian Galligan. *Citizens Without Rights: Aborigines and Australian Citizenship*. Cambridge: Cambridge University Press, 1997.

Chesterman, John, and Brian Galligan, eds. *Defining Australian Citizenship: Selected Documents*. Carlton South, Victoria: Melbourne University Press, 1999.

Chesterman, John, and Brian Galligan. "Indigenous Rights and Australian Citizenship." In *Individual, Community, Nation: Fifty Years of Australian Citizenship*, edited by Kim Rubenstein, 64–72. Melbourne: Australian Scholarly, 2000.

Clark, Bruce. *Native Liberty, Crown Sovereignty: The Existing Aboriginal Right of Self-Government in Canada*. Montreal & Kingston: McGill-Queen's University Press, 1990.

Clark, Jennifer. "'The Wind of Change' in Australia: Aborigines and the International Politics of Race, 1960–1972." *The International History Review* 20, no. 1 (March 1998): 89–117.

Cunneen, Christopher, and Terry Libesman. *Indigenous People and the Law in Australia*. Sydney: Butterworths, 1995.

Curran, James. *The Power of Speech: Australian Prime Ministers Defining the National Image*. Carlton, Victoria: Melbourne University Press, 2006.

Curran, James, and Stuart Ward. *The Unknown Nation: Australia After Empire*. Parkville, Victoria: Melbourne University Press, 2010.

Curthoys, Ann. "An Uneasy Conversation: The Multicultural and the Indigenous." In *Race, Colour and Identity in Australia and New Zealand*, edited by John Docker and Gerhard Fischer, 21–36. Sydney, NSW: UNSW Press, 2000.

Davidson, Alastair. *From Subject to Citizen: Australian Citizenship in the Twentieth Century*. Cambridge: Cambridge University Press, 1997.

Davis, S. Rufus, ed. *Citizenship in Australia: Democracy, Law and Society*. Carlton, Victoria: Constitutional Centenary Foundation, 1996.

Denis, Claude. "Indigenous Citizenship and History in Canada: Between Denial and Imposition." In *Contesting Canadian Citizenship: Historical Readings*, edited by Robert Adamoski, Dorothy E. Chunn, and Robert Menzies, 113–26. Peterborough, Ontario: Broadview Press, 2002.

Docker, John, and Gerhard Fischer, eds. *Race, Colour and Identity in Australia and New Zealand*. Sydney, NSW: UNSW Press, 2000.

Dodds, Susan. "Citizenship, Justice and Indigenous Group-Specific Rights-Citizenship and Indigenous Australia." *Citizenship Studies* 2, no. 1 (1998): 105–19.

Dodson, Michael. "First Fleets and Citizenships: The Citizenship Status of Indigenous Peoples in Post-Colonial Australia." In *Citizenship in Australia: Democracy, Law and Society*, edited by S. Rufus Davis, 189–223. Carlton, Victoria: Constitutional Centenary Foundation, 1996.

Durie, M. H. *Te Mana Te Kāwanatanga—The Politics of Māori Self-Determination*. South Melbourne, Victoria: Oxford University Press, 1998.

Dussault, Justice René. "Citizenship and Aboriginal Governance: The Royal Commission's Vision for the Future." In *From Subjects to Citizens: A Hundred Years of Citizenship in Australia and Canada*, edited by Pierre Boyer, Linda Cardinal, and David Headon, 211–16. Ottawa: University of Ottawa Press, 2004.

Dutton, David. *Citizenship in Australia: A Guide to Commonwealth Government Records*. Canberra: National Archives of Australia, 1999.

Dutton, David. *One of Us? A Century of Australian Citizenship*. Sydney: UNSW Press, 2002.

Ebbeck, Genevieve. "A Constitutional Concept of Australian Citizenship." *Adelaide Law Review* 25 (2004): 137–67.

Elkin, A. P. "Australian Aboriginal and White Relations: A Personal Record." *Journal of the Royal Australian Historical Society* 48, part 3 (July 1962): 208–31.

Fleras, Augie. "Rethinking Citizenship Through Transnational Lenses: Canada, New Zealand, and Australia." In *Citizenship in Transnational Perspective: Australia, Canada, and New Zealand*, edited by Jatinder Mann, 15–48, Politics of Immigration and Citizenship Series. New York: Palgrave Macmillan, 2017.

Fleras, Augie, and Jean Leonard Elliott. *The "Nations Within": Aboriginal—State Relations in Canada, the United States, and New Zealand*. Toronto: Oxford University Press, 1992.

Fleras, Augie, and Paul Spoonley. *Recalling Aotearoa: Indigenous Politics and Ethnic Relations in New Zealand*. Auckland: Oxford University Press, 1999.

Fletcher, Christine. "Living Together but not Neighbours: Cultural Imperialism in Australia." In *Indigenous Peoples' Rights in Australia, Canada, & New Zealand*, edited by Paul Havemann, 335–50. Auckland: Oxford University Press, 1999.

Foster, Cecil. "Multiculturalism as Second Reconstruction: The Continuing Quest for Fraternal Membership in North American Liberal Democracies." *Canadian Review of American Studies* 43, no. 3 (2013): 323–51.

Foster, Hamar. "'Indian Administration' from the Royal Proclamation of 1763 to Constitutionally Entrenched Aboriginal Rights." In *Indigenous Peoples' Rights in Australia, Canada, & New Zealand*, edited by Paul Havemann, 351–99. Auckland: Oxford University Press, 1999.

Gabriel, Christina. "Citizens and Citizenship." In *Critical Concepts: An Introduction to Politics*, edited by Janine Brodie and Sandra Rein, 157–69. Toronto: Pearson, 2009.

Gagnon, Alain-G., ed. *Contemporary Canadian Federalism: Foundations, Traditions, Institutions*. Toronto: University of Toronto Press, 2009.

Galligan, Brian. "Australian Citizenship in a Changing Nation and World." In *Citizenship in Transnational Perspective: Australia, Canada, and New Zealand*, edited by Jatinder Mann, 79–96, Politics of Citizenship and Immigration Series. New York: Palgrave Macmillan, 2017.

Godfery, Morgan. "Whose Citizenship Anyway?" *Set: Research Information for Teachers* 3 (2009): 4.

Goldlust, John. *Understanding Citizenship in Australia*. Canberra: Australian Government Publishing Service, 1996.

Goodall, Heather. *Invasion to Embassy: Land in Aboriginal Politics in New South Wales, 1770–1972*. St Leonards, NSW: Allen & Unwin, 1996.

Goot, Murray, and Tim Rowse. *Divided Nation: Indigenous Affairs and the Imagined Public*. Carlton, Victoria: Melbourne University Press, 2007.

Gorman, Daniel. *Imperial Citizenship: Empire and the Question of Belonging*. Manchester: Manchester University Press, 2006.

Granatstein, Jack L. *Canada 1957–1967: The Years of Uncertainty and Innovation*. Toronto: McClelland and Stewart, 1986.

Green, Joyce. "The Impossibility of Citizenship Liberation for Indigenous People." In *Citizenship in Transnational Perspective: Australia, Canada, and New Zealand*, edited by Jatinder Mann, 175–88, Politics of Citizenship and Immigration Series. New York: Palgrave Macmillan, 2017.

Griffiths, R. T., and S. Ward, eds. *Courting the Common Market: The First Attempt to Enlarge the European Community*. London, England: Lothian, 1996.

Haebich, Anna. *Spinning the Dream: Assimilation in Australia, 1950–1970*. North Fremantle, WA: Fremantle Press, 2007.

Harris, Aroha. *Hikoi: Forty Years of Maori Protest*. Wellington: Huia, 2004.

Harris, Paul, and Stephen Levine. With Margaret Clark, John Martin, and Elizabeth McLeay, eds. *The New Zealand Politics Source Book*, 2nd ed. Palmerston North: Dunmore Press, 1994.

Havemann, Paul, ed. *Indigenous Peoples' Rights in Australia, Canada, & New Zealand*. Auckland: Oxford University Press, 1999.

Havemann, Paul. "Indigenous Rights in the Political Jurisprudence of Australia, Canada, and New Zealand: Parallel Chronologies." In *Indigenous Peoples' Rights in Australia, Canada, & New Zealand*, edited by Paul Havemann, 22–64. Auckland: Oxford University Press, 1999.

Hill, Richard S. *Maori and the State: Crown-Maori Relations in New Zealand/Aotearoa, 1950–2000*. Wellington: Victoria University Press, 2009.

Hill, Richard S. "Maori and State Policy." In *The New Oxford History of New Zealand*, edited by Giselle Byrnes, 513–36. South Melbourne, Victoria: Oxford University Press, 2009.

Hudson, Wayne, and John Kane, eds. *Rethinking Australian Citizenship*. Cambridge: Cambridge University Press, 2000.

Hudson, Wayne, and John Kane. "Rethinking Australian Citizenship." In *Rethinking Australian Citizenship*, edited by Wayne Hudson and John Kane, 1–11. Cambridge: Cambridge University Press, 2000.

Humpage, Louise. "Revision Required: Reconciling New Zealand Citizenship with Māori Nationalisms." *National Identities* 10, no. 3 (September 2008): 247–61.

Hutching, Megan. *New Zealanders by Choice*. Wellington: Identity Services, 1998.

Igartua, José. "'Ready, Aye, Ready' No More?" In *Rediscovering the British World*, edited by Phil Buckner, 48. Calgary: University of Calgary Press, 2005.

Igartua, José. *The Other Quiet Revolution: National Identities in English Canada, 1945–1971*. Vancouver: UBC Press, 2006.

Irving, Helen. *To Constitute a Nation: A Cultural History of Australia's Constitution*. Cambridge: Cambridge University Press, 1997.

Irving, Helen, ed. *The Centenary Companion to Australian Federation*. Cambridge: Cambridge University Press, 1999.

Ivison, Duncan, Paul Patton, and Will Sanders, eds. *Political Theory and the Rights of Indigenous Peoples*. Cambridge: Cambridge University Press, 2000.

Jayasuriya, Kanishka. "From British Subjects to Australian Values: A Citizenship-Building Approach to Australia-Asia Relations." *Contemporary Politics* 14, no. 4 (December 2008): 479–95.

Jenson, Jane. "Citizenship Claims: Routes to Representation in a Federal System." In *Rethinking Federalism: Citizens, Markets, and Governments in a Changing World*, edited by Karen Knop, Sylvia Ostry, Richard Simeon, and Katherine Swinton, 99–118. Vancouver: UBC Press, 1995.

Johnston, Darlene. "First Nations and Canadian Citizenship." In *Belonging: The Meaning and Future of Canadian Citizenship*, edited by William Kaplan, 349–67. Montreal & Kingston: McGill-Queen's University Press, 1993.

Jones, Carwyn, and Craig Linkhorn. "'All the Rights and Privileges of British Subjects': Māori and Citizenship in Aotearoa New Zealand." In *Citizenship in Transnational Perspective: Australia, Canada, and New Zealand*, edited by Jatinder Mann, 139–58, Politics of Citizenship and Immigration Series. New York: Palgrave Macmillan, 2017.

Jordens, Ann-Mari. *Promoting Australian Citizenship, 1949–71*. Canberra, Administration, Compliance and Governability Program, 1991.

Jordens, Ann-Mari. *Redefining Australians: Immigration, Citizenship and National Identity*. Sydney: Hale & Iremonger, 1995.

Jordens, Ann-Mari. *Alien to Citizen: Settling Migrants in Australia, 1945–75*. St. Leonards, NSW: Allen & Unwin, 1997.

Jordens, Ann-Mari. "The legal and non-legal aspects of immigration and citizenship." In *Individual, Community, Nation: Fifty Years of Australian Citizenship*, edited by Kim Rubenstein, 84–91. Melbourne: Australian Scholarly, 2000.

Joseph, Philip A. *Constitutional and Administrative Law in New Zealand*. Sydney: The Law Book Company, 1993.

Kaiser, Wolfram. *Using Europe, Abusing the Europeans: Britain and European Integration, 1945–1963*. London: Macmillan, 1996.

Kalantzis, Mary. "Multicultural Citizenship." In *Rethinking Australian Citizenship*, edited by Wayne Hudson and John Kane, 99–110. Cambridge: Cambridge University Press, 2000.

Kaplan, William, ed. *Belonging: The Meaning and Future of Canadian Citizenship*. Montreal & Kingston: McGill-Queen's University Press, 1993.

Kaplan, William. "Who Belongs? Changing Concepts of Citizenship and Nationality." In *Belonging: The Meaning and Future of Canadian Citizenship*, edited by William Kaplan, 245–64. Montreal & Kingston: McGill-Queen's University Press, 1993.

King, Michael. *The Penguin History of New Zealand*. Auckland: Penguin Books, 2003.

Knop, Karen, Sylvia Ostry, Richard Simeon, and Katherine Swinton, eds. *Rethinking Federalism: Citizens, Markets, and Governments in a Changing World*. Vancouver: UBC Press, 1995.

Knowles, Valerie. *Forging Our Legacy: Canadian Citizenship and Immigration, 1900–1977*. Ottawa: Citizenship and Immigration Canada, 2000.

Krieken, Robert Van. "Between Assimilation and Multiculturalism: Models of Integration in Australia." *Patterns of Prejudice* 46, no. 5 (2012): 500–17.

Kukathas, Chandran, ed. *Multicultural Citizens: The Philosophy and Politics of Identity*. St Leonards: The Centre for Independent Studies, 1993.

Kymlicka, Will, and Wayne Norman. "Return of the Citizen: A Survey of Recent Work on Citizenship Theory." *Ethics* 104 (January 1994): 352–81.

Kymlicka, Will, and Wayne Norman, eds. *Citizenship in Diverse Societies*. Oxford: Oxford University Press, 2000.

Kymlicka, Will, and Wayne Norman. "Citizenship in Culturally Diverse Societies: Issues, Contexts, Concepts." In *Citizenship in Diverse Societies*, edited by Will Kymlicka and Wayne Norman, 1–41. Oxford: Oxford University Press, 2000.

Labrum, Bronwyn. "Developing 'the Essentials of Good Citizenship and Responsibilities' in Maori Women: Family Life, Social Change, and the State in New Zealand, 1944–70." *Journal of Family History* 29, no. 4 (October 2004): 446–65.

Lamonde, Yvan, and Gérard Bouchard, eds. *La Nation Dans Tous Ses États: Le Québec en Comparaison*. Montreal: Harmattan, 1997.

Langton, Marcia. "The Nations of Australia." In *From Subjects to Citizens: A Hundred Years of Citizenship in Australia and Canada*, edited by Pierre Boyer, Linda Cardinal, and David Headon, 191–209. Ottawa: University of Ottawa Press, 2004.

Lunt, Neil, Paul Spoonley, and Peter Mataira. "Past and Present: Reflections on Citizenship Within New Zealand." *Social Policy & Administration* 36, no. 4 (August 2002): 346–62.

Maaka, Roger. "Maori and the State: Diversity Models and Debates in New Zealand." In *Belonging? Diversity, Recognition and Shared Citizenship in Canada*, edited by Keith Banting, Thomas J. Courchene, and F. Leslie Seidle, 285–318. Montreal: The Institute for Research on Public Policy (IRPP), 2007.

Maaka, Roger, and Augie Fleras. "Engaging With Indigeneity: Tino Rangatiratanga in Aotearoa." In *Political Theory and the Rights of Indigenous Peoples*, edited by Duncan Ivison, Paul Patton, and Will Sanders, 89–109. Cambridge: Cambridge University Press, 2000.

Macintyre, Stuart. *Winners and Losers: The Pursuit of Social Justice in Australian History*. Sydney, NSW: Allen & Unwin, 1985.

Macklin, Audrey. "From Settler Society to Warrior Nation and Back Again." In *Citizenship in Transnational Perspective: Australia, Canada, and New Zealand*, edited by Jatinder Mann, 285–314, Politics of Citizenship and Immigration Series. New York: Palgrave Macmillan, 2017.

Mann, Jatinder. "The Evolution of Commonwealth Citizenship, 1945–48 in Canada, Britain and Australia." *Commonwealth and Comparative Politics* 50, no. 3 (July 2012): 293–313.

Mann, Jatinder. "The Introduction of Multiculturalism in Canada and Australia, 1960s–1970s." *Nations and Nationalism* 18, no. 3 (July 2012): 483–503.

Mann, Jatinder. "'Leavening British Traditions': Integration Policy in Australia, 1962–1972." *Australian Journal of Politics and History* 59, issue 1 (March 2013): 47–62.

Mann, Jatinder. "Anglo-Conformity': Assimilation Policy in Canada, 1890s–1950s." *International Journal of Canadian Studies* 50 (December 2014): 253–76.

Mann, Jatinder. *The Search for a New National Identity: The Rise of Multiculturalism in Canada and Australia, 1890s–1970s*. New York: Peter Lang, 2016.

Mann, Jatinder, ed. *Citizenship in Transnational Perspective: Australia, Canada, and New Zealand*. Politics of Immigration and Citizenship Series. New York: Palgrave Macmillan, 2017.

Mann, Jatinder. "The Redefinition of Citizenship in Canada, 1950s–1970s." In *Citizenship in Transnational Perspective: Australia, Canada, and New Zealand*, edited by Jatinder Mann, 97–116. Politics of Citizenship and Immigration Series. New York: Palgrave Macmillan, 2017.

Mann, Jatinder. "The End of the British World and the Redefinition of Citizenship in Australia, 1950s–1970s." *Chinese Journal of Australian Studies*, Issue 2 (December 2018): 41–75.

Mann, Jatinder. "The End of the British World and the Redefinition of Citizenship in Canada, 1950s–1970s." *Asian Journal of Canadian Studies* 24, no. 2 (December 2018): 17–53.

Mann, Jatinder. "The End of the British World and the Redefinition of Citizenship in Aotearoa New Zealand, 1950s–1970s." *National Identities* 21, no. 1 (2019): 73–92.

Markus, Andrew. *Australian Race Relations 1788–1993*. St. Leonards, NSW: Allen & Unwin, 1994.

Markus, Andrew. "Australia's Immigrants: Identity and Citizenship." In *Citizenship in Transnational Perspective: Australia, Canada, and New Zealand*, edited by Jatinder Mann, 225–44, Politics of Citizenship and Immigration Series. New York: Palgrave Macmillan, 2017.

Marotta, Vince. "The Ambivalence of Borders: The Bicultural and the Multicultural." In *Race, Colour and Identity in Australia and New Zealand*, edited by John Docker and Gerhard Fischer, 177–89. Sydney, Australia: UNSW Press, 2000.

Marshall, T. H. *Class, Citizenship, and Social Development: Essays by T. H. Marshall*. Westport, Connecticut: Greenwood Press, 1964.

Martin, Jean I. *The Migrant Presence: Australian Responses 1947–1977*. Hornsby, NSW: Allen & Unwin, 1978.

McAloon, Jim. "Unsettling Recolonization: Labourism, Keynesianism and Australasia from the 1890s to the 1950s." *Thesis Eleven* 92 (February 2008): 50–68.

McAloon, Jim. *Judgements of all Kinds: Economic Policy-Making in New Zealand, 1945–1984*. Wellington: Victoria University Press, 2013.

McKinnon, Malcolm. *Immigrants and Citizens: New Zealanders and Asian Immigration in Historical Context*. Wellington: Institute of Policy Studies, Victoria University of Wellington, 1996.

McMillan, Kate. "Developing Citizens: Subjects, Aliens and Citizens in New Zealand Since 1840." In *Tangata Tangata: The Changing Ethnic Contours of New Zealand*, edited by Paul Spoonley, Cluny Macpherson, and David Pearson, 267–89. Southbank, Victoria: Thomson, 2004.

McMillan, Kate. "From 'the Commonwealth's Most Dutiful Daughter' to 'Young Multicultural Nation': Non-Citizen Voting Rights and New Zealand's Citizenship Regime." In *Citizenship in Transnational Perspective: Australia, Canada, and New Zealand*, edited by Jatinder Mann, 117–38, Politics of Citizenship and Immigration Series. New York: Palgrave Macmillan, 2017.

Meaney, Neville. "'In History's Page': Identity and Myth." In *Australia's Empire*, edited by Deryck M. Schreuder and Stuart Ward, *The Oxford History of the British Empire series*, general editor Wm. Roger Louis. Oxford: Oxford University Press, 2008.

Metge, Joan. *A New Maori Migration: Rural and Urban Relations in Northern New Zealand*. London, England: The Athlone Press, 1964.

Metge, Joan. *Rautahi: The Maori of New Zealand*. London, England: Routledge, 2004.

Mulgan, Richard. "Multiculturalism: A New Zealand Perspective." In *Multicultural Citizens: The Philosophy and Politics of Identity*, edited by Chandran Kukathas, 77–90. St. Leonards: The Centre for Independent Studies, 1993.

Neice, David C. *Ethnicity and Canadian Citizenship: A Metropolitan Study*. Ottawa: Citizenship Registration Branch, Department of the Secretary of State, January 1978.

Ongley, Patrick, and David Pearson. "Post-1945 International Migration: New Zealand, Australia and Canada Compared." *International Migration Review* 29, no. 3 (Autumn 1995): 765–93.

Pearson, David. "Theorising Citizenship in British Settler Societies." *Ethnic and Racial Studies* 25, no. 6 (November 2002): 989–1012.

Pearson, David. "Rethinking Citizenship in Aotearoa/New Zealand." In *Tangata Tangata: The Changing Ethnic Contours of New Zealand*, edited by Paul Spoonley, Cluny Macpherson, and David Pearson, 291–314. Southbank, Victoria: Thomson, 2004.

Pearson, Lester. "Symbols and Realities." In *Mike: The Memoirs of the Right Honourable Lester B. Pearson: Volume 3, 1957–1968*, edited by J. A. Munro and A. I. Inglis. London: Victor Gollancz, 1975.

Perham, Elisabeth Rose. "Citizenship Laws in the Realm of New Zealand." *The New Zealand Yearbook of International Law* 9 (2011): 219–40

Peterson, Nicolas, and Will Sanders, eds. *Citizenship and Indigenous Australians: Changing Conceptions and Possibilities*. Cambridge: Cambridge University Press, 1998.

Pfeiffer, Rolf. "New Zealand and the Suez Crisis of 1956." *The Journal of Imperial and Commonwealth History* 21, no. 1 (1993): 126–52.

Pillai, Sangeetha. "The Rights and Responsibilities of Australian Citizenship: A Legislative Analysis." *Melbourne University Law Review* 37, no. 3 (January 2014): 736–85.

Pocock, J. G. A. *The Discovery of Islands: Essays in British History*. Cambridge: Cambridge University Press, 2005.

Pouarahi, Jozie Karanga. "We be Iwi before We be Kiwi: The Price of Citizenship for Indigenous People of Aotearoa." *Just Policy*, no. 45 (October 2007): 45–8.

Pryles, Michael. *Australian Citizenship Law*. Sydney: The Law Book Company, 1981.

Rees, Anthony M. "T. H. Marshall and the Progress of Citizenship." In *Citizenship Today: The Contemporary Relevance of T. H. Marshall*, edited by Martin Bulmer and Anthony M. Rees, 1–23. London: UCL Press, 1996.

Referendums to be held...27th May, 1967...Arguments For and Against. Canberra: Australian Government Publishing Service, 1993.

Rice, Geoffrey W. ed. *The Oxford History of New Zealand*, 2nd ed. Auckland: Oxford University Press, 1992.

Roughan, Nicole. "Te Tiriti and the Constitution: Rethinking Citizenship, Justice, Equality and Democracy." *New Zealand Journal of Public and International Law* 3, no. 2 (November 2005): 285–301.

Rowley, C. D. *The Destruction of Aboriginal Society: Aboriginal Policy and Practice—Volume I*. Canberra: ANU Press, 1970.

Rowse, Tim. "Diversity in Indigenous Citizenship." *Communal/Plural* 2 (1993): 47–63.

Rowse, Tim. "Indigenous Citizenship and Self-Determination: The Problem of Shared Responsibilities." In *Citizenship and Indigenous Australians: Changing Conceptions and Possibilities*, edited by Nicolas Peterson and Will Sanders, 79–99. Cambridge: Cambridge University Press, 1998.

Rowse, Tim. "Indigenous Citizenship." In *Rethinking Australian Citizenship*, edited by Wayne Hudson and John Kane, 86–98. Cambridge: Cambridge University Press, 2000.

Rowse, Tim. "Indigenous Citizenship and the Historical Imagination." In *Citizenship in Transnational Perspective: Australia, Canada, and New Zealand*, edited by Jatinder Mann, 159–74, Politics of Citizenship and Immigration Series. New York: Palgrave Macmillan, 2017.

Rubenstein, Kim, ed. *Individual, Community, Nation: Fifty Years of Australian Citizenship*. Melbourne: Australian Scholarly, 2000.

Rubenstein, Kim. *Australian Citizenship Law in Context*. Pyrmont, NSW: Lawbook, 2002.

Rubenstein, Kim. "The Lottery of Citizenship: The Changing Significance of Birthplace, Territory and Residence to the Australian Membership Prize." *Law in Context* 22, no. 2 (2005): 45–61.

Rubenstein, Kim. "The Vulnerability of Dual Citizenship: From Supranational Subject to Citizen to Subject?" In *Citizenship in Transnational Perspective: Australia, Canada, and New Zealand*, edited by Jatinder Mann, 245–62, Politics of Citizenship and Immigration Series. New York: Palgrave Macmillan, 2017.

Sawer, Geoffrey. "The Australian Constitution and the Australian Aborigine." *Federal Law Review* 2, no. 1 (1966): 17–36.

Spoonley, Paul, Cluny Macpherson, and David Pearson, eds. *Tangata Tangata: The Changing Ethnic Contours of New Zealand*. Southbank, Victoria: Thomson, 2004.

Spoonley, Paul. "Renegotiating Citizenship: Indigeneity and Superdiversity in Contemporary Aotearoa/New Zealand." In *Citizenship in Transnational Perspective: Australia, Canada, and

New Zealand, edited by Jatinder Mann, 209–24, Politics of Citizenship and Immigration Series. New York: Palgrave Macmillan, 2017.

Stasiulis, Daiva. "Respatializing Social Citizenship and Security Among Dual Citizens in the Lebanese Diaspora." In *Citizenship in Transnational Perspective: Australia, Canada, and New Zealand*, edited by Jatinder Mann, 49–78, Politics of Citizenship and Immigration Series. New York: Palgrave Macmillan, 2017.

Stephens, Mamari. "'A Useful and Self-Respecting Citizenship'—Maori as Citizens in the Quest for Welfare in the Modern New Zealand State." In *Citizenship in Transnational Perspective: Australia, Canada, and New Zealand*, edited by Jatinder Mann, 189–208, Politics of Citizenship and Immigration Series. New York: Palgrave Macmillan, 2017.

Stretton, Pat, and Christine Finnimore. "Black Fellow Citizens: Aborigines and the Commonwealth Franchise." *Australian Historical Studies* 25, no. 101 (October 1993): 521–35.

Thomson, Dale C. *Louis St. Laurent: Canadian*. New York: St. Martin's Press, 1968.

Thornton, Margaret. "Legal Citizenship." In *Rethinking Australian Citizenship*, edited by Wayne Hudson and John Kane, 111–20. Cambridge: Cambridge University Press, 2000.

Tratt, Jacqueline. *The Macmillan Government and Europe: A Study in the Process of Policy Development*. Basingstoke, Hampshire: Macmillan, 1996.

Turner, Bryan S., ed. *Citizenship and Social Theory*. London: Sage, 1993.

Turner, Bryan S. "Contemporary Problems in the Theory of Citizenship." In *Citizenship and Social Theory*, edited by Bryan S. Turner, 1–18. London: Sage, 1993.

Walker, Ranginui. *Ka Whawhai Tonu Matou—Struggle Without End*. Auckland: Penguin Books, 1990.

Walker, Ranginui. "Maori People since 1950." In *The Oxford History of New Zealand*, 2nd ed., edited by Geoffrey W. Rice, 498–519. Auckland: Oxford University Press, 1992.

Ward, Alan, and Janine Hayward. "Tino Rangatiratanga: Maori in the Political and Administrative System." In *Indigenous Peoples' Rights in Australia, Canada, & New Zealand*, edited by Paul Havemann, 378–99. Auckland: Oxford University Press, 1999.

Ward, Stuart. *Australia and the British Embrace: The Demise of the British Ideal*. Carlton South, Victoria: Melbourne University Press, 2001.

Ward, Stuart. "The 'New Nationalism' in Australia, Canada and New Zealand: Civic Culture in the Wake of the British World." In *Britishness Abroad: Transnational Movements and Imperial Cultures*, edited by Kate Darian-Smith, Patricia Grimshaw, and Stuart Macintyre, 231–63. Carlton, Victoria: Melbourne University Press, 2007.

Widders, Terry, and Greg Noble. "On the Dreaming Track to the Republic: Indigenous People and the Ambivalence of Citizenship." *Communal/Plural* 2 (1993): 95–112.

Williams, John M. "Race, Citizenship and the Formation of the Australian Constitution: Andrew Inglis Clark and the '14th Amendment.'" *Australian Journal of Politics and History* 42, issue 1 (June 2008), 10–23.

INDEX

Studies in Transnationalism

Jatinder Mann, *Series Editor*

This series is designed to advance the publication of interdisciplinary research in transnationalism from scholars in history, literature, politics, sociology, geography, and related disciplines in the social sciences and humanities. The series seeks to publish works that trace the ways in which concepts and ideas are expressed across national borders, focusing on imperialism, globalism, cosmopolitanism, diaspora, and other themes of interest in transnational studies. It embraces both established and innovative methodologies and welcomes submissions in various formats, including monographs, textbooks, colloquia, and reference books.

For additional information about this series or for the submission of manuscripts, please contact:

Peter Lang Publishing
Acquisitions Department
29 Broadway, 18th floor
New York, NY 10006

To order books in this series, please contact our Customer Service Department:

800-770-LANG (within the U.S.)
212-647-7706 (outside the U.S.)
212-647-7707 FAX

Or browse online by series at:

www.peterlang.com